Confederate
Cabinet Departments
and Secretaries

# Confederate Cabinet Departments and Secretaries

Dennis L. Peterson

McFarland & Company, Inc., Publishers
*Jefferson, North Carolina*

LIBRARY OF CONGRESS CATALOGUING-IN-PUBLICATION DATA

Names: Peterson, Dennis L., 1954– author.
Title: Confederate cabinet departments and secretaries / Dennis L. Peterson.
Description: Jefferson, North Carolina : McFarland & Company, Inc., Publishers, 2016. | Includes bibliographical references and index.
Identifiers: LCCN 2016015436 | ISBN 9781476665214 (softcover : acid free paper) ∞
Subjects: LCSH: Confederate States of America—Politics and government. | Confederate States of America—Officials and employees—Biography. | Cabinet officers—Confederate States of America—Biography. | Davis, Jefferson, 1808–1889—Friends and associates. | Confederate States of America—Biography.
Classification: LCC E487 .P49 2016 | DDC 973.7/13—dc23
LC record available at https://lccn.loc.gov/2016015436

British Library cataloguing data are available

**ISBN (print) 978-1-4766-6521-4**
**ISBN (ebook) 978-1-4766-2514-0**

© 2016 Dennis L. Peterson. All rights reserved

No part of this book may be reproduced or transmitted in any form or by any means, electronic or mechanical, including photocopying or recording, or by any information storage and retrieval system, without permission in writing from the publisher.

Front cover print titled Jefferson Davis and His Cabinet; Confederate flags, 1896 (both images Library of Congress)

Printed in the United States of America

*McFarland & Company, Inc., Publishers*
  *Box 611, Jefferson, North Carolina 28640*
  *www.mcfarlandpub.com*

To my parents, Ralph and Hazel Peterson,
who encouraged this book but never lived to see it,

and to Connie, my wife,
who is the inspiration and love of my life

# Table of Contents

| | |
|---|---|
| *Preface* | 1 |
| *Acknowledgments* | 5 |
| *Introduction: The Birth of the Confederate Nation* | 7 |
| 1. Jefferson Davis's Selection of a Cabinet | 11 |

### Part I. Justice Department

| | |
|---|---|
| 2. Overview | 29 |
| 3. Judah P. Benjamin | 40 |
| 4. Thomas Bragg | 47 |
| 5. Thomas Watts | 50 |
| 6. Wade Keyes, Jr. | 54 |
| 7. George Davis | 56 |

### Part II. Treasury Department

| | |
|---|---|
| 8. Overview | 61 |
| 9. Christopher Memminger | 73 |
| 10. George Trenholm | 79 |
| 11. John Reagan | 83 |

### Part III. War Department

| | |
|---|---|
| 12. Overview | 89 |
| 13. Leroy Pope Walker | 130 |
| 14. Judah P. Benjamin | 139 |
| 15. George Randolph | 143 |

| | |
|---|---|
| 16. James Seddon | 148 |
| 17. John C. Breckinridge | 154 |

### Part IV. Navy Department

| | |
|---|---|
| 18. Overview | 165 |
| 19. Stephen Mallory | 186 |

### Part V. Post Office Department

| | |
|---|---|
| 20. Overview | 197 |
| 21. John Reagan | 202 |

### Part VI. State Department

| | |
|---|---|
| 22. Overview | 211 |
| 23. Robert Toombs | 226 |
| 24. Robert M. T. Hunter | 237 |
| 25. Judah P. Benjamin | 242 |
| *Conclusion. A Final Assessment of Davis's Cabinet* | 245 |
| *Appendix A. The Constitution of the Confederate States of America* | 251 |
| *Appendix B. Governors of the Confederate States* | 262 |
| *Chapter Notes* | 263 |
| *Bibliography* | 275 |
| *Index* | 283 |

# Preface

The Library of Congress estimates (the latest figures are for through 2002) that it has about 70,000 books on the American Civil War, or the War Between the States. (Some sources estimate the total number of books out there on that topic to be in the hundreds of thousands.) And about one new book on the topic is published every day. This author does not know if either of those estimates is accurate, but he does know that there are more books on the Civil War than any person could read.

So why do we need yet another one? More particularly, why do we need *this* book?

Most of the 70,000—or hundreds of thousands—of books on the Civil War deal with some factor associated with the causes of the war or the military aspects of the war—the battles; the generals; the campaigns; the strategies and tactics; the various departments or branches of military involved; specific units; the everyday life of soldiers, sailors, or civilians in the war; etc. Relatively few of those books, however, focus specifically on the civil government of the Confederacy, on the individual members of Jefferson Davis's cabinet, or on the individual departments within the cabinet (other than the War Department). Some biographies have been written on a few of the more prominent cabinet secretaries (e.g., Robert Toombs and John C. Breckinridge), but they were also generals of note and were connected with several famous battles. Very few books, however, have attempted to tell the many stories of the entire Confederate cabinet, sketching each secretary's life and activity in the cabinet and discussing the organization, workings, strengths, and weaknesses of each department.

Perhaps the three "classic" works that did do this—J.L.M. Curry's *Civil History of the Government of the Confederate States* (1901), Burton Hendrick's *Statesmen of the Lost Cause* (1939), and Rembert Patrick's *Jefferson Davis and His Cabinet* (1944)—were published many years ago. Beyond those sources, if one wants to learn about the Confederate cabinet, he must search many different sources. (A quick glance at the bibliography of this book will demonstrate just how many—and there are many others to which this author did not have ready access.) *Those* are reasons why *this* book is needed.

But it is also needed for another reason: most Americans, including even some people who otherwise "know their history," know essentially nothing about this particular topic. Few can list the six cabinet departments in the Confederate executive branch. Even fewer can name the men who headed those departments. And still fewer can tell anything about what those officials did during their time in office, let alone tell anything more of their lives.

While researching this book, the author happened upon an online history trivia quiz that asked users to name all of the men who had served in Jefferson Davis's cabinet. The average score, the site explained, was something like 19 percent. (The author was surprised that it was even that high!) He took the quiz himself and—in spite of being in the midst of doing extensive reading about those very men—missed one! (He tries to excuse himself based on the results of aging, but it is proof of the need for more widely available information on the subject.)

The author began working on this book truly from the standpoint of a novice. Having taught American history for a number of years on the junior high/high school level and as an occasional substitute teacher on the college level, he was familiar with most of the names of the men about whom he was reading, but his knowledge of them was indeed shallow. Recognizing his ignorance, he began his research as the typical student today might do—he googled the names of the individual department secretaries and the names of each department. He checked out Wikipedia for some general information, knowing that not everything from that source is credible but also knowing that it could give some ideas for where to find reliable information. He checked out and read works that recurred in his reading during his preliminary research survey. He then checked the sources cited in the bibliographies of those books and read many of them. He discovered gaps, contradictions, and differences of opinion. He became convinced that another book was needed that gathered much of that scattered information and the various opinions regarding those people. And somewhere during that process the topic became an obsession with him. The book you now hold in your hand is the outcome of that obsession.

In writing this book, the author was seeking to answer, primarily for his own benefit but secondarily to share with others who might be interested—not merely academics who study such stuff regularly as professionals but also average "buffs" of the War Between the States and Southern history—answers to the following questions:

## Preface

- Who were the men who made up the civilian executive departments of the Confederacy?
- What were their strengths and weaknesses?
- What made them tick? What did they have in common with each other that made them cast their lot with the Confederacy?
- What motivated their service on the side of the South?
- What contributions did they make to the Confederate cause?
- How did they get along with Jefferson Davis? With each other?
- What happened to them after the war?
- What evaluation can be made of them in hindsight?

This book is by no means perfect. No book is. Not everyone will agree with many of the conclusions and opinions the author reaches. That is not unusual in the field of history, where numerous historians can examine the exact same information and yet reach divergent opinions. And not everyone will be satisfied with the topics covered. Some people will think that the author spends too much time on one person or department; other people will think that the author should have paid *more* attention to the same person or department. But the reader must remember that this is not intended to be an exhaustive, definitive academic textbook on the Confederate cabinet. It is merely a survey, an attempt to provide in one place basic information about the Confederate government that rarely is covered elsewhere.

But what the author has covered is what *he* thought was important and interesting—*to him*. It is based on the information that he discovered in his exploratory journey. And he hopes that he can share that interest and enthusiasm for the topic with whoever might choose to read this book.

Special efforts were made to balance available newer source materials with older sources, but little attention has been paid—past or present—to the cabinet departments as a whole. Perhaps this effort to gather some of the scattered available information into one source will prove beneficial to others who have the same curiosity and who seek the same information. And the author hopes they will go even further in their study than he did in his, thereby adding even more to the knowledge base on this topic.

The book's 25 chapters are divided into six parts, one for each of the Confederate cabinet posts. Within each part, the first chapter is devoted to a general overview of that department and its bureaus or sub departments, workings, problems, failures, and successes. Each of the subsequent chapters of each part provides a biographical sketch of a head of that department. The length of these chapters varies greatly based on both the length of time the person served in the post and the amount of information available about him.

# Acknowledgments

The process of writing this book and getting it published has taken between four and five years. Research, reading, note taking, outlining, organizing, and writing were sporadic because of numerous other work, family, and church responsibilities. During that time, many people have contributed to making this book possible—and better than it might have been without their assistance.

The quest to produce this book really began when I was taking occasional university history classes and was unable to take the much-in-demand History of the South course taught by the esteemed Dr. Carl Abrams at Bob Jones University. I happened to mention that problem in a casual conversation with Dr. Abrams, and he volunteered to discuss the problem with the dean of the School of Arts and Sciences. A few days later, Dr. Abrams contacted me and said that he had worked out an agreement with the dean whereby Dr. Abrams would offer the class just for me, on a one-on-one basis, after regular class hours. The two of us met in his office every two weeks for the whole semester. During each two-week period between our meetings, I read two books on various aspects of Southern history from a long list that Dr. Abrams provided and then wrote a paper on one of them. Half of the books were ones that Dr. Abrams required; the other half were those that I chose from the list. When we met in his office at the end of each two-week period, we discussed the two books that I had read during the preceding two weeks.

At some point during that semester, Dr. Abrams offered perhaps the best piece of advice I've ever received from a professor: Examine the books listed in the bibliography of every book you read, and then read many of those closely. This practice, once applied, became a never-ending cycle for me and lit the spark that ultimately led to my undertaking this book project. Thank you, Dr. Abrams!

Many other people have helped make this book possible. Rita Mitchell, head of the Photo Acquisition and Text Permissions Department at BJU Press, and Sylvia Gass, also of that department, were of great assistance in helping me learn how to find and acquire photographs and deal with text-permissions issues. Rita even volunteered to locate many hard-to-find photos herself. (It was less trouble for her to do that than to have me continually interrupting her work with myriad e-mailed questions.) Sylvia gave me valuable advice concerning sources in the public domain and fair use of printed materials.

My mother and father, Ralph and Hazel Peterson, sacrificed much to help me get through college, indulged my thirst for history, and encouraged my love of books and reading, even when they thought that I could have put my money toward "more important things" than "another book." In their quiet way, they both encouraged me to write about what I was learning. I only wish that they could have lived to see the day when their little boy got his first book published.

My wife Connie also put up with a lot of late nights and early mornings while I was researching and writing this book. And she, too, tolerated the many times that I interrupted her concentration as she worked on her own lesson plans and teaching preparations to hear me read some fascinating (to me) fact or bit of information that I had encountered in my research. She was the impetus behind the first article I had published when, after hearing me read an iteration of it for the umpteenth time, she exclaimed, "I don't want to hear it again! Either submit it to a magazine for publication or never mention it to me again!" That hurt—but it worked. I submitted it to an academic journal. It was published. And I've been writing ever since. And after all these years of reading and writing—and reading aloud to her—she still agreed to critique the first draft of this book. She caught many things that I, being so close to the material, would never have seen. Most important of all, she believed in me. Thank you, Connie. I love you!

Finally, I want to give praise to the One who has made all things possible. He loved me enough to send His Son, Jesus Christ, to die for me. I thank Him for giving me the desire to learn, enabling me to write, providing me a supportive family, leading me to the right publisher, and sustaining me through the entire process. If anything good comes as a result of this book, it is to His glory alone.

# Introduction: The Birth of the Confederate Nation

The Confederate States of America officially came into being as a sovereign government on February 4, 1861, when six of the first seven states to secede from the United States government—South Carolina, Georgia, Alabama, Mississippi, Louisiana, and Florida—met in Montgomery, Alabama, and formed a provisional government. (Texas's delegation would arrive later.) The provisional government was to exist for one year, giving it time to write and approve a constitution; elect a president, a vice president, and a congress; organize the requisite departments; select officials to run those departments; and hire the necessary personnel for each department.

The delegates elected Jefferson Davis, former U.S. senator from Mississippi, as the first (and what proved to be the *only*) president of the Confederacy. The new president had a sad, solemn, unsmiling face that betrayed constant pain and looked as though it would break if he attempted to smile. His deep-set eyes were shaded by heavy brows. He sported a wisp of a goatee and less noticeable hair on his lower jaw.

Alexander Stephens, formerly one of Georgia's U.S. representatives, was elected vice president. His face was pale, thin, and expressionless. He had a long, thin nose; sad, dull eyes; and a beardless, almost child-like face. His frame was slight and frail, giving him a boyish appearance and giving others the impression that he was too young, too small, and too weak a man for such a big job as was being thrust upon him.

Unlike the old U.S. Constitution, the Confederate Constitution extended the terms of the president and vice president to six years, but it forbade them to succeed themselves.

Today, the name Jefferson Davis produces, as it did then, mixed reactions.

Some of the terms used by his contemporaries in describing him included *aloof, arrogant, cold, conceited, disdainful, egotistical, hypocritical, narrow-minded, obstinate, vain,* and *vindictive.* On the other hand, others who encountered him used such terms as *attentive, cordial, gentlemanly, patient,* and *polite.* The irony is that he was all of these characteristics.

Jefferson Davis, President of the Confederate States of America (Library of Congress).

At least part of the cause of Davis's perceived inability to get along with people was his multiple health problems. He always seemed to be in fragile health. He had had malaria (the same disease that had killed his first wife in 1835), and it recurred regularly, causing him severe discomfort. He was virtually blind in his left eye. He might have suffered from neuralgia, which nauseated him and caused intense pain. He also had various digestive ailments (possibly including acid reflux or a stomach ulcer) that bothered him repeatedly. He lost his appetite, often did not eat, and deteriorated physically during the war.[1] No doubt the normal stress of such a responsible position, to say nothing of the added stresses of leading a nation at war, complicated his health issues. These perpetual difficulties undoubtedly contributed to his peevishness.

The convention delegates wrote and adopted in March 1861 a constitution that was for the most part identical to that of the U.S. Constitution. (See Appendix A.) It set up a national government with legislative, executive, and judicial branches. It did, however, have several important differences.

- The president was limited to one six-year term, and he could not succeed himself.
- Cabinet members had seats in the Senate and could enter into floor debate, although they could not vote.
- The Confederate Congress could not issue bounties, levy a protective tariff (long a bone of contention between the North and the South), or

appropriate funds for any internal improvements (another major factor in the regional divisiveness).
- A two-thirds vote by both houses of the national legislature was required for the admission of any new states to the Confederacy.
- Congress could make no appropriations that the department heads, through the president, had not requested.
- The president had the power to use a line-item veto whereby he could reject single items in appropriations bills or write in a substitute, or alternate, amount.
- Although the new Constitution protected the institution of slavery, it forbade the slave trade.

To assist the president, Congress authorized the following six departments to make up his cabinet: the State Department, the Treasury Department, the War Department, the Navy Department, the Post Office Department, and the Justice Department. The president had power to appoint the heads (secretaries) of these departments, but Congress had to confirm them. (Details about each of these departments and biographical sketches of their respective secretaries are presented in subsequent chapters.)

As has already been stated, the Constitution set up, in addition to the executive branch and its various cabinet departments, a congress with legislative authority. The judicial system left in place the respective state courts and added several circuit courts. It also provided for a supreme court, but none was ever formally organized. Therefore, rulings by the various attorneys general, the heads of the Confederate justice department, served as the final authority in the absence of a supreme court.

The Confederate Constitution represented what George Rable called "a paradox."[2] It sought to protect the states' sovereignty and rights while also creating a central government that was strong enough to protect the nation during a war. The Constitution's authors, like the Founders of the American republic, feared strong government and unlimited power, and they sought to protect against corruption and concentrations of governmental power. They also sought to avoid needless pork-barrel spending. These factors affected their outlook toward taxes, government spending (especially internal improvements), checks and balances, and executive authority.

The Constitution gave the new nation a comparatively strong president. The drafters of the Confederate Constitution also sought to remove the president from political party influence and pressure. The president, the founders believed, should be a leader of support for Southern independence, not the leader of a particular political party. This absence of party spirit actually was the desire of George Washington, and he had warned about allowing partisan political influences ("factions," he called them) to infect the new republic after he left office. But political parties had, indeed, swept the spirit of unity from the government long before the issues of the internal improvements, the protective tariff, or slavery entered the picture. The founders of the Confederacy again sought to restore the spirit of nonpartisanship to government.

One of Davis's first priorities as president of the Confederacy was to select people to fill each of the six cabinet-level positions in the government. Although the men he chose have been heavily criticized for their many and various failings (if those men have not indeed been virtually forgotten), most of them actually were capable men and, under the circumstances, comprised as good a cabinet as was possible. As subsequent chapters will demonstrate, they were never "mere political hacks."[3]

CHAPTER 1

# Jefferson Davis's Selection of a Cabinet

Jefferson Davis claimed that his nominations for cabinet positions were based on "considerations of the public welfare only."[1] He claimed to have had friendships with none of his nominees before he named them to cabinet positions; he had never even met two of them.

In *A Short History of the Confederate States of America*, Davis had relatively little to say about his individual cabinet members. He failed to mention at all four of his nominees—Hunter, Trenholm, Watts, and George Davis. In his larger *Rise and Fall of the Confederate Government*, he devoted only one short chapter (and that only three pages long, and one page of which was a collage of photos of the six original cabinet members) to the selection of his cabinet.[2] Surprisingly, considering that Davis ultimately named Judah Benjamin to three different cabinet posts during the existence of the government, Davis mentions Benjamin only as having been nominated to the cabinet (along with the names of the other nominees and their departments) and as having departed from the Davis party shortly before Davis's capture by Union forces. He mentions Memminger only in the list of his nominees. He mentions Reagan only as accompanying him in his flight from Richmond near the end of the war. He mentions Randolph and Mallory only in connection with the evacuation of Norfolk. He also notes that Mallory pushed for completion of the ironclads *Louisiana* and *Mississippi* in New Orleans before that city fell. The name that Davis mentioned most often in the book is that of Breckinridge, but all of the instances are in relation to his military service, not to his short time as secretary of war.

This conspicuous lack of apparent interest in his supposedly most trusted advisors seems to indicate a man who was self-centered and egotistical. Davis was known as a hands-on micromanager of every detail. Historian William Davis wrote that Jefferson Davis had a "penchant for doing everything for himself."[3] He could not delegate, or, once he did delegate, he could (or would) not leave that person free to do the required work.

Only two of Davis's 17 cabinet officers wrote memoirs of note. Few biographers have written accounts of the individual cabinet members and their work. Only three major works have been written on the cabinet collectively—Curry, *Civil History of the Government of the Confederate States* (1901); Hendrick, *Statesmen of the Lost Cause* (1939); and Patrick, *Jefferson Davis and His Cabinet* (1944).

Davis began thinking of possible cabinet nominees shortly after his election. He obviously had thought about it a lot, but apparently he kept his thoughts to himself. Speculation and rumors abounded as people wondered who his selections would be. A flood of names were recommended to him as possible nominees. William Lowndes Yancey of Alabama and Howell Cobb of Georgia were frequently mentioned. Other names included Georgia U.S. representative Francis S. Bartow, Georgia Supreme Court justice Henry Benning, journalist and former ambassador John Forsythe, South Carolina Senator James Henry Hammond, Mississippi Senator John Hemphill, ambassador Henry Jackson of Georgia, Georgia governor Herschell Johnson, South Carolina U.S. representative Laurence Keitt, South Carolina U.S. representative Porcher Miles, Mississippi Senator Robert Walker, and Texas Senator Louis Wigfall.

Although ambitious men clamored after positions in the new government, and although Davis was inundated by office-seekers, many of the men he preferred did not want positions. Some of them actually turned down his offers of high office. One man even rejected his approaches three times before finally submitting to entreaties by Davis and numerous friends whom Davis had solicited to convince the desired nominee. Once several of the original secretaries were in office, however, many of them changed their minds and resigned. Others resigned after intense public (especially congressional) criticism. Still others resigned because of their frustrations in trying to work with Davis.

Davis had no political debts to consider in selecting cabinet secretaries. Curry said that "the absence of cliques and personal rivalries and party claims, enabled the President to look only to capacity."[4] Davis had no friends to reward with an office. He had no enemies that he sought to punish by preventing their gaining office. He merely wanted men who had both character and conviction.[5] Therefore, "this executive duty, with ... suggestions of innumerable persons with varying degrees of fitness, causing much sectional and personal disappointment and ill feeling, was discharged with ease and to general satisfaction."[6]

## 1. Jefferson Davis's Selection of a Cabinet 13

Although Davis claimed to have no political motives for his cabinet nominees and based them on only the needs of the public, he actually did have several political considerations. Historian George Rable showed that Davis at the same time tended to lean toward Democrats and secessionists (although he judiciously avoided rabid secessionists) as he considered people for his cabinet.[7] Another of Davis's considerations was the felt need to ensure that each of the original six states that made up the Confederacy be represented on the cabinet. That consideration was designed to placate the states, prevent jealousies, and ensure broad support for the administration. Nine of the 11 states that ultimately made up the Confederacy had representatives in the Cabinet at some point during the life of the Confederacy. Only Tennessee and Arkansas never were represented in the cabinet. In striving for a broad state representation in his cabinet, Davis was looking to the need of the Confederacy to present a civil, orderly, and legitimate face to the nations of the world from whom the new government sought economic intercourse, military aid, and diplomatic recognition. Interestingly, the only one of the original seven states not represented in the original cabinet, Mississippi, was represented by Davis himself in the executive branch.

A third factor in the selection of cabinet members was Davis's desire to have the cabinet made up of moderates, not rabid secessionists. Consequently, Davis considered the economic and political factions of the South in making his selections. He also had to consider the former Whigs and the moderate Unionists. Therefore, he first sought men of ability. Then he wanted men who represented the various political factions and the individual states. He considered recommendations made by not only the various congressional delegations but also by private citizens. But sometimes his appointments went against what the state delegations or individuals had suggested.[8] Because of Davis's concern about state representation, Hendrick referred to Davis's selection process as having "a 'pork-barrel' basis."[9]

Although Davis sought to include only moderates in his cabinet, he was concerned about how the radical leaders of the secession movement would react when he passed over them in making his cabinet nominations. He was especially concerned about the reactions of Robert Barnwell Rhett and William Lowndes Yancey. Surprisingly, Davis did not personally seek input from any of the state delegations. Men who thought they should have been consulted but were not became resentful. Davis himself was a moderate, neither a fire-eater nor a Unionist, and his choices therefore likely reflected his own views. He realized that the best course lay in moderation, where most of the popular support was, not with either extreme.[10]

Davis had only a few personal interviews with individuals to whom he would offer cabinet posts. Instead, he preferred to send telegrams, especially if he was already familiar with a person's background. His first interview was with Yancey. But Yancey suggested instead that Davis consider Leroy Walker for secretary of war. As for himself, Yancey did not think that he could be part of a government that was controlled by moderates and conservatives and thought that it would limit his independence. He preferred, instead, to run for the Alabama state legislature.

Next, Davis met with Robert Barnwell Rhett, whom Davis wanted for the State Department. But Rhett, too, turned him down, saying that he was sick of politics. Rhett did, however, suggest Howell Cobb of Georgia and Christopher Memminger of South Carolina for cabinet posts.

Davis then conferred with Alexander Stephens, his vice president and a Georgian. Stephens discouraged any nomination for the Cobbs, but he lobbied Davis on behalf of Robert Toombs and Herschel Johnson. Toombs had just missed being elected president, so, although Davis and Toombs did not like each other, Davis felt obligated to offer Toombs a post as a way of smoothing any ruffled feathers and mending any broken fences. He offered him the post of secretary of state, but Toombs declined. Later, Davis approached Toombs with the offer again, but again Toombs declined. He viewed a place in the cabinet as meaningless flattery.[11] Yet, while refusing, he suggested that he was willing to take the position temporarily until someone else could be found. Davis took that as an acceptance and moved on to filling the next secretarial position in his cabinet.

Davis offered the Treasury Department to Christopher Memminger, and Memminger readily accepted. He offered the War Department to C.C. Clay, but Clay declined because of poor health.

Davis's cabinet—especially certain departments—had a high turnover rate. The composition of the cabinet was always changing. During the short life of the Confederate States of America, 17 people were at one time or another members of the executive's cabinet. Fourteen people filled six posts in four years. Davis had six different secretaries over the War Department alone. One nominee, Benjamin, served in three different departments—attorney general, secretary of war, and secretary of state. Ironically, two of the longest-serving cabinet members—John Reagan and Stephen Mallory—we know relatively little about because not as much has been written about them, and neither man kept especially detailed records or wrote about his experiences in the Confederate government. Only Mallory held one post, the Navy Department, the entire life of the government and only that position. (Reagan filled the postmaster general position for the life of the government, but he also served as acting secretary of the treasury during the last days of the war.)

## Characteristics of the Original Cabinet Members

A brief look at the characteristics of the various men who served in the cabinet is instructive.[12]

*Age*: The average age of a cabinet member was 48. The youngest was Reagan at 42. The oldest was Memminger at 58.

*Place of birth*: Three of the cabinet members were not born in the United States. Benjamin was born in the Danish West Indies (now the Virgin Islands); Memminger was born in Württemberg, Germany; and Mallory was born in Trinidad, British West Indies.

*Occupation*: Most (13) of the men who held cabinet positions were lawyers, including many of those who were politicians at the time Davis tapped them for his cabinet.

*Slavery*: All of them were, or had been, slave owners and plantation owners.

*Political experience*: All of the cabinet members were experienced in one or more aspects of state or national politics. One (Breckinridge) had been vice president of the United States. Another (Hunter) had been Speaker of the House of Representatives. Five had been members of the U.S. House. And six had been U.S. senators.

*Education*: Nine cabinet members were college graduates. Four of those who were not college graduates nonetheless had one or more years of college education.

*Religion*: All three of the great religions—Protestant, Catholic, and Jewish—were represented on the cabinet.

*Politics*: Both Democrats and former Whigs were on the cabinet. The one political commonality among the various original nominees was that they had all supported John C. Breckinridge in the 1860 presidential race. The followers of Stephen Douglas and Constitutional Unionist John Bell had no representative on the cabinet.

*Overall competence*: One must beware of judging the members of Davis's cabinet by modern-day expectations for officeholders. All of his cabinet members were, by that day's standard, well-educated and well-trained, and they were better prepared to lead by far than the average man.[13] This is not to say that they were all the best men available for their respective jobs, but they were men of proven ability.

*Social standing*: Few cabinet members were aristocrats. Reagan's father was a tanner, and Reagan himself had once been an overseer. Mallory had helped his mother run a boarding house for sailors in Key West, Florida. Memminger was the son of a German immigrant family and spent his early years in an orphanage in Charleston. Benjamin was the son of a small Jewish merchant. The only true aristocrats among the cabinet nominees were Hunter, Toombs, Walker, Randolph, Seddon, and Breckinridge. Randolph was the grandson of Thomas Jefferson.

Davis submitted his cabinet nominees—some of whom he had not even informed of their nomination—to Congress for confirmation. For the most part, Congress rubber stamped Davis's nominees, giving the president the benefit of the doubt and waiting to see how they performed in office before making any judgments about them.

Although Davis did not have to deal with political party pressures in his cabinet selections, he did have pressures applied to him during the selection process. From the time the Confederate government was founded, the provisional capital of Montgomery was awash with people seeking positions in the new government. They wrote letters to Davis. They visited him in person. If they were not seeking positions for themselves, they were pleading the case for others among their families and friends. Ever gracious, Davis felt that he must see or reply to each of them.

Davis made his original appointments with the same assumption that became his pattern, getting little or no counsel from others and presuming "that loyalty to the Confederate cause provided sufficient qualifications" for all positions.[14] This practice would in many instances cause Davis and the Confederacy untold trouble.

The absence of political parties led Davis to believe that every state should be represented in the cabinet. With six cabinet departments and six states in the original cabinet, this task seemed easy enough. Davis, of course, represented Mississippi, and Vice President Stephens represented Georgia. Robert Toombs of Georgia was selected for secretary of state. Stephen Mallory of Florida was tapped for secretary of the navy. Judah Benjamin of Louisiana was named attorney general. For secretary of war, Davis preferred Braxton Bragg, but, deferring to the principle of civilian control of the military, he chose Leroy Pope Walker of Alabama instead. John Reagan of Texas (Texas entered the Confederacy shortly after the Confederate Congress first met) got the nod for the Post Office Department. And Christopher Memminger of South Carolina became the secretary of the treasury. As other states joined the Confederacy, officials from those states got non-cabinet positions so that no state would feel slighted.

In an odd quirk of Southern political thinking, Congress established a Navy Department that was separate from the War Department rather than merely a subsection within the department. The nomination of Mallory as the navy secretary was the only original Davis appointee whose confirmation was delayed by Congress. The reason was that some congressmen doubted Mallory's commitment to secession. But Davis had good reasons for choosing him, and those qualifications will be covered in the chapter devoted to Mallory's life.[15] (Interestingly, Mallory was one of only two members of the original cabinet who stayed with Davis throughout the life of the Confederacy, John Reagan, the postmaster general, being the other long-termer.)

Former U.S. senator Judah Benjamin of Louisiana, Davis's choice for the post of attorney general, became a sort of jack of all trades for the Confederacy. He served as head of not only the justice department (for about nine months) but also the War Department (for about six months) and the State Department (for a little more than three years). His first post as attorney general, however, proved to be, for Benjamin, a "minor job [for a] major figure."[16]

For the Treasury Department, Davis acted on Barnwell's recommendation and named Christopher Memminger of South Carolina. Memminger had "a conservative but quick financial mind" and was "frugal."[17]

The State Department would be critical in the attempt to gain foreign diplomatic recognition of the fledgling Confederacy and to acquire legitimacy for conducting trade around the world. It would spearhead "King Cotton diplomacy." To head this important department, Davis actually wanted Robert Barnwell. But Barnwell declined. Davis turned instead to Robert Toombs, the former secretary of state for Georgia.

The sixth and final cabinet office was the Post Office Department. Davis named John Reagan to be postmaster general. As was mentioned earlier, Reagan was only one of two original cabinet nominees to remain in the position for which he was selected throughout the entire life of the Confederacy. He also did double duty as treasury secretary in the end.

Following the secession of Virginia, the Confederate government voted to move the national capital to Richmond. The fledgling government and its officials and clerks took along with them all of their baggage and the papers of the cabinet departments. The move was not only a huge logistical task but also a move that greatly influenced Confederate military strategy and decision making. The attention of the administration and the War Department was destined to be from that point focused on the Eastern Theater. The Western Theater was relegated almost to an afterthought, a "side show of the big show," as Sam Watkins termed it in *Co. Aytch*, his popular book about his war experiences there.[18]

If Davis thought that he was bombarded with office-seekers in Montgomery, it was as nothing compared with the deluge that hit him in Richmond. According to Rable, even otherwise dignified members of the Confederate Congress went about trying to get government positions for relatives and favorites.[19]

With Davis's original cabinet members in place, one might have expected that the president would devote his attention to providing general direction to the executive branch of the new government, laying out broad policies, and providing general oversight of each cabinet department while leaving the details of putting those policies into action in the hands of the respective department secretaries. Not Davis. He had to have his hand in everything, large and small.

Davis bogged himself down with insignificant paperwork on every imaginable topic that came in when he should have let clerks handle them.[20] He did not have to do that; he *chose* to do it. He simply could not bring himself to delegate. He was afraid that if he did, something might not be handled right. In short, he did not trust his secretaries enough and thought too highly of his own abilities.

This is not to say that he did not confer with his secretaries. He did. In fact, he met with individual secretaries practically every day and with the entire cabinet two or three times a week. Meetings of the full cabinet could last for as much as five hours, sometimes longer. The problem was that such meetings rarely saw anything accomplished. Josiah Gorgas, who was the chief of the Ordnance Bureau in the War Department, lamented that Davis was wasting precious time and energy in senseless talk and began to think that perhaps Davis was not up to the job. At the same time, he despaired of finding anyone better.[21]

Yet, Davis worked long hours and hard. He was, in the words of War Department clerk John Jones, "'indefatigable in his labors.'"[22] Most of his time and energy, as one might expect of a chief executive during wartime, was taken up with military matters. Early in the war, he was a frequent visitor on battlefields (e.g., in the waning minutes of First Manassas). He was sometimes even under fire. Because the protection of the capital was a paramount concern for Davis, he often rode over the Richmond defenses, inspecting them, so he knew those defenses well. McPherson concluded, "No other chief executive in American history exercised such hands-on influence in the shaping of military strategy."[23]

Davis's direct involvement in the other cabinet departments was much less. The main areas over which he exercised micromanagement dealt with military strategy and tactics, none of which was clearly defined, leaving it to himself to define. (More will be said of his definitions of the Confederate strategy and tactics in Chapter 12.) But some of the other secretaries, as well as their subordinates, complained of Davis's heavy-handed style of administration. For example, Joseph Jones of the Medical Department complained that Davis "placed too high an estimate upon his own individual military genius, and failed to grasp in all its bearings the problem of the terrible death struggle of the young nation."[24]

# 1. Jefferson Davis's Selection of a Cabinet

**Table 1. Cabinet Members of the Confederate States of America**

| DEPARTMENT | SECRETARY | STATE |
| --- | --- | --- |
| Justice | Judah P. Benjamin* | Louisiana |
|  | Thomas Bragg | North Carolina |
|  | Thomas Watts | Alabama |
|  | Wade Keyes, Jr. | Alabama |
|  | George Davis | North Carolina |
| Treasury | Christopher Memminger* | South Carolina |
|  | George Trenholm | South Carolina |
|  | John Reagan | Texas |
| War | Leroy Pope Walker* | Alabama |
|  | Judah P. Benjamin | Louisiana |
|  | George Randolph | Virginia |
|  | James Seddon | Virginia |
|  | John C. Breckinridge | Kentucky |
| Navy | Stephen Mallory* | Florida |
| Post Office | John Reagan* | Texas |
| State | Robert Toombs* | Georgia |
|  | Robert M.T. Hunter | Virginia |
|  | Judah P. Benjamin | Louisiana |

* Charter member of the cabinet

## Alexander Stephens

Although Alexander Stephens technically was not a member of Davis's formal cabinet, he, as the vice president, was potentially a major advisor to and influence upon the Davis administration. In fact, Stephens was selected by the Confederate Congress meeting in Montgomery to head the Committee to Organize the Executive Department. As such, he consulted Davis practically every day during the selection of the cabinet.[25] This position, and his subsequent words and actions after his falling out with Davis, warrant his inclusion—albeit brief—in this work.

Alexander Stephens, Vice President of the Confederate States of America (Library of Congress).

Stephens was born on February 11, 1812, near Crawfordville, Georgia. He became an orphan at age 14, and he and his brother Linton were sent to live with relatives. "Little Alec," as Stephens was called, like Davis, had numerous health problems and a "melancholic disposition."[26] He threw himself into his studies, however, and graduated from Franklin College in 1832. Two years later, he was admitted to the bar and began practicing law. As happens with many in his profession, he became interested in politics.

In 1836, Stephens was elected as a Whig to the Georgia state legislature, and he served in that capacity for the next seven years. During that time of political training, he became acquainted with Robert Toombs, and their friendship lasted as long as the two men lived. In 1843, Stephens was elected to the U.S. House of Representatives, and he continued in that position until 1859.

Stephens was an ardent advocate of states' rights and a defender of slavery, but, as a Whig, he also supported a federally funded national program of internal improvements. Upon the demise of the Whig Party, he reluctantly became a Democrat. In spite of his support of slavery and states' rights, however, he opposed secession, not because he did not think it was a state's right but because he did not think it was a wise move at that time. He thought that the best way for Southerners to defend their rights was from within the Union; secession was only a last resort, and, even then, a state should secede only in cooperation with other Southern states. He maintained that view until Georgia seceded in January 1861. His state selected him among nine others to be a delegate to the Provisional Confederate Congress in Montgomery. Because of his outspokenness in trying to preserve Southern rights within the Union, he was chosen vice president, which also meant that he would serve as president of the Senate.

It seems incongruous that Davis and Stephens would be serving together as president and vice president; they were different in so many ways. One was a wholehearted Democrat, and the other was a half-hearted Democrat who was formerly a wholehearted Whig. An attacker of Stephen Douglas and popular sovereignty was paired with a supporter of Douglas and his plan. Rabun asked the obvious question: Why should one expect these men to work together any better as president and vice president than they had before, when they were continually opposing each other?[27] Apparently, Congress thought that the two men *could* work together—or would be a check and balance to each other.

That assumption seemed to prove itself true in the first four months of the new government. During the cabinet-selection process, Davis consulted regularly with Stephens. Stephens was instrumental in getting Robert Toombs to accept the secretariat of the State Department. Davis also asked Stephens to work extensively in convincing other Southern states to join the original seven states in the Confederacy. And Davis turned to Stephens to lead a peace commission to Washington to negotiate the nonviolent transfer of forts in Charleston and Pensacola to Confederate hands. Acting on Stephens's advice, Davis named Robert E. Lee to strengthen the defenses along the Atlantic coast.

But somewhere along the way Stephens began to be disaffected with Davis, and the rift only grew with time. Stephens thought that the whole idea of a peace commission to Washington was futile, so he declined to accept the position. When Davis later asked him to go to Arkansas to convince that state to secede, he declined that assignment, too. Similarly, Davis asked him, upon the request of Virginia governor John Letcher, to go to Virginia on the same kind of mission. Stephens was finally prevailed upon by the cabinet members to go to Virginia. He came back with a treaty that made Virginia a member of the Confederacy.[28]

Stephens spoke often on behalf of the new government, encouraging unity and support for the government loans. And he prophesied military success as the reward for such national unity.[29] All seemed to be well between the two men, but then, once the war began in earnest, Davis became absorbed in its details and consulted Stephens less than before. Stephens, increasingly disgruntled, stayed away from Richmond more and more, and he was seldom around when Davis might have wanted his advice. But Rabun marks the point at which Davis and Stephens irrevocably split as early as the day the seat of government was moved from Montgomery to Richmond.[30] It was downhill from there. At first, it was not an open or active hostility but rather a passive, foreboding indifference. Feeling increasingly slighted and marginalized, Stephens began a gradual withdrawal from Davis. Granted, many of Stephens's periods of absence were legitimate, when he was away on government business. But during his absences, Davis was turning more and more to others—notably Judah Benjamin—for advice.

But Stephens, too, was being influenced by others, most notably Robert Toombs, whom Stephens greatly admired and respected; Georgia's governor Joseph Brown; and Stephens's brother Linton. Linton began the war as a lieutenant colonel in a Georgia regiment serving in northern Virginia, and all he seemed to write about in his letters to brother Alec were his complaints about the army's administration. The vice president's brother was always complaining fiercely about the leadership in the army.[31] According to Linton, nothing in the army was done right. Alec did not respond in agreement, but neither did he deny, dispute, or disprove the accusations.

Meanwhile, Toombs was becoming disaffected with Davis, who never seemed to accept or follow his advice. Toombs was especially disgruntled over what he perceived as Davis's bias in favor of West Pointers. He grumbled and groused to anyone who was willing to listen. And Stephens certainly did that.

Governor Brown tangled with Davis almost from the beginning. He never passed up a chance to criticize or hinder efforts of the administration.[32] He was especially sensitive to any action by the Davis government that threatened Georgia's rights. He insisted on handling his state's defense with Georgia's troops rather than surrendering them to Confederate command. He obstructed tax collection within the state. And he made sure that everyone, especially Linton and Alexander Stephens, knew it when he disagreed with the Davis government.

Two issues were particularly sensitive to Davis's opponents, especially to Brown and Stephens: conscription and the suspension of the writ of *habeas corpus*. (These issues are covered in greater detail in Chapter 2.) Stephens spoke against these measures but never did anything in his official capacity to stop them.

Eventually, Stephens's opposition to Davis became so pronounced and intense that his imagination ran wild. Always suspicious of Davis, he began to suspect Davis's motives, imagining him to be masterminding various conspiracies to keep the war going by avoiding any reasonable (to Stephens's mind) negotiated peace, by ensuring Lincoln's reelection, and even working to become a dictator. Meanwhile, the man who suspected a Davis-led conspiracy was, in fact, engaging in one himself. Governor Brown and the Stephens brothers orchestrated a well-planned public campaign against Davis. The governor fired the opening salvo by calling the Georgia legislature into special session during which he made a scathing speech against Davis. Linton Stephens introduced several resolutions in the Georgia House decrying the Confederate conscription acts and the suspension of *habeas corpus*. And then the vice president offered the coup de grace with a three-hour speech to the legislature essentially seconding his brother's resolutions.

A few Southern newspaper editors wrote that if Stephens could not support the administration, he should resign, following the example of Vice President John C. Calhoun when he disagreed with Andrew Jackson over the tariff and the Force Bill. Others supported Stephens, recalling Thomas Jefferson's open disagreements with John Adams. Overall, however, Stephens's attacks greatly influenced the public, which for many years after the war blamed Davis for the South's defeat. Only later was Davis's public image restored in the Lost Cause narrative.

Davis refused to respond in kind to Stephens. After trying in letters to resolve their dispute, Davis maintained a discreet public silence over the rift and dropped the dispute.[33] In a gesture of good will and showing a lack of animosity, Davis asked Stephens to be part of the Hampton Roads peace delegation. Stephens attended, but when the conference failed, he essentially complained, "I told you it wouldn't work." To the end of the war—and even after in his book *A Constitutional View of the Late War Between the States*—he blamed Davis for the South's decline and demise. Davis said nothing in response.

Both Davis and Stephens were arrested and imprisoned at the end of the war. Shortly after Stephens was released, the Georgia legislature elected him to the Senate, but the Radical Republicans refused to allow him to take the seat. He was, however, elected and seated as a U.S. representative in 1873 and served in that capacity until 1882, when he was elected governor. Only a little more than a hundred days into his term, however, he suddenly died.

## *The Confederate Civil Service*

Working under each department head appointed by Davis and confirmed by the Confederate Congress were large numbers of civilian employees ("civil servants") whose hiring was the responsibility of the individual department secretaries. Over the course of the war, more than 70,000 people worked in the Confederate Civil Service, the vast majority (57,124 of them) under the War Department.[34] In contrast, the State Department employed only about 30 civilians. The Treasury Department had multiple sub departments and had to hire numerous civilians as accountants, auditors, tax collectors, customs agents, and numerous other positions, amounting to a total of about 2,780 employees.

Once Jefferson Davis named his cabinet members and they were confirmed by Congress, each secretary had to organize his department from scratch. This task was perhaps easiest for John Reagan, the postmaster general. His first action was to write letters and send an emissary to officials in the U.S. Post Office who hailed from the South, offering them equivalent or higher positions in the Confederate postal system. Postal employees who were already working in Southern positions under the U.S. system simply continued their duties but for a different employer, the Confederacy.

The task was much harder, however, for all of the other department heads. They tried to make their task as easy as possible by adopting as much of the U.S. Constitution as they could. Where that was not possible, they adapted the new document to reflect their views. Many office holders in the Federal government left those posts and went south expecting to get the same, or better, positions in the Confederate government. Federal officeholders already in the South stayed in those positions but worked for a new employer.[35] The Confederate secretaries eagerly encouraged such new hires. But the task was especially hard for the secretary of war. For every soldier serving the Confederacy, dozens of civilian workers were required to support the armies.

All told, the Confederate Civil Service employment probably was, according to Van Riper, as high as 70,257. The largest department, as has been noted, was the War Department with 57,124. The Engineering Bureau and the Niter and Mining Bureau combined accounted for about 25,000 of that number. The department with the fewest civilian employees was the State Department, which employed less than 30. The Justice Department had 125, the Treasury Department 2,780, the Navy Department 1,016, and the Post Office Department 9,183.[36] The number of civilian employees in each department at first grew as the Confederate government got established and up and running, but as the war turned against the South and as Northern armies captured more Southern territory, the figures declined until the end of the war and the dissolution of the Confederate government.

Much of our information about the inner workings of the Confederate government, especially the cabinet departments and the bureaus operating under the departments, comes from diaries written by members of the Confederate Civil Service. Two of the most prominent first-hand accounts by such civil servants are *A Rebel War Clerk's Diary* by J. B. Jones and *Inside the Confederate Government* by Robert Garlick Hill Kean. These two primary sources will be quoted periodically throughout this work.

## *Preliminary Assessment of Davis's Cabinet*

Although the members of the Confederate cabinet were, as individuals, talented and capable men, they were not particularly effective. The cabinet really never worked well together as a team. Some of them did not stay in office long enough to be effective. Others, arguably, were not effective because they stayed too long. One cabinet member, Judah Benjamin, although effective enough, might have been even more effective had he found his niche and been allowed to stay there. He held three cabinet posts—attorney general, war, and state—during the four-year life of the Confederacy. Arguably the two most effective cabinet secretaries, Stephen Mallory and John Reagan, were the only two who remained in one department for the entire life of the government, thereby giving those two departments the requisite stability to function well.

Although all cabinet members had their respective strengths and weaknesses, one consistent theme throughout the workings of the entire cabinet, regardless of department or person, was the influence of President Jefferson Davis. He, too, had his strengths and weaknesses, but they were magnified in his interactions with the various cabinet members. Many of the cabinet members, especially those who served as secretary of war, concluded that they could not get along with Davis's constant interference and micromanagement and ultimately resigned. One consistent critic of Davis was Robert G. H. Kean, the head of the War Bureau within the War Department. Kean constantly complained about how Davis ran his departments with a tight rein, how he refused to delegate authority, especially military matters, and how he got bogged down in minutia.[37] He described Davis as a "very slow worker," and said that both Randolph and Seddon grumbled about their never-ending, tedious, and unproductive meetings with Davis when they were secretaries of war.[38]

Kean admitted Davis's honesty and patriotism but decried his lack of administrative ability and pure judgment when it came to appointing people to positions of responsibility. He especially hated how Davis had treated Walker, Randolph, and Seddon but catered to Benjamin. He rested his case on that latter complaint.[39] He complained that Davis was "fickle" in how he "dealt with the *honorable* men" who had worked for him in the War Department (referring to secretaries Randolph, Seddon, and Walker)—and categorized his acceptance of Benjamin as "the strongest fact against his good sense and capacity as a President I know."[40] Perhaps Kean's last two statements provide the foundation evidence for the inability of the cabinet to work together or to get along with Davis.

Part I

Justice Department

CHAPTER 2

# Overview

One of the least discussed aspects of the Confederate States of America is its justice system. Battles, troop movements, naval strategy, weapons and ordnance, and even mail delivery seem to be more compelling subjects than writs, lawsuits, and courtrooms. Yet, the justice system was as vital to the Confederacy's survival as any of these other aspects of its government.

The foundation of the whole legal system of the Confederacy was its constitution. It did not take the delegates of the Provisional Congress long to draft a constitution because they already had a near-perfect model to work from: the U.S. Constitution. And the men who drafted the Confederate version "exhibited the powers of the best minds the learning of juris-consults, the legislative experience of the members, and the convictions of what the history of the United States had shown to be weaknesses or failures of the old system."[1]

The drafting committee was composed of two delegates from each state of the Confederacy. The committee chairman was Robert Barnwell Rhett of South Carolina. The goal of the committee was "to devise a system which would stand the test of antagonism and result in the welfare of the people and the safeguarding of human rights."[2]

The committee presented its report to the full Provisional Congress on February 26, 1861. The document was debated briefly, and they were "frequent, sparkling, earnest, learned, [and] conducted in the best spirit."[3] The main goal was "reformation of the Union," and "many of the changes were verbal, introduced for clearness, to prevent ambiguity and to settle controversy."[4] The proposed constitution was adopted unanimously on March 11, 1861. It was then ratified by each state.

With a few minor changes (although the founders of the Confederacy did not think they were minor!), the delegates adopted the U.S. version almost *in toto*. After all, "the seceding States were not dissatisfied with the Constitution, but with its administration, and their avowed and manifest purpose was to restore its integrity and secure in the future its faithful adherence."[5] The only changes made "were explanatory of the well-known intent of the authors, remedial of the evils which had provoked secession, purgative of the vicious interpretations of selfish majorities, and to secure the accomplishment of the true ends of the Confederacy."[6]

The differences between the two constitutions were as follow.

## Article I

- Perhaps the most obvious difference was that the Confederate Constitution granted that "the principal officer in each of the Executive Departments" would have "a seat upon the floor of either House, with the privilege of discussing any measures appertaining to his department."
- The Confederate Constitution forbade appropriations for "any internal improvements intended to facilitate commerce; except for the purpose of furnishing lights, beacons, and buoys and other aids to navigation upon the coasts and the improvement of harbors and the removing of obstructions in river navigation."
- The Confederate Post Office was required to pay its expenses from its own revenues after a certain date (March 1, 1863).
- The importation of slaves was forbidden.
- The Confederate Constitution required a two-thirds vote of both houses of Congress for any appropriation of money from the Treasury, and the appropriations had to give the precise amount and the purpose for it.

## Article II

- The president and vice president of the Confederacy would each serve a six-year term and could not succeed themselves.
- The president could remove any cabinet member at his pleasure, but he had to report any removal to the Senate along with his reasons for terminating the person.
- No presidential appointee who was rejected by the Senate could be resubmitted during the ensuing recess.

## Article III

- There were no essential differences between the two constitutions on the third article, but it is discussed separately below.

## Article IV

- Protection was granted for a person's right to travel among the states with his property, including slaves.

### Article V
- Members of the Confederate Congress could propose amendments to the Constitution, and they would be considered in a convention called for the purpose.
- Amendments had to be ratified by a two-thirds vote of the state legislatures or a two-thirds vote of state conventions.

### Article VI
- All laws passed by the Provisional Congress would remain in force until "repealed or modified."

### Article VII
- The Confederate Constitution was to become effective upon ratification by five of the original Confederate states, upon which elections for president, vice president, and Congress would be held.
- The states that ratified the Confederate Constitution were specifically named.

The third article of the Confederate Constitution provided for a judiciary headed by an attorney general, who was a member of the president's cabinet. It gave the judiciary complete jurisdiction over the following areas: "(1) all cases affecting ambassadors, other public ministers and consuls; (2) all cases of admiralty and maritime jurisdiction; (3) controversies to which the Federal [i.e., Confederate] government shall be a property; (4) controversies between two or more states; and (5) between citizens claiming land under grants of different states."[7]

The judiciary recognized all existing state courts and state supreme courts as the foundation of the system. "Secession brought no changes in them, save for the temporary increase in jurisdiction during the interregnum between the two Federal judiciaries."[8] Congress eliminated the circuit courts and transferred their jurisdictions to the existing district courts. These courts still referred to and accepted in their proceedings the precedents established in the United States courts. The Constitution also provided for a national Supreme Court that "was to be composed of all of the district judges sitting annually at the seat of government [first Montgomery and later Richmond]."[9]

In addition to these major courts, the judiciary included a Court of Claims, under which was the Board of Sequestration Commissioners, the Court of Admiralty and Maritime Jurisdiction, the Territorial Courts of Arizona, and the Indian extraterritorial courts for the District of Tush-ca-hom-ma (the Choctaw, Chickasaw, and Indian Reserve west of the Chickasaws) and the District of Cha-lah-ki (the Creek, Seminole, Cherokee, Osage, Quapaw, Seneca, and Shawnee tribes). Over all of this system was the attorney general, and, under him, one assistant attorney general. The attorney general also was responsible for the works of the Patent Office, which was headed by the commissioner of patents; the Bureau of Public Printing, which was headed by a superintendent; and the Law Office, which was headed by a law clerk.

During the life of the Confederate States of America, four men served as attorney general, heading the Justice Department, and one as interim attorney general. These men are listed in Table 2.

Table 2. Attorneys General of the Confederacy

| Attorney General | Dates in Office | Opinions Written |
|---|---|---|
| Judah P. Benjamin | March 5, 1861–November 21, 1861 | 13 |
| Thomas Bragg | November 21, 1861–March 18, 1862 | 7 |
| Thomas Watts | March 19, 1862–October 1, 1863 | 99 |
| Wade Keyes, Jr. (interim) | October 2, 1863–January 1, 1864 | 24 |
| George Davis | January 2, 1864–end of Confederacy | 75 |

Each of the full-time attorneys general will be discussed later in separate chapters. Wade Keyes, the interim attorney general, served the shortest amount of time and will therefore be discussed in this overview of the Justice Department rather than in a separate chapter.

Although the Judiciary Act of 1861 provided for a supreme court (made up of the various district court judges from all of the Confederate states) and was included in the Constitution, the Confederacy never got around to organizing one. Attempts to organize the Court were repeatedly postponed and delayed. A bill for this purpose was passed by the Senate on March 19, 1862, but it never made it through the House. A similar bill was passed by the House in April 1862. Attorney General Watts strongly pleaded with Congress to pass a bill for organizing the court on January 1, 1863. And President Davis and various other members of his cabinet repeatedly urged the same action. The final attempt was made on March 14, 1865. But it never passed because it faced fierce opposition. In the absence of a supreme court, the Confederate attorney general became the de facto "supreme court," and his "opinions were the final legal authority for all federal officials."[10]

The key opponents of a supreme court were William Yancey of Alabama, Louis Wigfall of Texas, Robert Barnwell of South Carolina, and Henry Burnett of Kentucky. Their main objection seemed to be the Court's supremacy over the states' courts. Yancey claimed that the state courts were the backbone of the Confederacy; Wigfall said that he would never vote for a supreme court as long as the system gave that court appellate jurisdiction over the state courts.[11] Some congressmen opposed the court because they were afraid of who might be named to sit on it or who would exert the greatest influence over who its justices would be. Other opponents simply feared men of ambition. The general population was also apathetic about the establishment of a supreme court, so one could not expect their representatives to care about it. Another reason for the lack of interest in forming a supreme court was that most people simply were too preoccupied with the war and the activities of organizing and running the other departments of government engaged in waging that war.[12]

"In the absence of a Supreme Court, the Attorney General spoke for the Confederacy," Robbins explained.[13] Each of the five Confederate attorneys general issued formal, written advice to the Confederate president and his cabinet members or their aides at various times. The attorney general's office issued a total of 218 judicial opinions, which were recorded in the "Opinion Book" of the office (published 1950, Rembert Patrick, ed.). Most of those opinions were addressed to the secretary of war and the secretary of the treasury. Other large numbers of opinions were addressed to the president and the secretary of the navy. The Confederate courts also continued using and referring to precedents established in cases that had been heard before the United States courts.

General Robert E. Lee suggested that Congress institute, in addition to the civilian courts, "a series of permanent military courts to be composed of three high ranking officers chosen for eminent judicial attainments."[14] Congress approved the idea and established military courts-martial as follows: one for each corps; one for each geographical division; one for each cavalry division; and one for each of the states' home guard reserves.

## *Major Issues for the Confederate Courts*

The Confederate judicial system dealt with many different issues, just as the U.S. courts had done, but the three most important issues involved (1) *habeas corpus*, conscription, and exemptions from conscription; (2) impressments of military stores or equipment; and (3) contractual disputes. Also included were numerous disputes concerning the authority and limitations of the states' militia and home-guard troops.

### *Habeas Corpus* Cases

Many people thought that the war that was soon to break out between the states would be a relatively short affair, and they assumed that existing state militias and volunteers would more than supply the need for soldiers. Large numbers of men did volunteer, especially after Lincoln called for 75,000 Northerners to help him put down the "rebellion" of the seceding states. But it soon became obvious that the little rebellion was going to be much bigger and last much longer than most people had at first thought. Both sides would need large armies, and they would be needed for an extended length of time. Many of the volunteers soon tired of camp life, constant drilling, and military rigor and discipline, and they left as soon as their terms of enlistment were up or soon after they first tasted combat and found that it was not all glory but included a lot of gory. Both sides soon resorted to conscription, or the draft—forced military service.

The Confederate Congress passed the first conscription act on April 16, 1862. It stated that "every able-bodied white man between the ages of eighteen and thirty-five [was] subject to military service."[15] If anyone eligible for the draft could not or did not want to serve, he could hire a substitute. Five days after this conscription act was passed, Congress passed a supplemental exemption act that removed "Confederate and state officials as well as many engaged in professional and industrial pursuits" from the obligation to serve.[16]

A second conscription act was passed on September 27, 1862. It raised the upper age limit for conscription from 35 to 45. Later, a third conscription/exemption act was passed, further delineating who was and was not eligible for the draft. A December 28, 1863, act made hiring of substitutes illegal. Another act, passed January 5, 1864, abolished all exemptions for those who had hired substitutes earlier. And capping all of these laws was the suspension of the writ of *habeas corpus*. Much of the litigation coming before the Confederate court system involved these conscription and exemption laws and their interpretation and application to individuals.

Among the foremost opponents of conscription were Henry Foote, Jr., John Orr, Robert Toombs, and even Confederate vice president Alexander Stephens. These men were pitted against the primary supporters of conscription, which included Governor Joseph Brown, Barnwell Rhett, Louis Wigfall, and William Yancey. The majority in Congress, of course, believed the conscription acts to be constitutional, or they would not have passed them in the first place. The attorney general also ruled them to be constitutional. But it was in the courts that the greatest problems became evident. People gave little heed to the Confederate district courts, but they kept a close eye on what the state supreme courts did.[17]

The first court ruling on conscription came from Texas in the case of *Ex parte Coupland*. Upholding the constitutionality of the law, the Texas judges established the doctrine that how the government went about raising and maintaining its armies had essentially no limits.[18] It also ruled in 1864 that Congress had the right to draft someone who had already provided himself a substitute.[19]

The next major rulings came from the court of Georgia. In the appeals case *Jeffers v. Fair*, the court unanimously agreed "not to consider whether the conscription acts constituted a violation of the spirit of the Constitution," thereby upholding a lower court ruling denying a petitioner's *habeas corpus* request and implying that Congress had unlimited power in its raising of armies.[20] It also ruled that no offensive war on foreign soil could employ the militia and that the militia was not to be absorbed into the Confederate army.[21] That portion of the ruling held significant implications for the use of the Georgia militia by the Confederate army. It did, however, declare that the Confederate government could not require state officers to serve in the army. Furthermore, the court stated that exemption from the draft was a privilege, not a right, and therefore the legislature that granted an exemption could also revoke it at will.[22]

Two other cases involved individuals who had first volunteered but later hired substitutes, but then they were drafted after their discharge. In both of those cases, the court ruled that exemptions were conditional.

Alabama's court ruled in two cases to uphold the constitutionality of the conscription and exemption acts. It said that a state court and Confederate courts had concurrent jurisdiction when determining whether someone escaped the draft by obtaining a substitute and thereby had been discharged and also whether that discharge then exempted him from all other liability to serve.[23]

Virginia was a relative latecomer to the legal wrangling over conscription. Its court did not rule on the issue until January 1864, when it declared that Congress had the authority to raise armies, by force if necessary. However, Congress could not coerce state officers to serve in the military. The state government was the entity that determined whether officers were necessary to the functioning of the state government.

All of these cases mentioned heretofore were interpreted and upheld by the courts of Alabama, Georgia, Mississippi, and North Carolina, and they established precedents for future litigation. But nowhere was the argument about the constitutionality of the conscription and exemption laws greater than in North Carolina. That state had been lukewarm toward the Confederacy from the start, and it was the perfect battleground for controversy over these issues. Although more North Carolinians volunteered than the people of any other state, it enforced the conscription laws more strictly than the other states, and North Carolinians reacted fiercely against such coercion. The Appalachian counties in the western part of the state were especially noted during the war as havens for deserters and draft dodgers. Efforts to chase down such evaders led to intense violence and recrimination throughout the war.

Chief justice of the North Carolina Supreme Court R. M. Pearson seemed to signal that he was leaning contrary to earlier rulings that had upheld the constitutionality of conscription and exemption. In other of his rulings, he had released deserters who had been arrested by the militia, declaring that the state's executive lacked the authority to arrest deserters. Of 30 *habeas corpus* cases heard in North Carolina between the state's secession and June 22, 1863, 27 had been before Pearson. Word spread—inaccurately, as it turned out—that Pearson had ruled that the conscription acts were unconstitutional. The assistant secretary of war, John Campbell, wrote to a military official, "'The decision ... is not regarded by the Department as a sound exposition of the act of Congress and you will not regard it in your official action as such.'"[24] Furthermore, Secretary of War James Seddon wrote to North Carolina governor Zebulon Vance asking him to hold back what he considered an overeager contrary involvement of the North Carolina judicial officials in cases of military service.

These entreaties had no effect on Pearson. He reaffirmed his opinions from earlier cases and declared that the conscription act did not include substitutes. He retorted that the Constitution had not given the secretary of war authority as a judge and that Congress had no power to make the secretary a judge. These issues, he said, were matters for the courts—and only the courts—to decide. Who could or could not be conscripted and who could and could not be exempted were decisions for the courts.

As the disagreement between the state and the Confederate authorities intensified, the case of Edward S. Walton came before the court. Walton had requested a writ of *habeas corpus* because he had obtained a substitute and was therefore exempt from conscription. The Confederate government, however, said that he was not exempt and had tried to draft him. After hearing the case, Pearson declared the conscription and exemption acts to be void because they violated a contract. He ordered Walton released from conscription and asked that the case be reviewed by a higher court. This case prompted President Davis to ask Congress for the power to suspend the right of *habeas corpus*. When the Walton case was heard on appeal, Pearson's ruling was reversed, and both acts were declared to be constitutional.

## Impressment Cases

The first impressment act was passed on March 26, 1863, and granted authority to seize goods for military use. A second impressment act was passed the following year. Although these acts were widely unpopular, they led to only three court cases, all of them in Georgia. In two cases, the acts were declared constitutional, but the way that the particular cases were handled was determined to be illegal because the plaintiffs had not been justly compensated. In the third case, the court ruled that there was no constitutional right to impress *structures*.

### Militia and Home Guard Cases

Several court cases resulted from disputes involving the state militia and the home guard troops. Some of the cases dealt with the liability or exemption from duty to serve in those organizations. These cases also revealed gross inconsistencies in the practices among the states regarding state officers and their liability to or exemption from the Confederate draft. Similarly, the various state courts sometimes cited other state courts' earlier decisions as precedent, but just as often the various decisions disagreed with each other. Nonetheless, by mid–1864, the states' courts had come to accept the power of the Confederate military.

During this evolution of legal opinion, the judicial system of the Confederacy made several adjustments. Perhaps the three most important were these: continuances were allowed in cases where lawyers were serving in the military, suing of soldiers for debts was forbidden during their time of service, and cases requiring a jury were suspended.[25]

Two attorneys general, Wade Keyes and George Davis, would not review the constitutionality of the various state laws because they believed that once a bill became law they could not rule on it. Keyes also thought that the power of the Court "to supersede state law was not unlimited," especially in contract disputes, as some people thought, thereby going along with the philosophical position of states' rights.[26]

Perhaps the best assessment of the Confederate judicial system was offered by Hamilton, when he stated, "The wonder is that so much uniformity of construction was finally attained and the Confederate government so generally upheld."[27] One could conclude that the various backgrounds and views of the large number of attorneys general only increase that wonder, as their respective biographical sketches in subsequent chapters might suggest.

## *The Patent Office*

Almost an afterthought in the attorney general's office was the matter of patents. The Confederate Congress authorized the filing and issue of patents on March 4, 1861. By August of that year, the rules and regulations for doing so were established, following closely, as most of the operations of the Confederate administrative branch did, the practices of the U.S. Patent Office. One difference, however, was that the Confederate patent office allowed foreigners to apply for and obtain patents—if their respective governments had granted the Confederate government diplomatic recognition.

When the Patent Office was organized, it was operated by "a chief clerk, two assistant examiners, two clerks and a messenger, as well as [its commissioner, Rufus R.] Rhodes."[28] Rhodes, a native Mississippian, had worked in the U.S. Patent Office before offering his services to his state and the new Confederacy.

Many of the records of the Patent Office were destroyed during the war, but enough facts are available to give one an idea of how the office operated and the kinds of inventions that the South considered. In the first partial year of its existence, the Patent Office received 304 applications for patents (fewer than other nations' patent offices received) and issued 57 patents. Many of those patents were for agricultural implements, "from hoes to a steam plow, textile machines, maritime and civil engineering implements."[29] But, according to Rhodes's 1861 annual report, the largest single category was for "'fire arms, or other destructive implements of war,'" including even a machine gun.[30] That category included patents for "cannon, cartridges and devices for making cartridges, fuses, breech-loading guns, submarines, torpedoes, camp cots, revolving pistols, swords, sabres [sic] and lances."[31]

Among the first patents the office issued was one for the submarine *H.L. Hunley*. The *Hunley* was completed and tested and became the first submarine to sink an enemy warship, although in so doing it suffered catastrophe itself, at the cost of its entire crew. (The *Hunley* was eventually recovered and is undergoing restoration in Charleston, South Carolina.) Other patents were issued for such notable inventions as a method of using photography to make maps (R.S. Sanxay and Adolph Gomert, 1864), a steam-powered gun (Charles Dickenson and Ross Winans), copper percussion caps for firearms (James C. Calhoun), electric torpedoes (Matthew F. Maury), and a "coal bomb" (Thomas E. Courtenay).

As the war dragged on and shortages resulted, many patents sought to provide substitutes for scarce items, including wooden-soled shoes, for which four patents were issued in 1863. As the wounded began to return home, several patents were issued for implements designed to make life easier for them, including many patents for prostheses.

Rhodes admitted that he was more lenient in granting patents than the U.S. Patent Office was. "Mindful of the maxim that 'it is better to err on the safe side,' I have, from the day the office was organized, acted upon the principle of giving the benefit of all doubt to the applicant."[32] Rhodes believed that Southerners were very creative. They should have the freedom to invent. He proposed to see results by having liberal patent policies. The South certainly needed all of the ingenuity and inventiveness its people could muster.

Perhaps the most notable controversy over patent rights during the Confederacy was that concerning who had rights to the design and engineering of the *Virginia*, the renovated former U.S.S. *Merrimack*. Those rights were claimed by both John M. Brooke, a Navy Department employee, and J.W.H. Porter, a ship's carpenter. In the end, Brooke got the patent in his own name.

Rhodes was the Patent Office's only commissioner, serving in that capacity throughout the war. The staff of the office remained small throughout its lifetime. The office began laying off employees, operating with a greatly reduced staff, late in 1864, but it continued to function right through to the end of the war. Many of its records were destroyed in the ruins of Richmond as the war neared its end. And after the war, when paper was scarce, many Patent Office documents were sold to be used as newsprint.

CHAPTER 3

# Judah P. Benjamin

President Jefferson Davis's choice for the Confederacy's first attorney general was a man who would fill more different cabinet posts than any other and one of only three of his original cabinet picks who would still be on the cabinet when the end of the Confederacy came. That man was both one of the most respected and one of the most vilified men in the Confederate government. He was Judah P. Benjamin.

Judah Benjamin was born August 6, 1811, to Jewish parents on the island of St. Croix, Virgin Islands. When he was two years old, the family moved to Wilmington, North Carolina. Four years later, they moved to Fayetteville, North Carolina, where they lived for five years. There he attended a common public school until the president of the Hebrew Orphan Society helped him get into the Fayette Academy, a private school. Later, his family moved to Charleston, South Carolina, where Benjamin spent his youth. He was intelligent and congenial.[1]

In 1825, when Benjamin was 14, he enrolled at Yale. Although he was

**Judah P. Benjamin, Attorney General (and later Secretary of War and Secretary of State) (Library of Congress).**

40

the youngest student there, he excelled, ranking near the top of his class. But he mysteriously and quickly left Yale. Later, a classmate suggested that his sudden departure might have had something to do with his fondness for gambling.[2] By the time he was 17, Benjamin had returned to the South and was living in New Orleans, where he was getting a fresh start. He got a job in a mercantile business and tutored students on the side while he was also studying French and the law. In 1832, he was admitted to the bar and began practicing.

Benjamin married Natalie St. Martin the following year, but it turned out to be a less-than-harmonious marriage. He was a Jew, but he was one purely by heritage, not by any intensity of belief or even depth of knowledge of the religion. He actually knew little of Old Testament Judaism and was not especially religious. His wife, on the other hand, was a devout Catholic. Furthermore, he was interested in "bookish" things, and they bored her easily. She became increasingly more interested in his money than in him, and she spent it freely and lavishly.[3]

By the time Benjamin reached his mid-twenties, he already had built a lucrative practice, had acquired quite a large fortune, and was considered a legal scholar. He had even published a book, a compendium of Louisiana superior court decisions. He also began a lifelong involvement in politics. He ran at age 30 for city alderman as a Whig, but he was defeated. The next year, however, he ran for the state legislature and won. In 1844, he was elected a delegate to the state constitutional convention, where he pushed hard for improved public education.

Meanwhile, he became part owner of Belle Chase, a sugar plantation, with its 140 slaves. He studied and learned the sugar industry so thoroughly that he was soon a nationally known expert on it. But his wife soon tired of plantation life, and, in the summer of 1845, she headed to Europe with her brother, daughter, and a black servant. With the exception of a brief return to Washington after Benjamin was elected to the U.S. Senate, she remained in Europe, seeing her husband only during his brief annual visits to Europe. In her absence, he brought his mother, sister, and a niece to live with him in a 20-room mansion he had built. He lost it all, however—plantation, wife, and much of his wealth—during the war.

Benjamin's interests also included railroads. He promoted Southern railroad expansion with the dream of uniting the North, the South, and the West by rail. In this sense, he had more in common with northeastern business interests than with his own planter class.

Despite Benjamin's intense involvement in railroad promotion and plantation operations, his interest in politics continued unabated. He began his political career as a Whig. He was defeated in his first political race, an attempt to become a city alderman, when he was 30. The next year, 1842, he was elected to the lower house of the Louisiana legislature, where he established a reputation as an orator. He then ran for and was elected to the state senate in 1851 and began to be mentioned as a likely candidate for the U.S. Senate. The legislature indeed elected him to the U.S. Senate in 1852, and he became the only Jew in the U.S. Senate that session and only the second one in the history of the Senate to that time. (The first Jewish senator was David Levy Yulee, a Democrat from Florida, who served from 1845 to 1851 and from 1855 to 1861.)

As the Whig Party imploded and declined, Benjamin moved closer to the views of the Democrats. He finally switched parties in 1856, when he was reelected to the Senate as a Democrat. It was in the Senate that he became acquainted with Jefferson Davis, then a senator for Mississippi. At one point, the relationship was anything but cordial. Benjamin thought that Davis had insulted him during one of Davis's floor speeches, and he wrote Davis a note challenging him to a duel. Davis, realizing how his speech had been taken and, being a proper gentleman, tore up the note and offered an immediate and public apology, and the episode was over. The men became friends thereafter. This bond might have been part of the reason Davis retained Benjamin in his cabinet, even if it meant moving him from one position to another.

Physically, Judah Benjamin was a big man. His heavy frame seemed ready to burst from his clothes. He combed his dark hair neatly, unlike the slightly disheveled appearance of some of his colleagues. His beard was modest but neatly trimmed, and he had no moustache. On his mouth was the perpetual hint of a smile that made some people suspicious and prompted other people to wonder what he saw or knew that others around him did not.

Both personally and politically, Benjamin was an enigma. Meade referred to him variously as "a subtle and often highly complex character," "the only genius in the Confederate cabinet," and "the most incomprehensible of all the Confederate leaders."[4] Yet, his influence over Jefferson Davis was greater than that of any other cabinet member. He was quiet, never entered into confidences, and seldom revealed his thoughts to anyone. His conversations were never about himself, and from that reticence one might conclude that he had no past. He lived in "an inner sanctuary," and "that made the world suspicious, critical, even at times denunciatory."[5]

Benjamin was skilled at hiding things.[6] His tendency toward secrecy concerning himself extended even after the war in that he had been careful not to leave a paper record behind. He habitually burned documents and correspondence. Once he had read a letter, he destroyed it. As he neared the end of his life, he became obsessed with tracking down any of his correspondence and burning it.[7]

Benjamin had no strong beliefs regarding secession or Southern independence. In fact, Mapp points out that one day in 1860, Benjamin was "opposed to secession except as a last resort," but only three days later, he opined that trying to stay in the Union was hopeless.[8] Louisiana seceded on January 26, 1861, and Benjamin resigned from the Senate on February 4, 1861. During the war, he seemed more willing to abandon slavery and to arm the slaves and to support taking both actions more quickly than did other Southern leaders. His critics seemed to sense what they interpreted to be a noncommittal attitude toward the Southern cause. "With him nothing went deep."[9]

But to his credit, Benjamin was a hard worker, putting in longer hours than anyone who worked for him, but he also seemed adept at employing the strategy of "work smarter, not harder," for he never seemed to tire and was never in a hurry. A Charleston paper wrote that "[Benjamin] dispatches more business in one hour than most men could accomplish in a day."[10] Varina Davis once asked him how he always remained calm, unruffled, and energetic when all around him were agitated and fatigued. He replied that he always carried with him a little snack, and when he began to feel tired and stressed, he would eat that and be refreshed.

Although Benjamin was an eternal optimist, he saw and accepted realities. Perhaps his reputation for hard work and optimism came from the fact that when he had a job to do, he spared no effort to accomplish it, but, once it was achieved, he did not waste time enjoying the success but rather got busy with something else. If he failed in the task, he wasted no time feeling sorry for himself or wondering why he had failed. He just moved on to another task.[11]

Benjamin studied Davis carefully, flattered him, knew (and took advantage of) his likes and dislikes, and deferred to him. As a result, he clearly was closer to Davis than was any other cabinet member. Yet, he was not a yes man. He sometimes disagreed with Davis, but if the president overruled him or decided on a different route than Benjamin preferred, he did not pout or get angry.[12] Perhaps that was why others criticized Davis behind his back, undermined his policies, or resigned whereas Benjamin remained on good terms with Davis and was trusted and relied on by the president.

Benjamin was first nominated to be attorney general. After all, he was an immensely successfully attorney and was familiar with the courts. He had published a book on superior court decisions in Louisiana in his twenties, and he was widely considered to be a legal scholar. He also had gained experience arguing cases before the U.S. Supreme Court. He was intelligent and well educated, "beyond most of his time."[13]

Benjamin was a jack-of-all-trades, and he served in Davis's cabinet as not only the attorney general—the original position for which he was chosen—

but also later as secretary of war and secretary of state. Patrick referred to him as "the brains of the Confederacy."[14] Curry lauded Benjamin's speaking prowess, saying that he was "in the foremost rank of the parliamentary orators of [the] time."[15] Moreover, Curry continued, Benjamin had "the versatility of a self-originating intellect, a retentive memory, command of immense resources, strongest conviction of the rightfulness of the Confederate cause, [and] he managed matters committed to his hands, when the house was tumbling about his ears, with a cheerful courage and hopefulness that made him a wonder and a stimulating example in times of adversity and peril."[16]

Perhaps it was because of all these admirable qualities that many people, including Jefferson Davis, admired Benjamin. Mary Chesnut, who was never reluctant to confide her deepest feelings about the subjects of her journal writing, said of Benjamin, "Everything [he] said we listened to, bore in mind, and gave heed to it diligently."[17]

But not everyone felt that way toward Benjamin. To some people, he was a symbol of all that was wrong with the Confederacy. Many such people were in the Confederate military and developed their opinion of Benjamin while he was secretary of war.

For example, Robert G. H. Kean did not say that Benjamin was foolish but rather that he was "the least *wise*" of the cabinet members.[18] Kean, who later worked under Benjamin in the War Department as head of the War Bureau, declared that Benjamin was reluctant to accept the position of secretary of war and finally took it only on the condition that Davis handle all military matters.[19] Davis was only too willing to indulge his request. Kean, along with many others, believed that Davis heeded Benjamin's advice more than that of any other cabinet member, but no one else seemed to trust Benjamin.[20]

Overall, Benjamin was an unpopular secretary of war. People of both the North and the South tended to distrust Benjamin. Part of the reason was his Jewishness.[21] Many people had a racial bias against the man because he was Jewish. Relatively few Jews lived in the United States at the time; people knew little about Judaism as it was practiced, only what they read in the Bible; and people naturally tend to be suspicious of the unknown. He also sent mixed signals on various issues. His opponents said that he could argue whichever side of an issue paid him, "with serene indifference to the right and wrong of it."[22]

Benjamin did not seem to help people get to know him either. He "kept his personal life and views somewhat hidden."[23,24] Whenever his detractors and critics disparaged him and let their prejudices show, "he almost never answered, but simply retained what observers called 'a perpetual smile.'"[25]

Benjamin was not even the overwhelming favorite of the Louisiana legislature when it elected him to the U.S. Senate. When his term in the Senate was nearing its end and he faced reelection, the legislature had to cast 40 votes before the majority agreed to reelect him—and then by only one vote.

In the Senate, Benjamin spoke on the issue of popular sovereignty and opposed secession except as a last resort. Just three days after publicly opposing secession, however, on December 11 [, 1860], he had changed his mind and argued the opposite.[26] Louisiana seceded on January 26, 1861. Benjamin resigned the U.S. Senate on February 4.

Shortly after Jefferson Davis was inaugurated as president, he nominated Benjamin to be the Confederacy's first attorney general. Benjamin was not Davis's first choice for the office, but Davis liked Benjamin's "pleasing manner, … methodical habits, promptness, and attention to his duties."[27] Benjamin accepted the post, choosing "obscurity," because he thought "he could best serve the South by serving Davis and remaining in the presidential shadow."[28] The Congress confirmed him unanimously on March 5, 1861, but fellow cabinet members were not so congenial. They ridiculed him for predicting a long war and for recommending that immediate preparations be made for such a war. He also rankled them because he opposed moving the seat of government from Montgomery to Richmond. But he worked hard on this own departmental responsibilities, and within a month, he had the Justice Department organized and all judges in place. He was certainly not a "yes man"; he realized how the president and his secretaries should interrelate. And he became known for his "singular frankness and directness."[29] The president did not always agree with him, but whenever Davis overruled him or chose to disregard his advice, Benjamin did not pout or respond in anger.

Love and admire or despise and detest him, one could not ignore Benjamin. Serving in three cabinet positions and having the ear and confidence of the President, Judah Benjamin's fingerprints were all over the Confederate government. Regardless of what one thought of Benjamin's views on politics or religion or how one liked or disliked his personality, one had to concede that he was a hard worker. He was always busy and was good at it, getting much accomplished.[30] Varina Davis, the President's wife, reported that Benjamin typically spent about 12 hours a day with her husband, always working on government matters, and not only dealing with matters of his particular department but also offering general advice. He was "capable of enormous labor," and "went right at a job and finished it."[31] He operated by system and was an able administrator. Furthermore, "he knew how to handle men. He watched character perpetually, studied the motives of others, their wants, their weaknesses, knew how to adapt himself to them."[32]

But a man of such "energy and versatility" as Benjamin was too big for the office of attorney general.[33] He became bored. He yearned to be in a position where he could make positive contributions rather than merely being a lightning rod for Davis's critics. And Davis was eager to have him serve; he respected Benjamin's judgment enough not to want to lose him. So when Leroy Pope Walker's health failed and Walker temporarily stepped down as secretary of war on September 17, 1861, Davis appointed Benjamin to be acting secretary. He was nominated to the full post as secretary of war in March 1862. But that is a story for a later chapter.

CHAPTER 4

# Thomas Bragg

Judah Benjamin was succeeded as attorney general by Thomas Bragg. Bragg was born in Warrenton in Warren County, North Carolina, on November 9, 1810. Thomas was one of six sons born into the family. A brother destined to become more famous than Thomas was Braxton, who later became a leading Confederate general.

As a youth, Thomas attended school at the Warrenton Academy. He later attended and graduated from Captain Partridge's American Scientific & Military Academy (now known as Norwich University). Afterward, he studied law, being taught by John Hall, an associate justice on the North Carolina Supreme Court. He passed his bar examination and was admitted to the bar in 1833 at the age of 23. He then opened a law office in Jackson, North Carolina, and soon became quite successful.

Bragg struggled to get his political career in motion because he was a Democrat in a Whig-dominated district. Although he was elected to the state legislature in 1842,

**Thomas Bragg, Attorney General (North Carolina Museum of History / Public Domain).**

he served only that one term because he was defeated in his bid for reelection. He returned to law and served as the Northampton County prosecuting attorney. During the 1840s, he became increasingly more involved in party politics, serving as a delegate at the national Democratic conventions of 1844, 1848, and 1852, and gradually made a name for himself as he became more prominent.

In 1854, he ran for governor of North Carolina against Alfred Dockery and won by a margin of only a little more than 1,400 votes out of more than 94,700 votes cast. He ran for reelection in 1856 and won handily against John Gilmer, the candidate of a weak and dying Whig Party. Bragg's two terms as governor were characterized by a combination of Whig and Democratic issues. The requirement that one own land to vote was reduced (manhood suffrage), and most of the new voters supported the Democrats. Bragg promoted internal improvements, especially railroads, and improvements to the state banking system.

Physically, Bragg was a quiet, simple, and unpretentious man.[1] As for his social character, he refused to kowtow to his superiors or to be rude to his subordinates, and he did not venture into matters that were outside his area of authority or expertise.[2] He had a strong, logical mind, and the advice he offered tended to be conservative and predictable.[3]

In North Carolina, as was the case throughout the other Southern states, the issue of state's rights and the prospect of secession kept the times uncertain. Bragg was a strong believer in state's rights, but he was cool toward secession. Although he believed that states had a right to secede if they thought it was necessary, he did not think it was necessary. He "saw no future success in leaving the Union."[4]

In 1859, the North Carolina legislature elected Bragg to the U.S. Senate. He was assigned to chair the Committee on Claims. The key issue, however, continued to be whether the Southern states should secede. Bragg made few public statements on the issue but privately expressed his opinion that secession would be a mistake. When the issue finally came to a head, he reluctantly supported secession.[5] When North Carolina voted, against Bragg's advice, to leave the Union, he, like many other Southern statesmen, stood by his state. Only this sense of honor compelled him to resign from the Senate in 1861 and side with his state when it seceded.[6] "'I will stand by the old State,'" he said, adding prophetically, "'and if the worst shall ultimately come, as I very much fear, I will go down with her, and when all is over I will do what I can to save what is left of her.'"[7]

A few months after Bragg got back to North Carolina, he was notified that Confederate president Jefferson Davis had nominated him to replace Judah Benjamin as attorney general. His duties began on November 19, 1861.

As attorney general, the opinions that he wrote were not as clear as those of either his predecessors or his successors. He was not a master of language or as good a writer as they were, but he was a strict constructionist who interpreted congressional laws literally and legalistically.[8]

Bragg wrote only one report to inform the Administration and Congress. It was only six pages long and was a general accounting of the work that had been done by the Justice Department. It included an impassioned plea that a Supreme Court be organized as the Constitution stipulated. Although Davis agreed with Bragg on the need for the Supreme Court, Congress did nothing to establish it.

Although Kean states that Davis had in Bragg one of his most loyal supporters in North Carolina, Bragg did not like what he found on Jefferson Davis's cabinet.[9] It "was fraught with political bickering."[10] Davis seldom consulted him. Bragg quickly discovered that although the Confederate Congress had no formal political parties, it was divided into distinct informal factions, each made up of ambitious and disgruntled men.[11] As a "strict legalist," he pushed repeatedly but unsuccessfully for the organization of a supreme court and against impressments.[12] And he presciently saw the Southern troops' lagging morale and civilian apathy growing long before Gettysburg. He soon had had enough. He resigned on March 18, 1862, having served only about five months. Precisely why he retired is unknown, but it does not take a great imagination to think of several good reasons.

As was the case with many leaders, both military and political, who cast their lot with the Confederacy, Bragg's life was nearly ruined by the war. He was nearly bankrupt by the end of the war. But he worked to get his legal practice back on track and "earned a reputation as a strong defender of constitutional law and personal liberty."[13] He also opposed the rising peace movement in North Carolina during the rest of the war and tried to moderate many of the ongoing disagreements between Davis and Governor Zebulon Vance.

In 1868, when the North Carolina Constitution was being rewritten to comply with the Radical Republicans' requirements for the state to be readmitted to the Union, Bragg opposed some of the changes being made. He was elected chairman of the North Carolina Democratic Party in 1870. He and the Conservatives did not like having the Radicals dictate to them. They particularly objected to many of the actions of Governor William Woods Holden, President Andrew Johnson's temporary appointee as governor. Holden ran for a full term in 1868 and won in an election in which all former Confederate leaders were barred from voting. In 1871, Holden was impeached, and a team of lawyers made up of Bragg, William Ham, and Augustus Merrimon was hired to prosecute him. Holden was the first governor ever to be impeached, convicted, and removed from office (although not the first to be impeached and convicted).

Bragg died at home less than a year later, on January 21, 1872.

CHAPTER 5

# Thomas Watts

Thomas Hill Watts, Jefferson Davis's nominee to succeed Thomas Bragg as attorney general, was not consulted about the job until after he had been nominated and then confirmed by the Confederate Senate. Davis just assumed that Watts would accept the position.

Watts was born on January 3, 1819, in Alabama Territory near the town of Greenville in Butler County. He was the oldest of 12 children in his family. Shortly before his birth, his parents had moved to Alabama from Georgia in search of richer farm lands.

Watts attended Airy Mount Academy in Dallas County before going to the University of Virginia to study law at his parents' expense but with the stipulation that in return he would have to forfeit all claim to the family fortune or estate. He graduated with honors in 1840, passed the bar, and opened a law office in Greenville. By 1848, his practice was prospering, and he moved it to Montgomery. He married twice and had ten children. He also owned extensive lands and 179 slaves in 1860.

Physically and socially, Watts

**Thomas Watts, Attorney General (Alabama Department of Archives and History).**

was attractive. He had "shiny black eyes and [a] perpetual smile."[1] He became known for his hospitality, especially for the luxurious and bountiful meals he served his guests.[2]

Meanwhile, Watts, a pro–Union Whig, ran successfully for the state legislature in 1842. He represented Butler County from 1843 to 1845. He was later elected to the state senate. The Whig Party, both locally and nationally, was dying, however, and like many other former Whigs, Watts linked up with the Know-Nothing Party.

The "Know-Nothing Party" was the nickname given to the American Party, which had its origins in the late 1840s and early 1850s. It began as a secretive group of American-born, white, Anglo-Saxon males who shared an aversion to immigrants, especially those who were Roman Catholics. The party proposed strict restrictions on immigration, exclusion of foreign-born people from voting or holding elective office, and high residency requirements for citizenship. The members of the party called themselves "Nativists," but because of their secretiveness, whenever anyone asked them about their party, they often responded, "I know nothing," giving cause for their nickname.

The American Party grew in popularity as the Whig Party declined. Many of the people leaving the Whig Party gravitated to the American Party. Although by 1855 the Know-Nothings had won elections (43 U.S. House members, five U.S. senators, and hundreds of state and local officials), they were not very successful at passing major legislation. So their effect on the big political picture of the period is doubtful.

In 1856, the first—and only—national convention of the American Party was held in Philadelphia. The delegates nominated as their candidate former president Millard Fillmore, but he finished a distant third behind John C. Fremont, the candidate of the fledgling Republican Party, and the winner, Democrat James Buchanan. After that election, the American Party declined rapidly, with antislavery members joining the Republican Party and proslavery members going over to the Democrats.

In 1850, Watts ran unsuccessfully for the U.S. Congress (as a Know-Nothing). During that campaign, however, he realized the popular appeal of the state's rights position, and he adopted a moderate position on the issue. (Historian William C. Davis, however, characterizes Watts as an "ultra" whose extremism approached that of Yancey.[3]) In the 1860 presidential campaign, Watts supported John Bell and the Constitutional Union Party. Although Watts favored secession if Lincoln was elected, he wanted Alabama to secede only in cooperation with other Southern states. On this position, he was elected a delegate to the Alabama secession convention and signed the secession ordnance. Following Alabama's formal secession, Watts raised the 17th Regiment of Alabama Infantry and served for a time as its colonel under the Confederate army.

Shortly thereafter, Jefferson Davis nominated him to replace Thomas Bragg as attorney general. He assumed that position on April 9, 1861. Because Bragg had already done most of the work of organizing the department, just about all Watts had to keep himself busy was to broadly supervise court proceedings and to keep track of the courts' account books. But he took his job seriously and insisted on knowing in detail about all claims.[4, 5]

The most important task of the Confederate attorneys general was the interpretation of various and sundry laws, and all of the attorneys general wrote opinions reflecting those interpretations. What distinguished Watts's opinions from those of his predecessors was that he cited precedents established earlier in the history of the U.S. courts. His opinions reflected a belief in a strict construction of the Confederate Constitution. As a strict constructionist, he believed that in the federal system of government the law had to be enforced. Precious experience gain from seeing what happened when the opposite path was followed taught him that the future of the Confederacy depended on the faithful execution of the law.[6] Perhaps his most controversial interpretation was his upholding of the Conscription Act of 1862, by which all white males aged 18 to 35 were liable for the draft.

Watts was concerned that his office ought to treat the citizens respectfully. Early on, he issued orders that for any of his subordinates to be uncivil to even the lowliest person would result in a demotion. He realized that everyone who was ill treated would become an instant critic of not only him personally and of his department but also of the entire Davis administration.[7]

In August 1863, Watts ran for governor of Alabama against John Gill Shorter, and Watts won. Consequently, he resigned as attorney general on October 1, 1863, to serve as his state's chief executive. As governor, he (like other Southern governors, notoriously Joseph Brown of Georgia and Zebulon Vance of North Carolina) struggled with the Confederate government over the centralization of power and the effort to maintain state's rights. Opposition to him in the state legislature, however, hindered his defense of Mobile. He fought the Confederate government especially hard over impressments and conscription of Alabama troops. Corrupt impressment officers and Confederate soldiers not infrequently stole or confiscated farm produce, livestock, or equipment and then sold it for a personal profit. Sometimes, frauds posed as impressment officers, paying with counterfeit certificates, thereby further soiling the already bad reputation of the real impressment agents. Although Watts had upheld the Conscription Act, he was continually at odds with the Confederate government over its drafting of Alabama troops.

The problem that bothered Watts most was Congress's failure to set up a Supreme Court. They never did, in spite of his and Davis's repeated frequent reminders of that responsibility. But the lack of the court seems not to have adversely affected the nation. If a state court ruled against the central government on a matter, the central government would abide by that decision within that state but do as it pleased in other states. When attorneys general ruled on a matter, the central government generally accepted that as the final say on the issue, so the attorney general's office was a *de facto* supreme court.

As the war turned more and more against the Confederacy, Watts struggled with the increasing sacrifices demanded by the state of its people, the resulting war weariness of the people, and the spreading lawlessness throughout the state. He had to fight not only the Union invaders but also Confederate deserters and domestic Unionists who periodically clashed with local secessionists.

Following Lee's surrender in April 1865, and as the war sputtered to a close, Union troops arrested Watts at Union Springs, Alabama, on May 1, 1865. He was briefly imprisoned and charged with treason. A few weeks later, they released him and took no further action on the charges. When he returned home to Montgomery, he discovered that Union troops had burned his cotton crop, and he had to sell much of his land to pay off debts.

As the U.S. Congress implemented Radical Reconstruction policies, Watts's resentment grew. He became a leading Democrat and fought against Congressional Reconstruction while practicing law. He died on September 16, 1892.

CHAPTER 6

# Wade Keyes, Jr.

Wade Keyes was born on his parents' estate in Mooresville, Alabama, on October 10, 1821. As was typical for children of wealthy Southerners of the time, he was educated by private tutors as a youth before attending first LaGrange College (now the University of North Alabama) and then the University of Virginia. Following his graduation, his parents arranged for him to take a grand tour of Europe before he moved to Lexington, Kentucky, to study law "with several noted Southern attorneys."[1]

In 1844, after completing those studies and being admitted to the bar, Keyes began practicing law in Tallahassee, Florida. He specialized in property cases. In 1851, he moved his practice to Montgomery, Alabama, and became known as a legal expert, authoring two books on the law in the mid–1850s. In 1853, he became chancellor of the Southern Division of Alabama, a position he held for the next six years.

Although Keyes had been elected chancellor and was a Democrat, he was not a politician. In fact, he avoided politics if he could. During his time as chancellor, he attracted the notice of Judah Benjamin, who was especially impressed by Keyes's "administrative abilities, legal intellect, and writing skills."[2]

As the sectional controversies of the period intensified, Keyes became a convinced secessionist. When Alabama seceded on January 11, 1861, Keyes volunteered for a combat role but was instead assigned a staff position in a Richmond office. Benjamin, whom President Davis had made attorney general of the Confederacy, recalled the impression Keyes had made on him when Keyes had been chancellor, and Benjamin named him the assistant attorney general on May 6, 1861. Keyes served faithfully in that position throughout the life of the Confederacy. (He also served briefly as interim attorney general between the end of Watts's tenure and that of George Davis.) He was so efficient that he actually did more of the daily tasks of an attorney general than Benjamin did and was practically the *de facto* attorney general. He has been called the "guiding force" of the Confederate Justice Department.³ For that reason, he is included in this discussion of the Confederate attorneys general.

Benjamin was soon replaced as attorney general by Thomas Bragg, but Keyes was retained. In fact, he served as attorney general *ad interim* from Benjamin's resignation on September 17, 1861, until Bragg officially took over the position on November 21, 1861. Bragg served until March 18, 1862, and Thomas Watts took over on that date and served until he was elected governor of Alabama, resigning as attorney general on October 1, 1863. Keyes again served as attorney general *ad interim* from that date until January 2, 1864, when George Davis became attorney general.

In summarizing the influence of Keyes on the Confederate Justice Department, Patrick noted that Keyes had worked under three attorneys general. Keyes saw what worked and what did not work, and, with the insights gained from that experience, he had developed into the stabilizing influence in the department.⁴

As assistant attorney general and during his times as attorney general *ad interim*, Keyes wrote 24 opinions for the government. In them, he cited U.S. laws as precedents. His opinions dealt with such issues as "the duties of the attorney general; the treatment of prisoners of war; and, drawing on his former area of expertise, the appropriation of personal property for the war effort."⁵ In his annual report to the president, submitted on November 18, 1863, Keyes complained that the courts of the Indian Territories still were not organized. He also noted the absence of penitentiaries in some states, proposed that convict labor somehow be used for the benefit of the Confederacy, emphasized difficulties in finding newspapers willing to print the text of laws passed (the primary reason being that the costs exceeded the payment allowed by law for that purpose), and noted the inadequacy of district court judges' salaries.⁶

Keyes was well-qualified to be attorney general. He had been second in ranking authority in the department from the beginning. He had served under three attorneys general and essentially had been doing most of the work anyway. He, as a trained legal scholar, was actually better qualified to write legal opinions than the secretaries themselves. And he had practical experience in the department's work, having filled in as acting secretary numerous times (two months in the fall of 1861, several weeks in December 1861, two months in the fall of 1862, during August 1863, and two months in 1864). But he is probably the least known of the generally unknown attorneys general.

After the war was over, Keyes returned to Florence, Alabama, where he resumed his legal practice. He died there on March 2, 1879.

CHAPTER 7

# George Davis

The Confederacy's last attorney general was George Davis (no relation to Confederate president Jefferson Davis). He was born at Porter's Neck, his father's New Hanover County Plantation near Wilmington, North Carolina, on March 1, 1820. He attended W. H. Harden's Pittsboro, N.C., school until he was 14 years old. He then enrolled in the University of North Carolina at Chapel Hill. He graduated in 1838, at age 18, as class valedictorian. He then studied law and was admitted to the bar in 1840. He specialized in corporate, maritime, equity, and criminal law and developed a reputation as a man who took great pains with his responsibilities and worked hard.[1] In 1842, Thomas married Mary Polk, and they had two children.

Although George Davis had definite, strongly held opinions, he was not "dogmatic" or "intolerant"; rather, as a "devout but unobtrusive Chris-

**George Davis, Attorney General (North Carolina Museum of History).**

tian, he was the soul of honor."[2] He came close to being the ideal Southern gentleman who "knew how to live graciously."[3]

Davis was selected to be a delegate to the Washington Peace Conference, which was conducted February 4–27, 1861. He was then elected a delegate to the Provisional Congress and afterwards to the Confederate Senate, where he served until 1864. Jefferson Davis nominated him to be attorney general in December 1863. The Senate confirmed him unanimously. He took office on January 2, 1864, and served until April 24, 1865.

George Davis was the only cabinet member never to have held political office before 1861 and the founding of the Confederacy. But he was politically active and followed Whig principles in spite of his district's overwhelming Democrat majority.[4] He was conservative and held to the belief that the Constitution limited federal authority despite his Whig political views, which included expansionism, supporting a national bank, and internal improvements funded by the taxpayers.[5] He missed being nominated for governor in 1848 by one vote.

Like Watts, Davis became a staunch Constitutional Unionist when the Whig party died. He spoke out against secession until Lincoln tried to force the seceded states back into the Union.[6] But he returned from the Washington Peace Conference fully convinced that if the Union were preserved, it would happen only by bringing reproach on the South.[7]

Davis was a Whig in a Democrat-dominated state, but he was elected a delegate to the Provisional Congress. The next year, he was elected to the Confederate Senate for a two-year term. As a senator, he strongly supported the administration. When Thomas Watts resigned as attorney general, President Davis nominated Senator Gustavus Henry of Tennessee, but Henry declined. Davis then offered the position to Judge Charles Jones Jenkins of Georgia, but he, too, refused the post. Finally, the president turned to George Davis on December 31, 1863, and Davis agreed to be Watts's replacement. The Congress confirmed him unanimously. But because Davis's wife was then in poor health, he could not assume the duties of the office. He did so soon thereafter, however, following her death. (Thomas Keyes served as attorney general *ad interim* until Davis was available to take over the position.) Davis started his duties on January 22, 1864, and he served as attorney general until the end of the war.

Davis was a man of character who "despised hypocrisy and hated demagoguery" but deeply appreciated "decorum."[8] Like Judah Benjamin, Davis never seemed to be discouraged by defeat.

As attorney general, just as he had done as a senator, Davis advised the President, and that is considered to have been his greatest contribution to the Southern cause.[9] Benjamin, Davis's predecessor, had established a logical way of presenting his opinions, and Davis continued to use it in writing his 74 legal opinions. He first stated the case, then presented his argument clearly and logically, and finally he issued his decision briefly and succinctly (sometimes in as little as half a page).[10]

However, Davis developed a somewhat unusual political philosophy regarding his responsibilities when it came to laws passed by Congress. He believed that he did not have a right to issue an opinion that struck down an act of Congress after the president had signed it. If it was unconstitutional, he should raise that issue during a cabinet meeting when Davis was asking for his counsel. After a bill had been passed by Congress and signed by the president, it was the law, Davis reasoned, and, he, as the attorney general, had the duty to enforce it.[11]

Davis's last act as attorney general was to counsel President Davis to accept the preliminary terms of surrender. Then, on April 26, 1865, he left Davis in North Carolina during the government's flight from Richmond. He was captured by Union authorities in Key West, Florida, on October 18, 1865. He was imprisoned at Fort Hamilton, New York, until January 1, 1866. Upon his release and parole, he returned home to Wilmington, remarried (Monimia Fairfax), fathered two more children (for a total of eight), and resumed his legal practice. He became quite an acclaimed regional speaker, especially railing against the measures pushed by the Radical Reconstructionists. He continually pushed to reform the state's radical constitution. Governor Zebulon Vance offered him the nomination to be chief justice of North Carolina's Supreme Court, but he declined. (He was the only citizen to decline such an offer.)

Davis's last public address was a stirring eulogy of Jefferson Davis at the former president's funeral in December 1889. He concluded the tribute by stating that his public career had risen and fallen with the Confederacy and would never revive. Having reviewed the events of that period, he recalled "with love and admiration" the men who played roles in that great struggle. The thing that the South could be most proud of during the whole of the war was not their military victories but that Jefferson Davis and Robert E. Lee, during the bitter period that followed the war, had never said or written anything but the truth, and "truth was the guiding star of both of them."[12]

George Davis died at his Wilmington home on February 23, 1896. The Wilmington bar passed the following resolution of tribute to his honor:

> Conservative in disposition, of sound judgment, never carried away by passion or prejudice, of large experience and familiar with all the methods of business, he was a safe, wise and judicious counsellor, as well as advocate. He was also a cultured scholar and deeply read in literature and other departments of learning.[13]

Part II

# Treasury Department

CHAPTER 8

# Overview

Perhaps the least understood cabinet department of the Confederacy is the Treasury Department. It is least understood because it dealt with the economy, and economics was and continues to be a little-understood subject. Nevertheless, the Treasury Department and the economic policies it pursued determined almost as much as the War Department, its generals, and the battles they ultimately fought the fate of the Confederate nation.

The first secretary of the treasury was Christopher C. Memminger of South Carolina. In staffing his department, he hired several people who had recently resigned from positions in the U.S. Treasury Department, notably Philip Clayton and Charles Jones. Clayton had been the U.S. assistant secretary of the treasury. He helped fill some positions in the Confederate department and helped organize it based on his previous knowledge and experience. Jones knew all the "business formulas" of the U.S. Treasury and brought with him to his new position in the Confederate Treasury samples of all the forms the department would need. Henry Capers, who was Memminger's private secretary during his tenure as treasury secretary, remembered, "We were more indebted [to Jones] than to any single individual for the rapid and perfect organization of the department in all of its details."[1] The Treasury Department was organized and fully operational within a month of Memminger's appointment to office.

The chief personnel of the department were as follows.
Executive Office:

- Secretary—Christopher C. Memminger
- Assistant Secretary—Philip Clayton
- Chief Clerk and Disbursing Secretary (and private secretary to Memminger)—H. D. Capers

- Warrant Clerk—J. A. Crawford
- Primary Clerks—Thompson Allan, J. W. Anderson, H. Kennenworth, J. H. Nash, Edmund Randolph, Henry Sparnick, and J. P. Stevens
- Comptroller: Lewis Cruger; John Ott, Chief Clerk
- First Auditor: Bolling Baker; W. W. Lester, Chief Clerk
- Second Auditor: W. H. S. Taylor; J. C. Ball, Chief Clerk
- Register: A. B. Clitherall; Charles T. Jones, Chief Clerk
- Treasurer: Edward C. Elmore; T. T. Green, Chief Clerk; Thomas Taylor, Cashier

Memminger allowed no influence by politics or personality in his hiring. Rather, Capers declared that Memminger "viewed the whole matter of appointments to office strictly from a business standpoint."[2] He set—and expected employees to keep—fixed business hours of 9:00 a.m. to 3:00 p.m. and evening hours if necessary. And he set the example, being "the most punctual and devoted among all of the officials" and usually "among the first to arrive and last to leave."[3] He strictly forbade correspondence with newspapers, and he closely guarded the dissemination of information to any others outside the department. These practices resulted in greater efficiency but also brought criticism.

Memminger and his staff had their Department up and running before all of the other cabinet positions were filled. Their work was interrupted briefly, however, when they moved the capital to Richmond in May 1861.

Under the supervision of the secretary of the treasury were the following bureaus: Engraving and Printing Bureau; Tithing, or War Tax, Bureau; Treasury Note Bureau; Cotton-Tax Office; and Produce Loan Bureau.

Throughout the life of the Treasury Department, several sub departments were added for greater efficiency. The Second Auditor's office was responsible for handling only the accounts of the War Department, and, with a war going on, that was more than a full-time job. The Third Auditor's office handled accounts for only the Post Office Department. And the Lighthouse Bureau was responsible for the upkeep of lighthouses and navigational aids.

The greatest obstacle that Memminger's clerical staff faced was having their personnel used for military purposes. Absence of clerks for these activities forced some offices to close for lack of personnel to run them. This was just one of many examples of the Confederate government's competing demands upon its various departments.

Other offices under Memminger's authority included the mints (although the Confederacy never minted a single coin![4]), customs houses (rarely, if ever, did they have more than 35 customs houses, and the number steadily declined as the Confederate armies lost territory), and depositories. The depositories were of two kinds—pay depositories, which had authority to make payments for the government, and funding depositories, which had authority to receive deposits paid to the government. Eventually, as the department grew to include multiple bureaus and offices, more than 150 clerical workers were employed.

The Confederate government started with no money at all and no central bank. It was able to float some loans from the State of Alabama and local banks and businesses to get started. The February 28, 1861, loan to the Confederacy was for $15 million specie by state and local banks. They allowed the Confederacy to use their state and local bank notes until the Confederacy could print its own. Beyond that, it had specie that it had confiscated from U.S. mints in the South, confiscated property of "alien enemies,"[5] and donations from private citizens.

During its brief life, the Confederacy had four sources of revenue: the tariff (import/export fees), direct taxation, loans, and treasury notes. The tariff was an unreliable and insufficient source of revenue. The United States had had the tariff as its primary revenue source since the nation's inception, but given the blockade and the limited number of harbors in the South, it was insufficient in that circumstance. Direct taxation alone also was insufficient for waging a war; besides, the people of the South were averse to any form of direct tax. Loans seemed to be Memminger's preferred revenue source, especially the Produce Loans. Congress, however, despite Memminger's repeated warnings against doing so, turned increasingly to treasury notes, or paper fiat money, for operating revenue.

The following table shows the percentage of the Confederacy's revenue obtained through various means.

**Table 3. Confederate Revenue Sources**[6]

| REVENUE SOURCE | REVENUE (%) |
|---|---|
| Printing press (treasury notes) | 60 |
| Bonds | 30 |
| Taxes (of all kinds, including tariff) | 5 |
| Miscellaneous (loans, donations, etc.) | 5 |
| Total | 100 |

The taxing organization and structure of the Confederacy was not in place for collecting taxes efficiently. The central government had to depend on the individual states to be its tax agents, and the state tax systems were as varied as the states themselves. Assessments were not the same in any two places. The army's constant and ever-increasing demands for men to serve as soldiers depleted the supply of able-bodied men who might have served as tax collectors. Besides, the government did not pay tax collectors enough to attract good men.

There were three kinds of loans available to the Confederacy. Specie loans were "gold and silver coins and sterling bills of exchange."[7] Produce loans were the use of cotton or other crops and products as the basis for establishing credit abroad and raising funds domestically. And funding loans involved "forcing the withdrawal of currency from circulation, exchanging it for Government bonds."[8]

The Treasury put forth three Produce Loans in the first year of the Confederacy, each a little different than the others. The first Produce Loan, issued on May 16, 1861, was for $15 million. By it, planters and farmers subscribed for a particular portion of their crops to be sold and the proceeds loaned to the government. After they sold, they were paid "in specie or foreign bills of exchange, receiving 8 per cent 20-year bonds in return."[9] (The length of time for the bonds indicates that as early as August 1861 at least some people expected a long, not a short, war.) The program was proclaimed a resounding success.

To operate the Produce Loan Program, Memminger named publisher James Dunwoody Brownson (J.D.B.) DeBow to be the chief commissioner. Serving gratis, DeBow appointed a General Agent for each state. Each state's General Agent, in turn, appointed several Subordinate-Agents. The agents and subordinate-agents persuaded planters and farmers to subscribe, or pledge, a portion of their crops and then collected the subscribed amount from the proceeds when the crops were sold. The agents received as compensation a percentage of what they collected. DeBow resigned in January 1862 to become the General Agent in New Orleans, and Memminger appointed Robert Tyler, Register of the Treasury, to take his place.

On August 19, 1861, the second Produce Loan was announced. It was for $20 million in treasury notes and $30 million in 8 percent bonds. It operated very much like the first Produce Loan, but it stated that "Treasury notes as well as specie and foreign bills of exchange" could be used to pay for "the proceeds of the portion of raw produce and manufactured articles subscribed to the loan."[10] One purpose of this loan was to help stabilize the rapidly inflating Treasury notes. This loan had mixed success, not being quite as successful as the first loan and failing to be the stabilizer that its promoters expected. DeBow reported that the second loan had the following amounts of crops and goods subscribed: cotton—417,000 bales; sugar—3,500 hogsheads; molasses—3,500 barrels; rice—270,000 bushels; wheat—5,000 bushels; tobacco—1,000 hogsheads; Treasury notes—about $500,000; and other produce—about $500,000.[11]

The last Produce Loan, issued on April 21, 1862, for $250 million, was a tax in kind, an exchange of goods for government bonds. Cash was in short supply for Southerners. But, the South being an agricultural society, most people had ready access to bacon, corn, cotton, flour, tobacco, wheat, or some other crop or product that they were willing to loan to the government. A few people were willing to loan an entire crop, but some subscribed only a quarter or so of their crop. But overall, fewer and fewer people were subscribing to the loan schemes. Some suspected the government of trickery. Others feared a forced or compulsory sale at ruinous prices. And as the war dragged on and the South lost valuable crop-producing territory to the enemy, fewer and fewer farmers were available or could afford to loan anything to the government. Another factor in declining subscriptions for the Produce Loans was the fact that, in doing their jobs, the General Agents often found themselves in competition with their Subordinate-Agents, "and both, in turn, competed with the various state and private agencies. As competition increased, prices rose, and with the rise of prices, many planters again refused to sell their commodity, hoping for a still higher price later."[12]

Some people proposed that the government buy the entire cotton crop at the price it averaged over the previous five years and give in return bonds and Treasury notes. Others thought that the government should pay planters an advance, placing a lien on the upcoming crop. Memminger, however, rejected such proposals of government aid as unconstitutional. He suggested, instead, solutions that did not involve government. One such suggestion was that the people switch from cotton production to the manufacture of clothing and other supplies needed by the armies and to plant winter crops, thereby helping offset the shortage of grain. Another of his suggestions was to rely more on the wealth in banks and held by private citizens by applying for loans.

By 1864, the South had lost large portions of its productive agricultural lands. Produce Loan agents were told not to buy cotton but rather to "preserv[e] the cotton already purchased."[13] Cotton was rotting while exposed to the elements. It was being stolen. And it was increasingly being traded with the enemy across the border before it could be sold and the proceeds given to the government. Nonetheless, the Produce Loan program did bring in for the Confederate government an estimated $34,476,400.

Perhaps the greatest foreign policy triumph and financial success for the Confederacy came in the winter of 1862–63 in the form of the negotiation of a $15 million loan, backed by Southern cotton, with the French banking firm of Emile Erlanger and Company of Paris. Coming as it did after repeated failures to gain diplomatic recognition of the Confederacy and increasing difficulties in breaking through the blockade, this success was a great encouragement. It was the only foreign loan the Confederacy was able to get, but it bolstered Confederate credit and enabled the purchase of more guns and other war materiel to keep the South in the fight a little longer. In the long run, however, it was futile in that the South still did not win its independence.

In the winter of 1862–63, the chances of Confederate military success were looking more positive than at any other time during the war. Emile Erlanger initiated the idea, proposing such a loan in the fall of 1862. A series of negotiations produced a final arrangement in January 1863, and Congress ratified the secret agreement. By the arrangements, Erlanger and Company would make available a 20-year loan for £3,000,000 by selling bonds in the European market. These bonds would yield an annual percentage rate of 7 percent and would be redeemable as certificates for cotton. The Confederate government agreed to deliver the cotton to within ten miles of a railroad station or navigable river. Erlanger would receive a 7 percent discount as an incentive to deliver the funds to the Confederacy early. They would also receive a 5 percent commission on the face value of bonds sold and a "1 percent bonus on interest and principal payments made to investors."[14] Erlanger guaranteed the sale of £300,000 of the bonds.

Erlanger issued the prospectus on March 19, 1863. For three days, the firm made bonds available for purchase in Amsterdam, Frankfort, Liverpool, London, and Paris, all major financial markets of Europe. In that short period, "the loan was oversubscribed more than five times."[15] The investors of Europe were bullish on the Confederacy!

But in late March the price for the bonds began to drop as demand for them subsided. Erlanger and Company began to buy bonds on the open market, trying to create the illusion of demand that would maintain the value of the bonds, but it did not work. On April 5, the company decided that it could not afford to continue buying to keep the market artificially high and announced that it would no longer do so. The price of the bonds really took a hit in mid-July to early August as news of the South's tragic loss at Gettysburg (July 1–3) and the Union's closing of the Mississippi to Confederate traffic by the capture of Vicksburg (July 4). The price of the bonds plummeted from 88–90 to as low as 45. After that, it became increasingly clear that the Confederacy could not win, and the program ceased.

The first sales of the bonds had netted £2,700,000. In its attempt to keep the program afloat, Erlanger and Company had bought back more than half the bonds. That resulted in a loss for the company of £544,827.[16] Yet, the program was not a total loss because "a large part of these sums were available for use by the Confederates in Europe during the critical eighteen months in 1863 and 1864 when other sources were nonproductive."[17] They made possible the Confederacy's ability to contract new debts. The plan did not produce as much money as authorities desired, and military losses destroyed investors' confidence. It was simply too little too late.

Although it seems that the Erlanger loan was an exercise in futility for the Confederacy, if there had been no Erlanger loan, the South would have been unable to buy arms, ships, or supplies and would have had no credit. The loan sustained the South, keeping its war effort going longer than it might otherwise have lasted without it, and it therefore extended the life of the Confederacy a little longer.

Congress also passed a war tax of one-half of 1 percent on "the chief articles of property."[18] But the people were so opposed to internal taxation that the new law was next to impossible to enforce and therefore virtually ineffective. Only three states ever collected the tax in Confederate treasury notes; the others paid them in state treasury notes, thereby effectively increasing the national debt. Memminger recommended to Congress "the old tithing system, levying a per cent upon all products needed for the supply of the army. Congress followed his advice and passed on April 24, 1863, the Tithe Tax, which was subsequently known as the 'tax in kind.'"[19] By its provisions, all farmers in the Confederacy were forced to pay a tithe, or one-tenth, of all "cotton, wool, and tobacco as a tax-in-kind."[20]

Of the various revenue sources, clearly the printing of interest-bearing and noninterest-bearing Treasury notes was Memminger's least favorite method of revenue acquisition. In his March 14, 1862, report to Congress, he warned the legislators that "this is the most dangerous of all the methods for raising money."[21] Noninterest-bearing notes became "the general circulating currency of the Confederacy."[22] Congress seemed to like the printing press, however, so it was not the last time that Memminger had to warn them of the dangers of the printing press. The printing press produced about $1.55 billion, but Memminger foresaw the problems of inflation, counterfeiting and the infiltration of U.S. paper money ("greenbacks").

The value of money is determined by how much of it is in circulation, whether the free market will accept it as tender, and whether it is backed by something of intrinsic value, such as silver or gold. When it is not backed thus and more of it is printed, the value drops and prices rise accordingly. The increase in the amount of money in circulation is called inflation, which results in higher prices because the value of the currency drops in direct proportion to the increase in the money supply.

Memminger clearly understood this basic economic principle, and he dutifully warned Congress of the dangers of pursuing it as policy. But Congress repeatedly ignored his warnings, kept the printing presses running, churning out more and more paper money, and the Confederacy suffered the consequent hyperinflation of prices. The government, "the largest purchaser of commodities," paid inflated prices and lost more in the transactions than it had raised by printing more money. It also hurt the average family, which had little purchasing power to begin with. Because printing more money seemed like an easy and convenient solution to the government's needs, the government was tempted to resort to that method repeatedly during the war with "disastrous consequences."[23] Memminger reportedly urged on Congress the need to *reduce* the amount of currency in circulation. He showed that "taxes alone have never been able to sustain a nation engaged in a great war; that loans are necessary; but in order to maintain the credit on which these loans rest, a tax must be levied sufficient to meet the interest of the loan '*in specie or its equivalent, whenever this interest becomes due.*'"[24] Nonetheless, Memminger went along with Congress's continued printing of currency, knowing full well that it was bringing economic ruin on the Confederacy.

**Table 4. Money Supply in the South**

**(January 1861–January 1864)**[25]

| Date | Money Supply ($ millions) |
|---|---|
| January 1861 | 94.6 |
| April | 121.8 |
| June | 120.4 |
| October | 170.8 |
| January 1862 | 239.8 |
| April | 282.1 |
| June | 309 |
| October | 468.8 |
| January 1863 | 649.6 |
| April | 818.8 |
| June | 904.8 |
| October | 1067.1 |
| January 1864 | 1094.9 |

The amount of money in circulation at the founding of the Confederacy in early 1861 was less than $100 million. Thanks to the Confederate Congress's early penchant for turning to the printing presses, that amount increased to more than $120 million by summer of that year. It surpassed the billion-dollar level by October 1863. The inflation rate quickly became higher than the return on government bonds, so it destroyed their value and reduced any incentive the people might have had to purchase them. "Under the circumstances," Lerner concluded, "pure patriotism was the only reason for buying government bonds."[26] Printed money became so abundant, and therefore nearly worthless, that "in desperation, Memminger recommended that the South resort to honoring counterfeits."[27]

Memminger also recommended setting up branches of the Treasury

Department in Europe and in the Confederate states west of the Mississippi River. On March 14, 1862, Fraser, Trenholm & Company became the Confederate Depository in Liverpool, England, and the next year, General Colin J. McRae began serving as the agent in France. On January 29, 1863, the Erlanger loan was authorized. Other depositories were established in Bermuda, Nassau, and Havana, Cuba. To serve the Treasury's interests west of the Mississippi, Congress created the Trans-Mississippi Department under the control of General Kirby Smith. Memminger then set up a branch of the Treasury Department at Marshall, Texas, with P. W. Gray as the agent. Once the Trans-Mississippi was cut off from the east, however, the Treasury branch in the west acted almost as an independent Treasury Department.

Congress authorized a new issue of notes "at the rate of two dollars for three of the old issue" to absorb all the old currency and reduce the overall currency in circulation, and that gave the economy "'a new starting point.'"[28] But the new currency still had no "foundation upon which rests all credit; a certain and permanent income in specie, or its equivalent."[29] States collected and paid the taxes with state paper money.

Memminger's final recommendation to Congress was to make a tax payable in Confederate treasury notes. Congress ignored his advice. He warned them again of the dangers of printing more fiat paper money and suggested that they enact "'a simple tax on property and on incomes'" but repeal the tax on agricultural products and "'on incomes from property taxed as capital.'"[30]

The congressmen either did not understand basic economic principles about inflation or, more likely, were pandering to the popular public opinion among their economically uninformed constituencies. Inflation has always seemed desirable to some people who look only at its immediate effects. They see more paper money in their wallets. They do not see, however, the devaluation of that money and the skyrocketing prices of everything they must purchase. When the market catches up with the printing presses, the people are no better off than they were before; rather, they are worse off, and they demand more paper money. It becomes a vicious cycle, culminating in hyperinflation.

Todd estimated that the following total revenues came into the Confederate Treasury:

**Table 5. Revenue Totals**[31]

| REVENUE SOURCE | AMOUNT ($ MILLIONS) |
| --- | --- |
| Loans | 712.0 |
| Treasury notes | 1,554.0 |
| Tariffs/taxes | 207.5 |
| Seizures/donations | 514.0 |

One of the biggest problems for the Treasury Department (and of all of the other Confederate cabinet departments generally) was the inability to budget realistically. Patto stated, "Since the Confederacy was born in a sense full-grown, no history of working relations, no trust, no experience from which to gauge consequences were available to guide budget decisions."[32] And Nevins pointed out that the Confederacy was a "crisis government," and, as such, it "'was never able to think of long-range plans because short-range necessities hammered at the door.'"[33]

From start to finish, the Confederacy was characterized by the following four variables.

1. *Poverty*—The Confederacy started from a poor financial situation that grew continually worse as time went on. Its economic activity was stunted because of the blockade and the devastations of war. Hyperinflation ate away at the heart of the entire economy.

2. *Economic uncertainty*—The Confederacy suffered from an inability to rely on its one big cash crop, cotton. It was also unable to get enough foreign loans. The value of its currency was continually declining. And it suffered the consequences of slow and inefficient responses of the government to the economic conditions that were occurring.

3. *Lack of dependable information*—Sound economic and budgetary decisions, efficient collection of data and taxes, and reasonably accurate estimates of anticipated revenues and expenditures must be based on dependable data, and the Confederacy just did not have it.

4. *Lack of "complex redundancy"*—The Confederacy did not have the "skilled manpower," sufficient monetary reserves, or political stability necessary for ensuring a stable economy.[34]

In a mature, stable, and wealthy government, the treasury has a historical financial record on which to base budgetary decisions. Department heads request funds for their respective departments based on what they spent the previous year and on what they anticipate spending needs to be for the coming year. Without that base of information, Confederate department heads were merely guessing. Most of the time, their guesses were not even educated guesses; they were wild guesses, mere shots in the dark. And they had no means of collecting (or the time to collect) the data needed to make those guesses. The events of the war occurred so quickly, that by the time some datum was collected, it was woefully outdated and useless.

Complicating the process was the fact that all of the departments were doing the same wild guessing in competition for a limited amount of revenue.

## 8. Overview

And the executive branch's estimation of revenues was as uncertain as the department heads' estimates of their expenditures.

Adding further to the uncertainties were the "exigencies of battle," the fog of battle, and the shifting sands of war. Political—and in battleground areas literally physical—security was unpredictable. The Confederate government faced increasing demands that it could not fill.

Yet another complication to any good-faith efforts to budget realistically was the growing problem of inflation. Department budget requests were invariably deficient because between the time budget requests were submitted and when the bills came due the value of the currency changed. The actual bills were always higher than the anticipated bills. The departments typically underestimated actual expenditures, and the Treasury Department typically overestimated actual revenue receipts.

The various departments—especially those that, like the Post Office Department, generated revenue—expected that the monies they had budgeted for their departments would be there, available for their own use, when the bills came due. But the Treasury Department put all revenues into one "community pot," so to speak, and withdrew it as any department had a need for it. Budgeted funds were not earmarked for specific things. No department had a "lock box" on its budgeted funds. So every department was competing with all other departments for limited financial resources.

Because Congress was bent on trying to solve its financial problems using the printing press, inflation very quickly became a raging problem, and it only increased as the war progressed. Inflation was actually a kind of real, though inverse, tax on the Confederate people. Despite Memminger's efforts to remove much of the paper money from circulation through taxation and the 1864 Compulsory Funding Measure (which devalued Treasury notes not exchanged for noncirculating government bonds) and thereby help check inflation, he was unsuccessful. The printing presses ran faster than the government could collect the revenue. No more than $27 million in specie was ever available to the Confederacy at any time, and the national debt shot to more than $700 million. Inflation was staggering. Estimates of the annual inflation rate vary widely, depending on the data used to calculate it, ranging from 6,000 to 9,000 percent! And wages did not keep up with inflation, so real income declined dramatically.

Perhaps the most illustrative data on inflation involves the prices of consumer commodities in particular places and over time. Take, for example, the Atlanta, Georgia, area, where most of the employees of the Western & Atlantic Railroad worked. On November 26, 1861, the wholesale price of a 150-pound sack of salt—which was a necessity as it was the only means of preserving food, especially meats—was $8.75. About two years later, on November 18, 1863, the price had risen to $101.25. In about a year—from May 6, 1862, to May 12, 1863—the price of bacon rose from 40 cents a pound to $1.00 a pound. Over the same period, the price of a gallon of molasses rose from $1.20 to $7.50. The supply of corn on the market actually increased during that period, so one might expect the price for it to decline, but it actually went up because of inflation from $1.75 a bushel to $3.50 a bushel. And the price of flour went from $12.25 a bushel to $40 a bushel. The wage paid to blacks who were hired out in May 1862 was $1 a day, or $30 a month. One year later, they were getting $45 a month. (This fact should be put in perspective by noting that the average common soldier's pay was only $11 a month, rising to only $18 a month.[35]) "In no year did average wages and salaries even keep up with that part of inflation arising out of the increase in the supply of money."[36]

Capers noted, "At no time was [Memminger] given an unlimited authority to act as his judgment alone would dictate in the management of the Confederate finances, either at home or abroad. On the contrary, he was never more than an officer executing the will of Congress.... The financial legislation of Congress was, in the most vital points, opposed to his judgment and contrary to his often-repeated and strongly urged recommendations."[37]

Because of this frustration, Memminger offered several times to resign. He finally did give Davis his letter of resignation on June 15, 1864. During his time as secretary, Memminger regularly conferred with notable business leaders concerning economic and fiscal matters but none more so than George Trenholm. When Memminger resigned, it was Trenholm whom Davis nominated to replace him.

Trenholm did his best, but the damage had already been done, and the South had passed the point of no return. Several economists and historians have offered suggestions about how the South could have developed a more sound financial system, but it is still doubtful "whether *any measure* short of military victory would have improved ... the financial status of the Confederacy."[38]

CHAPTER 9

# Christopher Memminger

The first secretary of the treasury in Davis's cabinet is in many ways an enigma, a bundle of contradictions. Christopher G. Memminger opposed nullification and immediate secession but came to see it as a necessity. When he reached that conclusion, he was not a fire-eater or an immediate secessionist but a cooperationist. Yet he was the primary author of South Carolina's ordinance of secession. Memminger owned no slaves. Yet he served one of the states with the most slaves and was a leader in a slave nation. He was a man of strong convictions, "conscientious and methodical," yet he "lacked the moral courage to fight for his convictions" in economic matters.[1] He believed in a sound monetary system that resisted and opposed inflationary measures, yet as treasury secretary he "pursued a financial policy of paper money that he knew was destined to failure."[2]

Christopher Gustavus Memminger was born on January 9, 1803, in Vairhingen an der Enz, Würtemberg, Germany, and was baptized the next day. His father, a professional sol-

**Christopher Memminger, Secretary of the Treasury (Wikimedia Commons).**

dier, was killed in combat only a week after his son was born. His mother, thinking that she and her young son had a better chance of succeeding in life outside of Germany, came to America with her parents. But not long after arriving in Charleston, South Carolina, the mother died of disease. The grandparents began rearing Memminger, but his grandfather soon moved to Philadelphia with the family, and left four-year-old Christopher at "the Orphans House of Charleston."[3] So Memminger essentially grew up without the benefit of a father or a mother.[4]

When Chris was 11, Thomas Bennett, who would later be elected the governor of South Carolina, took Chris in as a foster child. Bennett was wealthy, "a Christian gentleman," "devoted patriot," and "upright citizen."[5] He gave Chris the best education available in that day, hiring for him the best tutors.

Bennett was not only wealthy but also politically connected and influential in the community. In 1815, before Chris was 13 years old, Bennett got his foster son enrolled in South Carolina College, one of the South's foremost colleges. But it was not just political connections that won Chris the enrollment; he actually had what it took to excel. He passed the school's rigorous admission tests and then led his class scholastically. At only 13, Memminger was, to quote the Rev. John Graves, one of his classmates, "'the smallest in stature, ... the youngest in years'" in his class.[6] Although he looked like a youngster, he talked and thought like an adult, mature beyond his years.[7] He showed a spiritual bent, being always in attendance at the school's religious services and faithfully observed personal devotions twice a day.

Because Memminger was studious and applied himself, he ended up being the salutatorian of his graduating class in 1820. He continued that application into adulthood, as he passed the South Carolina bar exam and joined the law firm of his foster father's brother, Joseph Bennett. He never had a legal specialty as such, but his favorite areas were commercial and constitutional law. He became an American citizen in 1824. (Memminger was one of two foreign-born members of the Confederate cabinet. The other was Judah Benjamin. But Benjamin never renounced his British citizenship by becoming either a U.S. or a Confederate citizen, whereas Memminger did.)

Politically, Memminger identified with the Union Rights Party, and he was a delegate to the nullification convention. He opposed nullification, but it passed anyway. Nonetheless, his presence at the convention earned him name recognition that contributed to his election as a Charleston city alderman in the next election. In that capacity, he began to focus on the educational needs of the city's young people. He sought to reform education in the state by raising the standards and making the schools more efficient. Many of his reforms also focused on providing an education for the blind, the deaf, and the dumb. Traveling to the Northeastern and New England states to observe their public schools, he brought back ideas to improve South Carolina's schools. His reforms were not without opposition, but the state legislature believed in them enough to pass a bill authorizing Charleston's government to levy a school tax to implement them.

Memminger was elected to the South Carolina House of Representatives in 1836 and was assigned to the Ways and Means Committee, the Federal Relations Committee, and the Education Committee, of which he became chairman. The only important legislation he introduced was a bill to prevent circulation of mutilated bank bills. It did not pass. He also introduced a bill regulating liens. That bill failed in the first session but passed later, thanks to his persistent efforts. Memminger opposed the national bank, believing strongly in specie payments. But his view was not shared by the majority in the South Carolina legislature. In debate, he "never attempted the art and mannerism of an orator.... While he was often eloquent, his eloquence was the expression of strong thought, logically conveyed, convincing the mind and demolishing all opposition by the earnest manner in which it was delivered."[8]

When talk of secession first arose (in 1852, not just before the 1860 election!), Memminger urged cooperation with other Southern states. Although he firmly believed that each state had the right to decide for itself, he believed that it would be much more effective if the states worked together. Separate action, he thought, would lead to war. The key issue, then, was whether each state was prepared to go to war and take the consequences that such an action would bring.

In 1852, Memminger was appointed an elector to the Electoral College. He voted for Franklin Pierce for president and William King for vice president. He did not run for reelection to the state legislature in 1853 and 1854, but he did in 1855 and won. He was made chairman of the powerful and influential Ways and Means Committee.

Governor William Henry Gist called the South Carolina legislature into extra session on November 5, 1860, ostensibly to choose electors for the Electoral College but also to choose delegates for a secession convention in case Lincoln was elected president. The delegates were chosen on December 17, 1860, and Memminger was one of them. At the convention, he was appointed to a committee to draft "a statement of the *causes* which justified the secession of South Carolina."[9]

Once South Carolina seceded, followed by six other Southern states, Memminger was among eight South Carolinians chosen as delegates to a convention held in Montgomery, Alabama, for the purpose of forming a Confederate government. There, he was chosen chairman of a committee that would draft a constitution. On the fourth day of the convention, the delegates voted on and approved the Constitution of the Confederate States of America.

Between the convention's election of Jefferson Davis and Alexander Stephens as president and vice president, respectively, and their inauguration on February 18, Congress set up a revenue system for the new nation, organized an army and a navy, and undertook many other matters associated with founding a government. On the day of the inaugurations of Davis and Stephens, Memminger learned that he had been nominated to be secretary of the treasury. He had not been the only aspirant. Other names that were considered included Robert W. Barnwell, Robert Toombs, Robert Barnwell Rhett, and Howell Cobb, who had just resigned as the U.S. secretary of the treasury and was therefore a logical candidate. But Davis chose Memminger.

Memminger had a long, lean face and nose. He wore no beard or moustache. His penetrating eyes rested under a neatly combed shock of silver-white hair. He had a firm line for a mouth with understated lips. On the cabinet, Memminger, like Judah Benjamin, tended to be calm and collected amid the other members, who frequently got worked up over issues.

Memminger's first task as Secretary was to identify a building for the new Treasury Department. He wanted to get to work immediately. "'The world must know at once that we are at work,'" he said, "'and that we are in earnest.'"[10]

Memminger got a New York engraving company to contract the making of bonds and bank notes for the new government, but U.S. agents seized the plates as contraband of war although there was as yet no war. The Confederacy had to import engravers, using whatever equipment they could find and whatever paper was available. Often, that was newsprint or wrapping paper. After the capital was moved to Richmond, the Treasury Department finally settled on the firm of Hoyer & Ludwig as the government's official engravers.

The government started with no money at all. On February 8, 1861, the State of Alabama loaned the Confederate government $500,000. That was followed on February 28 by a $15 million specie loan by local banks and businesses of the South. These loans were intended to get the government up and running until it could arrange for more permanent revenue sources.

Personnel to staff the department had to be obtained, and in personnel hiring and management Memminger excelled. He hired several people who had recently resigned from positions in the U.S. Treasury Department, notably Philip Clayton and Charles Jones. Memminger seems to have been uninfluenced by politics or personality in his hiring. Rather, he looked upon the appointments as merely a business transaction.

Memminger immediately announced regulations by which the department would operate, and he began enforcing his expectations right away. Recognizing the expectations and responsibilities of public trust, he watched his clerks carefully. He set—and expected employees to keep—fixed business hours of 9:00 a.m. to 3:00 p.m. and evening hours if necessary. He set the example, being "the most punctual and devoted among all of the officials" and usually "among the first to arrive and last to leave."[11] Memminger also recognized the dangers of "loose lips." Correspondence with newspapers was strictly forbidden, and dissemination of information to any others outside the department was closely guarded. These practices resulted in greater efficiency but also brought criticism. For example, Kean thought that Memminger was intelligent but "tricky, shifty, and narrow."[12] And this was one of the milder criticisms offered of him.

Memminger and his staff had their Department up and running before all of the other cabinet positions were filled. Their work was interrupted briefly, however, when they moved the capital to Richmond in May 1861. (Further details of Memminger's tenure as secretary of the treasury were covered in the overview of the Confederate Treasury Department and will not be belabored here.)

Throughout the war, Memminger grew increasingly more frustrated with both efforts to provide a sound financial footing for the government and butting heads with both Davis and a stubborn Congress that was determined to resolve economic problems using the printing press. Because of these frustrations, he offered several times to resign. He finally did give Davis his letter of resignation on June 15, 1864.

During his time as Secretary, Memminger regularly conferred with notable business leaders concerning economic and fiscal matters but none more than George Trenholm. When Memminger resigned, it was Trenholm whom Davis nominated to replace him.

Memminger retired to his summer home in Flat Rock, North Carolina. (This home later became the home of famed poet Carl Sandburg.) While some Confederate leaders fled the country after the war, Memminger did not. He was not arrested after the war, but he suffered nonetheless. His home in Charleston was confiscated (ostensibly because he had "abandoned" it). The enemy turned it into "an 'Asylum for negro orphan children.'"[13] Memminger applied for a presidential pardon and appealed for the return of his home. He was allowed to return to live in his home, but he was charged rent for it. He later got it back and obtained a pardon.

Memminger eventually resumed his legal career with his old partner, William Jervey. He also helped found and served as president of the Sulfuric Acid and Superphosphate Company, which began manufacturing operations in December 1868. He was elected to the state legislature in 1877, where he introduced a bill for the reorganization of South Carolina College.

Memminger's wife died during that legislative session, and he left politics and public life. He did, however, become president of the Blue Ridge Railroad, which was planning the construction of a Spartanburg-to-Asheville rail line through Rabun Gap.

Memminger's strength failed with advancing age. On February 28, 1888, a marble bust of Memminger was unveiled in Charleston, but he was not present for the ceremony. He was, instead, at home near death. He died a few days later on March 7, 1888. His body was taken to Flat Rock and buried there.

Chapter 10

# George Trenholm

Several men, including Trenholm, were asked to become secretary of the treasury after Memminger resigned, but all of them turned it down. The last, Trenholm, believed that Congress's views on the subject were totally opposed to his; therefore, he would not dream of accepting the position.[1] But he finally accepted the position and was formally nominated on July 18, 1864.

George Alfred Trenholm was born on February 25, 1807, in Charleston, South Carolina. In 1822, when Trenholm was only 15 years old, he went to work as an accounting clerk for John Fraser & Company, a major cotton brokerage firm based in Charleston. The company specialized in shipping sea island cotton, a crop in which coastal South Carolina specialized.

Trenholm's merchant father died when Trenholm was still young, denying George the opportunity for an advanced education. But that lack of one opportunity meant other opportunities for him to work his way up in the company. By 1853, he was head of the company. He became a director of both the Bank

**George Trenholm, Secretary of the Treasury (Wikimedia Commons).**

of South Carolina, then the largest bank in the state, and a South Carolina railroad. He was a successful and "highly respected businessman" who was focused on his commercial pursuits. Although he was traditional in business methods, his success did not come from being conservative in business. Rather, he was sometimes radical in his methods; "he liked to think big."[2] That is how the fleet of ships in his import-export business expanded to 50 ships and his companies grew from John Fraser & Co. to include Fraser, Trenholm and Co. (Liverpool) and Trenholm Brothers of New York. So when Trenholm entered public affairs, it was "reluctantly."[3] He was elected to the South Carolina legislature, where he served from 1852 to 1856.

Trenholm had supported nullification during the Jackson-Calhoun controversy over the tariff bill. His states' rights views only intensified over the years, and he became an early supporter of secession.[4]

When war broke out, Trenholm built and donated to the Confederacy the gunboat *Chicora* and served on the Charleston Board of Commissioners to fortify the city. Within days of the firing on Fort Sumter, his various companies developed a mutually beneficial relationship with the Confederate government. The Liverpool portion of his businesses became the Confederacy's overseas depository in return for a commission of 0.5 percent. It "helped negotiate and manage" the Erlanger loan, the Confederacy's only major foreign loan. And it "advised Confederate purchasing and propaganda agents and gave them room to work at 10 Rumford Place."[5]

Trenholm advised the government to form its own commercial fleet of blockade runners so their ships could carry whatever goods the military needed rather than relying on private shippers, who preferred to carry lighter, less bulky consumer goods, which offered greater profits. But the Confederate government turned a deaf ear to his pleas. Too late, they tried to implement his idea.

Nonetheless, Trenholm's companies continued to help the Confederacy. For example, near the end of 1861, a slow, heavy ship loaded with more than 20,000 rifles and other military equipment was stuck in Nassau. There was no chance of its outrunning the blockaders. But Trenholm provided the Confederates two small but fast steamers that ran the blockade and got the supplies into Mosquito Inlet, Florida. This action was the beginning of the practice of offloading goods from large British ships to smaller but faster Confederate blockade runners. Trenholm's company in Liverpool also contracted with British shipbuilders to construct first eight and later six additional steamers, thereby expanding his steamship fleet and using it to run the Union's blockade.

Of course, Fraser, Trenholm and Company also earned a 4 percent commission for selling the Confederacy's cotton. Trenholm and his companies "did more for the Confederacy, in the spirit of patriotism, than any other [company]."[6]

Trenholm was a personal friend, confidant, and advisor of Christopher Memminger when the latter was secretary of the treasury. His various business enterprises provided valuable help to the Confederate cause both domestically and in Europe throughout the war. When Memminger resigned, Trenholm was the logical choice to be his replacement.

More charismatic than Memminger, he was treasury secretary from July 18, 1864, until his resignation (citing poor health) on April 27, 1865. Kean posited that Trenholm was oblivious to the true situation at the Treasury Department when he became secretary. However, he waged a propaganda war of sorts on two fronts, one with the public and the other with Congress.

Trenholm tried to use a public relations campaign to convince the public that the Treasury Department was not ruling *over* the people but was actually an organization *of* the people. He kept the public informed of department activities and carried on heavy correspondence with those who wrote, trying to reassure them of the solvency of the government and its currency. He discouraged speculation, pledged not to fuel inflation, and encouraged the purchase of Confederate bonds as the safest investment.

Concurring with Memminger and making a publicly visible gesture, Trenholm continued to push Congress to stop printing paper money and instead to raise taxes that would be paid primarily by plantation owners. He also tried to encourage the public to purchase bonds.[7] He urged the government, as had Memminger repeatedly before him, not to print more paper money but rather to issue bonds and raise taxes.[8] Those taxes would rest heavily on the large farming interest.[9] He essentially continued Memminger's policies. He agreed with Memminger's sound money principles and won the congressional opponents of Memminger to his support, but he had no more success in getting Congress to follow his ideas than had his predecessor.

He could do no more for the Confederacy than continue to warn Congress of the dangers of the inflationary practice of printing worthless paper money. In fact, although he received relatively little criticism from Congress, he often blamed Congress for the Confederacy's economic woes.

Overall, none of his propaganda campaign, whether with the public or with Congress, worked. He challenged Congress either to accept his program or to come up with a better plan of their own. The congressmen remained passive. Even if they had enacted his program in its entirety, it would not have saved the Confederacy.

By early 1865, the Confederate government owed Trenholm's companies £224,125 for cash advances and £645,550 "in warrants expected."[10] His ships had delivered untold tons of supplies to Nassau and Bermuda, but the cargoes sat on the wharves rotting or deteriorating because the Southern ships could not run—or would not risk attempting to run—the blockade.

Trenholm was loyal to the South to the bitter end, but he was not blind. At some point, he determined that the South's attempt to win its independence was doomed. That is when he began to look for ways he could earn a profit *after* the war. He saw the devastation of the South's plantations, industries, railroads, and cities. He knew that the people would need help rebuilding after the war ended. Fleeing from Richmond with Davis, he fell ill and tendered his resignation to Davis on April 27, 1865. He was arrested the next day in Charleston and imprisoned in Fort Pulaski near Savannah. He did not get out of prison until he was paroled on October 11, 1865.

After the war, his companies faced several lawsuits by people trying to find and liquidate all Confederate assets. The former Confederacy still owed Trenholm's firms £170,000. In May 1867, Fraser, Trenholm and Company declared bankruptcy. It had more than £1.2 million in liabilities but assets of only £290,000.[11] Union authorities sold off his company's assets to pay uncollected duties on goods that the company had imported during the war.[12]

Trenholm accepted his lot as God's will. Then he determined to "forget about politics and to go to work rebuilding the South."[13] He petitioned President Andrew Johnson for a pardon and finally got it in 1866. Wasting no time, he worked to promote construction of a Charleston-to-Cincinnati-via-Knoxville railroad in 1866. He helped Charleston recover, and he was elected to the South Carolina legislature. He died on December 9, 1876, at the age of 69 years.

Chapter 11

# John Reagan

The summary of the life and work of John Reagan is covered more fully in Chapter 21, which discusses his involvement in the department with which he is most closely associated, the Post Office Department. But he is also included here, among the Treasury Department secretaries, because he was the last person to be responsible for the Confederacy's finances in the final days of the war after Trenholm's resignation. How short was his tenure! How short, therefore, must be any chapter devoted to Reagan as treasury secretary. He had no *time* to do much of anything in that capacity.

Reagan's tenure as secretary of the treasury ran from the day he took over from Trenholm, April 27, 1865, until he was captured by Union cavalry on May 10, 1865—only two weeks. During that time, he was in flight and hardly had time or opportunity to do anything administratively, let alone constructively, for his department or the economy of the South. As he and Davis fled, they disguised themselves and traveled under assumed names. Davis posed as a congressman from Texas and Reagan as a Texas state judge.[1]

When Davis and his cabinet, including a still-sick Trenholm, met on April 26, 1865, at the home of William Elliott White in Charlotte, they discussed the terms of surrender that General William T. Sherman had offered to General Joseph Johnston. Post Office Department secretary John Reagan favored accepting the terms but with qualifications. He believed that if the Lincoln administration rejected the deal that Sherman had offered (as it later did), or if they refused to recognize the principle of local self-government (which it did), the Confederacy had a duty to keep fighting, no matter how lopsided the contest might be.[2] The other cabinet members agreed and, when it became clear that the Lincoln administration had no intention of allowing Sherman's terms to stand, sent orders to Johnston to disband his army with instructions to meet somewhere else and resume the fight. Johnston, however, saw the futility of such a course and surrendered his army instead of doing as ordered.

At that point, Attorney General George Davis resigned. Trenholm tried to continue the flight with the rest of the government but was unable because of his continuing illness. So he, too, resigned, but not before appointing Reagan to be acting treasury secretary. Judah Benjamin strenuously objected that it was, in his opinion, unconstitutional for Reagan to hold two cabinet positions simultaneously, but President Davis rejected Benjamin's argument. (Reagan's written commission paper appointing him to the post was the last known official signature that Jefferson Davis applied to any document of the Confederacy.) Davis and a small party of cavalrymen separated from the others while Reagan took care of department matters.

As futile as Reagan's actions were by that point, he kept meticulous accounts of the government monies that had suddenly been placed in his care, which amounted to about $288,022 in gold and silver coin and bullion. At Abbeville, South Carolina, he put the wagon train containing the Confederate government's monies under the cavalry escort and ordered them to see it safely to Washington, Georgia. Benjamin left the party at that point to attempt an escape.

Reagan received word from General John C. Breckinridge (who was also the secretary of war) that the cavalrymen assigned to guard the treasury had been promised payment from the monies the party was carrying, so Reagan authorized that distribution. He then authorized the burning of all of the Confederate currency and bonds they were carrying. He also oversaw and documented the disbursement of several other payments, including amounts to the quartermaster general, the soldiers and officers of President Davis's guard, and various individuals who had legitimate claims against the government for various services they had rendered. Furthermore, he disbursed $2,000 in coins to be transmitted to General Braxton Bragg for the operations in the Trans-Mississippi Department. Reagan kept receipts for all of these transactions as though the government were fully functioning and would continue in operation far into the future. He clearly wanted everything to be kept above board and transparent right up until the bitter end. But he also ordered that the remaining specie be secreted out of the country to pay the government's foreign creditors. Even in defeat, he did not want his government to default!

Reagan left Washington, Georgia, about 11:00 p.m. on May 4, and joined Davis's party the next morning. They were all captured near Irwinville, Georgia. Reagan was imprisoned, along with Vice President Alexander Stephens, at Fort Warren in Boston. For 22 weeks, Reagan was kept in solitary confinement.

During his imprisonment, Reagan read much in Northern newspapers about the animosity that had developed and that was deepening between the sections. That led him to write an open letter to the people of Texas, appealing for them to recognize the authority of the U.S. government, renounce secession, repeal slavery, and extend the vote to the freedmen. He warned that if they did not do so, it would result in an oppressive military dictatorship. Most Texans, however, rejected his advice and disowned him. They lived to see his dire prophecy come true, however, with the military occupation of the South during Reconstruction.

Periodically, the question arises as to what happened to the Confederate specie that was supposed to have been secreted from the country to pay for Confederate debts. Did it ever make it to the creditors? Did someone or some group of people steal it, hiding it somewhere within the States? If so, did they ever retrieve it? If not, where is it today? People are still trying to find it.

Captain M. H. Clark, the last acting treasurer of the Confederacy, wrote to the editor of the Clarksville, Tennessee, *Courier-Journal*, on January 10, 1882, seeking to set the record straight. He gave a day-by-day account of the government's flight from Richmond to Washington, Georgia, including a detailed accounting for every disbursal of money from the funds in the hands of the fleeing parties. He concluded that there essentially was no Confederate "treasure," that "the old Confederates brought nothing out of the war, save honor."[3]

That question, like many others concerning the Confederacy, remains unanswered.

PART III

# War Department

CHAPTER 12

# Overview

Of the six Confederate cabinet departments, more has been written regarding the War Department than about any other department—perhaps even more about it than about the other five departments combined. For that reason, this chapter, although it is lengthy, will give merely the barest of summaries of the department and its various sub departments.

Because the Lincoln administration refused to allow the seceded Southern states to depart from the Union peacefully, the Confederacy found itself buffeted by the winds of war almost immediately after Lincoln's inauguration. This made the Confederate War Department perhaps the most important of the cabinet departments. One would think, therefore, that President Davis would have made a special point of ensuring that his nominee for this position was someone to whom he could entrust the responsibilities of national self-defense and war-making without second guessing his every decision or constantly hovering over his shoulder.

But Davis did not do that. He thought so highly of his own knowledge and abilities as a former military leader—both as a veteran soldier with actual combat leadership experience who could see the tactical front-line realities of war and as a former U.S. secretary of war who could see the big strategic realities and organizational needs—that he apparently put little thought into his choice of who should lead the Confederate War Department. Consequently, five different men rotated through the doors of the War Department, none of them exceptionally successful because of both their own and Davis's particular weaknesses. The results were fatal for the Confederacy.

Davis, in choosing someone to fill the position of secretary of war, should have been capable of giving his employees the authority they needed to do their jobs and then have trusted them to do so, thereby ensuring his own success.[1] Ideally, Davis should have envisioned, delegated, and empowered. He should have articulated a broad strategic plan of action for his secretary of war. Then he should have chosen for that position someone whom he could fully trust to implement the stated strategy by making the decisions necessary for its accomplishment based on that strategic plan and occasional guidance from himself as president. Instead, Davis clutched the reins of decision-making power himself, thereby hamstringing his secretary of war and rendering him nothing more than a glorified clerk, as many people subsequently charged. He thought too highly of his own abilities as a military leader and too little of the abilities of his subordinates. This self-assurance caused him to belittle the decisions and capabilities of his subordinates, from the secretary of war himself to the generals in the field. As a result, no matter whom Davis chose to be secretary of war, that person would not have been able to exert influence on him. Davis was simply looking for someone who would do what he had already decided and take whatever criticism resulted from those actions, not someone with the ability to determine policy and conduct the war.[2]

Nonetheless, having been both Franklin Pierce's secretary of war and a leader of combat troops himself, Davis did bring to the presidency important knowledge and abilities for organizing the Confederacy's War Department. Much of the Confederate War Department organization was based on that of the U.S. War Department, and he did not have to reinvent the wheel.

As was mentioned earlier, the military roles of the Confederate president were not clearly defined, leaving it up to the president to determine for himself the definitions and his level of involvement in implementing those defined roles and responsibilities. McPherson set forth Davis's five major areas of responsibility that fell within the jurisdiction of the War Department:

1. *Policy*—the "political goals" of the government, the end results desired in waging war;
2. *National strategy*—the use of the nation's "political, economic, diplomatic, ... psychological [and] military resources ... to achieve those war aims";
3. *Military strategy*—the plans for using the "armed forces to win the war and fulfill the goals of policy";
4. *Operations*—"the management and movements of armies in particular campaigns to carry out the ... military strategy"; and
5. *Tactics*—the organization and conducting of the details in a specific military engagement.[3]

As muddled as many of Davis's policies might have been, his main policy was crystal clear: to achieve independence for the Confederate States of America.⁴ Even the matter of slavery was a secondary factor to nationhood. One would think that setting and ensuring the success of a broad national strategy for achieving that independent status for his nation would have ranked almost as high on his list of priority responsibilities, but Davis delegated the diplomatic and economic aspects to others and had comparatively little direct involvement with those matters. The results of that selective hands-on/hands-off style of management were mixed and overall unsuccessful.

Most of Davis's time and energy were devoted to military strategy and operations, matters that normally are left to the military experts and professional soldiers. His overemphasis on those matters and his micromanagement of them to the neglect of his other broader responsibilities were probably his greatest mistakes as president.

Davis's military strategy was based more on political pressure from the various states making up the Confederacy than from any commitment to military theory. (In fact, in many ways Davis's actions violated established military theory.) The states insisted that every state be protected simultaneously. Each governor considered his state's protection, of course, to be the most important. As a result, Davis's choice of strategy was a "dispersed defense," but he would rather have committed the nation to a strategy of "concentration," or an "offensive-defensive" strategy.⁵ But rather than concentrating most of the nation's military forces at key points—seaports, major rivers, arsenals, and manufacturing facilities or sources of raw materials or subsistence supplies—he was forced to defend the whole border of the nation, thereby spreading the available troops out very thinly all around the nation. Other names for this type of strategy were "perimeter," "cordon," or "extended" defense.⁶

As the war progressed, the various states complained that Davis was focusing more on the defense of Virginia and less on other areas that should have had his attention. And they might have had good reason for their complaints. Because the protection of the national capital at Richmond was a permanent concern for Davis, and because he was there most of the time, his focus might naturally have been for the safety and protection of his immediate surroundings. He frequently got letters and telegrams from governors and state legislatures reminding him that he had been elected president of the whole Confederacy, not of Virginia. As long as his focus seemed to be primarily on the Eastern Theater, specifically on Virginia, the other states were reluctant to send any more troops to the Confederate army lest their states be left shorthanded if they were attacked by the enemy on their own soil. Perhaps we will never know how different Davis's strategy or the success of Confederate arms might have been had the capital remained in Montgomery, deep in the heart of Dixie.

Davis signed a bill on February 26, 1861, that authorized the creation of the General Staff of the Regular Army. Included in the General Staff were the Adjutant and Inspector General's Department, the Quartermaster General's Department, the Subsistence Department, and the Medical Department. The director or head of each department answered to the secretary of war. Each bureau or sub-department also had several other organizations working under its authority. And, as generally happens in a government bureaucracy, the War Department grew throughout the war.

The six men listed in Table 6 served as the secretary of war during the life of the Confederacy. (Because Gustavus Smith served a mere four days as interim secretary, his biographical sketch is not included in this book.)

Table 6. Confederate Secretaries of War

| Secretary | Term of Office |
| --- | --- |
| Leroy Pope Walker | February 21, 1861–September 16, 1861 |
| Judah P. Benjamin | September 17, 1861–March 23, 1862 (served in acting capacity until confirmed on November 21, 1861) |
| George Wythe Randolph | March 24, 1862–November 17, 1862 |
| Gustavus W. Smith (interim) | November 17, 1862–November 21, 1862 |
| James A. Seddon | November 21, 1862–February 6, 1865 (served in acting capacity until confirmed on January 19, 1863) |
| John C. Breckinridge | February 6, 1865–May 5, 1865 |

The position of assistant secretary of war was more stable than the superior position in the War Department, only two men serving in that capacity during the war. The first was Albert Taylor Bledsoe, who served from April 2, 1862, until October 1, 1862. He was followed by John A. Campbell, who served from October 21, 1862, until the end of the war in April 1865.

The role played by each of the bureaus of the War Department will be discussed briefly in this overview of that cabinet position. Several of the key players in leadership over those bureaus, especially over the Ordnance and Commissary Bureaus, will also be discussed.

## *Adjutant and Inspector General*

An adjutant general is responsible for procedures affecting personnel procurement and for the maintenance of all personnel records. An inspector general is the auditor of all military operations and, as such, is tasked with ensuring that the army complies with all policies and procedures of the army. He is also supposed to investigate all allegations of fraud, waste, and theft of military supplies and equipment. In the Confederate War Department, the roles of both adjutant general and inspector general were combined. Only one man served in that capacity, Brigadier General Samuel Cooper (March 16, 1861–May 5, 1865).

Cooper was born in New Hackensack, New York, on June 12, 1798. When he was 15, he enrolled in West Point, graduating two years later (which was at that time the typical length of study). He was assigned duty as a brevet second lieutenant in the light artillery. Six years later, he was promoted to first lieutenant and five years after that to captain. He remained in the artillery until 1837, at which time he became chief clerk in the War Department. In 1838, he was made assistant adjutant general. He served in the Second Seminole War (1841–42) and the Mexican War (1846–48), after which he was promoted to colonel and appointed to the position of adjutant general in 1852. He was also acting secretary of war briefly in 1857.

Cooper had become close friends with Jefferson Davis when Davis was the secretary of war. Ironically, Cooper's last act as U.S. adjutant general was to dismiss from the army Brigadier General David Twiggs for surrendering his command in Texas and all of the command's supplies to Confederate forces. Less than a week later, on March 7, 1861, Cooper resigned his own commission in the U.S. army, traveled to Montgomery, Alabama, and accepted a commission as a major general in the Confederate army and appointment to the post of adjutant and inspector general. He served in that position throughout the war.

As adjutant and inspector general, Cooper was instrumental in organizing the War Department based on his years of valuable experience as the U.S. adjutant general. He was promoted on May 16, 1861, to the rank of full general. He was the first of only five men to hold that rank before the war, and only two more were promoted to it during the war. So at the start of the war, Cooper was the highest-ranking military man in the Confederacy, outranking even P.G.T. Beauregard, Robert E. Lee, Albert Sidney Johnston, and Joseph Johnston. He reported directly to President Davis.

Diarist and chief of the Bureau of War Robert G. H. Kean thought that Cooper was incompetent because during his years in office he never knew what was going on in the army and never required an accounting of information; he had absolutely no information from the Trans-Mississippi theater of operations.[7] Kean declared that at no time could the adjutant inspector general even guess as to how many soldiers were in the army, much less how many were ready and able for active combat. He complained that Cooper never decided anything, seldom reported anything, and in the few instances when he did report something, the document was short.[8] Kean also complained that Cooper was seldom present at work and was ill-informed of legislation that concerned the military, but Davis kept him in office anyway. Kean attributed this to "'Davis's irrepressible *West Pointism.*'"⁹

Although many Confederate military records were destroyed or lost during the war, Cooper did his best to preserve all records under his care and authority. He oversaw the removal of military records from Richmond near the end of the war. His last official act as the Confederate adjutant and inspector general was to turn over all official records to the U.S. government at the end of the war. These records, in turn, were a valuable asset in the assembling of the *War of the Rebellion, Official Records of the Union and Confederate Armies.*

## *Quartermaster General*

Whenever an army is mobilized for war, whether offensive or defensive, it must be supplied with the things it needs both to fight and to live. That involves the farms of the nation, the manufactories that make the munitions and other equipment, the various and necessary forms of transportation required to deliver the goods, and the numerous people required in performing each of those tasks. These were the responsibilities of the Subsistence, Commissary, Foreign Supplies, and Niter and Mining bureaus of the Confederate government. Each of those bureaus had to be staffed by trained supply officers, quartermasters, and teamsters to get the jobs done efficiently. All of these people and bureaus served under the Quartermaster General's Department.

The task of equipping and supplying the military necessities of the Confederate armed forces was the prevue of the quartermaster general. Once men had been recruited and mobilized, they had to be equipped. When the necessary equipment had been obtained, it had to be transported and distributed to the individual armies, divisions, regiments, and companies wherever they were. The farms and factories had to produce so that the armies could be fed. The financial institutions had to supply funding. Trains and wagons had to be obtained or built to transport the necessary goods. And once those goods got to the troops, they had to be distributed. Every regiment was assigned a quartermaster, usually a sergeant, whose job it was to ensure that supplies were distributed to the troops in his regiment. This involved procurement and logistics, all under the authority and oversight of the quartermaster general. It involved, as legendary Confederate cavalryman Nathan Bedford Forrest so colloquially summarized the office's task, "gittin' stuff."[10]

The quartermaster general's responsibilities encompassed "the widest-ranging function in the military."[11] In fact, it was so all-encompassing that the Confederate government quickly divided some of the quartermaster general's responsibilities with two other bureaus—the Commissary of Subsistence, which supplied foods, and the Ordnance Bureau, which handled procurement of weapons and ammunition.

The South had four major sources of supplies and equipment: domestic production, trade with foreign countries, trade through enemy lines (i.e., with the enemy), and supplies and equipment captured from or abandoned by the enemy. At first, much of the Confederacy's equipment came from the Federal arsenals and forts taken over at the time of secession. Usually, however, these resources were retained by the states where they were captured. Later in the war, because the four main sources were not yielding enough because of the loss of territories where they were manufactured or imported, the Confederate government turned to two other sources, both unpopular with the citizenry—impressment, or government confiscation, and tax-in-kind.

Although everyone, it seemed, complained about the local quartermaster, the real problem was not at that level. The quartermaster could distribute only what he received. The problem was in delivery, or logistics. In many instances, the necessary supplies were available, often sitting in warehouses or stacked on docks at rail stations, but trains or wagons and teams were not available for their distribution.

Two men served as quartermaster general: Lieutenant Colonel Abraham Myers (March 25, 1861–February 15, 1863) and Brigadier General Alexander Robert Lawton (August 10, 1863–May 5, 1865).

Abraham C. Meyers, the Confederacy's first quartermaster general, was born in South Carolina on May 14, 1811. He later moved to Louisiana. He graduated from West Point in 1833 and was an assistant quartermaster in the U.S. army during the Seminole Wars. He also served in the Mexican War, during which he became a captain and the chief quartermaster for U.S. troops in Mexico. In 1860, he was serving in the quartermaster's department with a rank of brevet lieutenant colonel. He resigned from the army in January 1861, seemingly ending a long and distinguished military career.

But Myers's career was *not* over after all. On March 15, 1861, he found himself appointed quartermaster general for the Confederate army with the rank of colonel on account of his having so much knowledge and experience from having worked in the U.S. Quartermaster Corps. Starting essentially from scratch, his responsibility was to organize the department so as to be able to provide everything the Confederate army needed by way of clothing, transportation, and other essentials.

Both Myers and Northrop of the Subsistence Bureau (discussed later) had similar problems of logistics and supply of equipment and food, respectively.

Criticism was inevitable. Not only historians but also Myers's contemporaries claimed that he was ineffective. Commanders complained about how slowly supplies were delivered, about how they arrived damaged or ruined—if they arrived at all—and about how insufficient amounts of the supplies were delivered. They were always short of something. Barry stated that Myers displayed an "inability to grasp the transportation piece of the supply logistics puzzle."[12] What he was referring to was the fact that the Confederate government allowed the railroads to remain in private hands and under civilian control. Myers did not favor government control of railroads. Only late in Myers's term did the Confederate government move to control the railroads. As with many other situations, this was too little too late.

But Myers was not totally inept. He did some good things to get his fledgling bureau up and running. He set up his headquarters in a Richmond, Virginia, warehouse and set about locating and requisitioning even more warehouses to stockpile the goods he knew would be needed by such vast armies as would be mustered. He appointed four assistant quartermasters general in strategic transportation centers throughout the Confederate states: Charleston, South Carolina; Montgomery, Alabama; New Orleans, Louisiana; and San Antonio, Texas. Within the regions where those cities were located, he set up regional depots. He also set up "receiving points" in port cities based on the assumption that the South would have to import many of its supplies.

Although Myers was an experienced officer, most of his military experience had been in the artillery. Considering what he had to work with and the vast scope of his responsibilities, he generally fulfilled his duty well. The duties of quartermaster general, however, simply overwhelmed him, and he resigned in August 1863. Congress liked Myers, but Davis did not. Behind his dislike of Myers was the fact that the two men's wives did not like each other![13]

Kean recorded in his diary that for a long time, Davis had not liked Myers,[14] and he warned that because Myers had a lot of popularity among the congressmen, his removal would anger friends.[15] Congress made Myers a brigadier general, but Davis replaced Myers with Brigadier General Alexander Lawton, another South Carolina native, allegedly "in the interest of efficiency," in August 1863.[16] (Lawton later asked to be relieved as quartermaster general because he thought that the controversy over Myers decreased his effectiveness.[17])

Davis's abrupt action resulted in a loud outcry from Congress. The Senate simply refused to confirm Lawton, but Davis kept him in the office anyway. The Senate then voted 15–9 that Myers was still the quartermaster general. Seventy-six members of the Confederate House of Representatives signed a letter to Davis calling for him to reinstate Myers, but Davis held firm. The Senate finally confirmed Lawton in February 1864, and Myers stepped down.

Although both Meyers and Lawton were at the time and since have been criticized by historians and armchair generals for their failure to adequately supply the South's armies, much of that criticism is unjust. Considering the circumstances under which they had to work—including a gradually diminished productive capacity as Union armies took over more and more territory, farm lands, and manufactories—they did an admirable job at what they did. If any aspect of Confederate supply can be faulted, it lies in the area of transportation.

Even when food, supplies, weapons, and ammunition were available in abundant quantities, it often could not be put into the hands of the fighting men because the means of transportation (railcars, locomotives, or wagons and horses) were unavailable or roads were impassable. In countless instances, perishable food items bound for hungry troops rotted on rail platforms or in warehouses because it could not be delivered to the men.

Not until late 1862 did the South's rail system fall under the control of the Confederate government. Until then, railroad executives, more concerned about the revenues they stood to gain from paying passengers and private freight customers than for the fighting forces, put profit before patriotism. And who is not to say that any one of us might have had the same priority? The fact remains that supply was not a problem of quantity so much as it was a problem of logistics.

Alexander Lawton was born November 4, 1818, in Beaufort, South Carolina, and graduated from West Point in 1839. He was a second lieutenant in the artillery until 1840, when he resigned to study law at Harvard. He graduated in 1842 and moved to Savannah, Georgia, where he practiced law, became involved in the Augusta and Savannah Railroad, and entered politics, serving as a representative in the Georgia statehouse from 1855 to 1856 and as a state senator from 1859 to 1860.

When Georgia seceded, Lawton became a colonel in the 1st Georgia Volunteers, which was engaged in the seizure of the federal Fort Pulaski. On April 13, 1861, he became a brigadier general in the Confederate army and was assigned to guard Georgia's coastline. He was later reassigned to serve in Virginia, leading a brigade during Stonewall Jackson's Valley Campaign. He also saw action in the Seven Days Battle and at Second Manassas and Sharpsburg. He was seriously wounded at Sharpsburg and had to convalesce at home for several months. At the end of his recovery period, he was named quartermaster general, having been personally sought out by President Davis. Although Lawton desperately sought to be returned to field command, he acquiesced to Davis's earnest pleas and accepted the new position.

By the time Lawton took over, however, the Confederate government was for all intents and purposes financially ruined. Lawton's task was made even more difficult by the steady loss of productive farmlands and factories as the Union armies executed the Anaconda Plan and occupied increasingly more of the South. But some historians say that the soldiers gained immediate relief, getting much-needed supplies, and that the general transportation situation improved greatly.[18] Lawton was especially credited with the speedy transfer of Longstreet's troops from Virginia to Georgia just in time to make a major contribution to the Confederate victory at Chickamauga. (It was unfortunate that the same could not be said for Longstreet's later move to Knoxville, Tennessee, before the battle of Fort Sanders.)

## *Commissary General of Subsistence*

The role of the commissary general of subsistence was to procure and distribute food for the War Department's many armies and all of their beasts of burden. And that was no small task. In fact, it proved to be "one of the most vexing problems faced by the Confederacy during the Civil War."[19] War was expensive business, not only when the troops were fighting but also when they were encamped. Unfortunately, the Confederacy's pockets were not deep and they developed holes as the war progressed. The people who at various times wore the pants—the department secretaries and War Department bureau chiefs—were unequal to the tasks they faced.

The commissary general of subsistence had to be able to deal with myriad types of people, from military commanders to civilian farmers to speculators to state governors. Moreover, he had to "somehow overcome the obstacles of internal corruption, food speculation, hoarding, balky superiors, military reverses, currency depreciation, and an inadequate transportation system."[20]

The first commissary general of subsistence was Colonel Lucius B. Northrop, who served from March 27, 1861, when Secretary of War Leroy Walker named him commissary general, to February 15, 1865. He was born in Charleston, South Carolina, on September 8, 1811. He graduated from West Point in 1831 and served in Indian Territory and in the Seminole Wars, during which he was wounded, ending his active service. He went on to study medicine in Philadelphia before returning briefly to the service again, serving in the Subsistence Department.

In 1848, Northrop was dropped from the army on the charge of practicing medicine on charity patients. Jefferson Davis, a West Point classmate, came to his defense and got Northrop reinstated. Northrop remained on inactive duty, however, and practiced medicine in Charleston until 1861. When South Carolina seceded, Northrop resigned his commission and offered his services to

## 12. Overview

the Confederacy. He was commissioned a lieutenant colonel in the Subsistence Department.

Northrop faced myriad obstacles from the very beginning, and in many ways the Subsistence Bureau was a dismal failure. Some historians point to failures in the Subsistence Bureau as the cause of the South's defeat because many Confederate armies were on the verge of starvation and could not reasonably be expected to be effective soldiers on empty stomachs. On the other hand, other historians say that the South produced sufficient food resources to feed not only all of its armies but also its civilian population. Supporting that claim, Sherman commented that during his march of destruction from Atlanta to Savannah through the heart of Georgia he saw ample crops. So how could armies be starving while the South produced amble crops?

The answer lies in the problems encountered in the area of logistics and the poor decisions that the leaders of the Confederacy made in their efforts to supply those resources. The Upper South produced "one-third of the wheat grown in the United States … plus oats, rye, barley and plenty of corn."[21] It also produced large numbers of hogs and cattle. Whereas more than a third of Northern cattle were dairy animals, the South raised beef cattle almost exclusively. However, the war drew the Southern farmer, whether by voluntary enlistment or conscription, away from the farm and into the armies, where he became "a consumer rather than a producer."[22]

But by the end of 1862, and especially by the end of 1863, much of the South's food-producing territory had been lost to Federal troops. The question then became how to get food, especially beef, from the other places (especially Florida and Texas) where it was raised in quantity to the Eastern Theater armies. Roads were little more than worn paths, and they became a morass of muddy teamster torment in wet weather and clouds of choking, blinding dust in the dry seasons. That left railroads and ships or boats as the only other transportation methods. Although the blockade was not completely successful, especially during the first year of the war, it nonetheless put a crimp in the logistical plans of the South. Besides, even if goods could get through the blockade, they still had to be transported inland to where they were needed most. Roads were unreliable, and rivers were navigable only so far inland.

That left the only other means of transport—railroads. Although the South had begun to express interest in railroad development during the antebellum period and actually had more miles of track in place than most of the "developed" countries of Europe, it still had far less than the North had. And railroad development in the South was incomplete and focused on purely local interests rather than on the needs of the entire region of the South. Railroad companies would identify a location that wanted goods shipped and another location that wanted to receive those goods, and they would build a railroad between those two points, ignoring the possibilities that existed for further development by linking to other peripheral locations. Therefore, the lines were often disconnected.

A further complication was the fact that there was no standard gauge of rail. Some railroads used a five-foot gauge; other railroads used a four-foot, eight-and-a-half-inch gauge. Sometimes two dissimilarly gauged railroads served the same town, but goods carried by each railroad had to be offloaded from one railroad, transported to the other railroad, and reloaded onto that railroad's cars. In some towns, the local teamsters exerted influence on the town officials to ensure that the railroads did *not* incorporate a standard gauge lest it put the teamsters out of work.

As the war progressed, railroad tracks, bridges, trestles, cars, and motive power wore out or were damaged. Because of the pressures and demands of the war on the railroads, this infrastructure was not maintained, and it fell into disrepair. Added to this natural deterioration were the ravages that the railroads incurred from the enemy, especially Sherman's troops as they tore up track, twisting and bending the rails beyond any possibility of future use. Union troops left "Sherman's neckties" all over the Southeast, especially through Georgia and the Carolinas.

Warehousing was another logistical nightmare for the South. Although regional warehouses were established and well stocked throughout most of the war, food often rotted there or on railroad station platforms because there were no cars to haul the produce or meat. Food rotten while men starved, often mere miles from the sustenance.

Like the quartermaster general's job, Northrop's job was thankless from the very beginning, and he was destined for not only criticism but also ultimately failure, not through any fault of his own but because of some of the same factors that made it next to impossible for Myers to successfully do his job.

Northrop also seemed to have had trouble getting along with people. Mary Chesnut called him "the most 'cussed' and vilified man in the Confederacy."[23] McPherson thought that "a man of congenial personality might have been able to overcome criticisms of the inevitable food-supply deficiencies in the Confederacy. North Carolina governor Zebulon Vance described Northrop's personality as 'peevish, obstinate, condescending, and difficult.'"[24]

When John C. Breckinridge became secretary of war, one of his first acts was to convince Davis that Northrop had to go. Northrop, seeing the handwriting on the wall, tendered his resignation, which Davis dutifully accepted. Northrop was succeeded on February 16, 1865, by "the able" Brigadier General Isaac Munroe St. John, who served in that capacity until May 5, 1865.[25]

Perhaps the best commentary on how the failure of the Subsistence Bureau contributed to the loss of the war for the South was General Robert E. Lee's final communication to President Davis immediately following his surrender to Grant at Appomattox. He reported to Davis his surrender of the Army of Northern Virginia and explained the reasons for it. He stated that he had retreated toward Amelia Court House, but "not finding the supplies order to be placed there, nearly four hours were lost in endeavoring to collect on the country subsistence for men and horses. This delay was fatal…. We had no subsistence for man and horse, and it could not be gathered in the country. The supplies ordered … could not reach us, and the men … were worn out and exhausted."[26]

## Surgeon General of the Medical Department

The Medical Department was authorized by the Confederate Congress on February 26, 1861, in the act that established the General Staff for the Confederate army. It provided for a surgeon general, four surgeons, and six assistants.[27] More personnel (assistant surgeons) could be added in the future if necessary. Similar provisions were made for the navy on May 16, 1861. (This showed that the congressmen had no idea of either the length of the coming war or the savagery and physical destructiveness to human bodies that the war would entail.) When the first battles were fought, however, with larger-than-expected numbers of soldiers engaged on both sides and suffering higher-than-expected casualties, Congress authorized a progressively larger Medical Department.

On August 22, 1861, Davis asked Congress to reconsider a bill it had passed authorizing the addition of one assistant surgeon for each regiment of the army.[28] He thought that it was an extravagant waste of money. He vetoed other similar measures that were designed to improve the medical services of the military. Nonetheless, the department did steadily improve in efficiency and increase in size as the war progressed. By 1864, the surgeon general's office had six medical officers on duty. Eighteen surgeons served in the field as medical directors and supervisors. Eight more directors served over hospitals, and six were field inspectors. Perhaps most importantly, five boards had been set up to examine appointees and assistant surgeons who had been recommended for promotion.[29] There were also 154 principal hospitals.

The head of the Medical Department was the surgeon general, who "was charged with the administrative details of the Medical Department—the government of hospitals, the regulation of the duties of surgeons and assistant-surgeons, and the appointment of acting medical officers when needed for local or detached service."³⁰ That task would seem to be almost overwhelming for one man even in peacetime; during war, it *was* overwhelming.

The first surgeon general, David C. DeLeon of Alabama, was ordered to serve as acting surgeon general beginning on May 6, 1861. Understanding that his tenure was merely temporary, he served a little more than two months, until July 12, 1861. On that date, he was relieved by Charles H. Smith, who was to be temporarily in charge of the medical bureau.[31] Again, the man understood that his orders were merely temporary. He was to fill in only until a suitable candidate could be found to take full charge of the department. That order came a little more than two weeks later, on July 30, when Samuel Preston Moore was ordered to duty as acting surgeon general. He was confirmed by the Senate on December 13, 1861, and remained in that office for the duration of the war. (Because of the short duration of DeLeon and Smith's time in office, they are not included in the more in-depth discussion of the Medical Department. Primary focus, instead, is on Moore.) The navy had its own chief medical officer, the top-ranking naval surgeon William A.W. Spotswood.

South Carolina-born Moore had graduated from the Medical College of South Carolina in 1834 and was appointed assistant surgeon in the U.S. army the following year. He served in various frontier locations and in the Mexican War over the next 14 years and was promoted to surgeon with the rank of major in 1849.

When South Carolina seceded, Moore resigned his commission and moved to Arkansas, where he established a private medical practice. He did not intend to get involved in the war that he knew he was coming; he did not want to fight the government to which he had sworn allegiance. But neither did he want to lift his sword against the state of his nativity. However, when Arkansas seceded and Jefferson Davis (whom Moore had met during the Mexican War) began urging him to offer his services to the Confederacy, he relented and accepted the position of acting surgeon general.

Moore was "intelligent, thorough, impartial, and industrious," but he was "extremely addicted to the formality of army discipline" and expected everything to be done by the book.[32]

The surgeon general had the rank of colonel, surgeons had the rank of major, and assistant surgeons were ranked as captains. They all had pay comparable to their corresponding ranks in the regular army. The navy had its own medical staff, and they were similarly organized. In addition, many private physicians were hired by contract. They were assigned no rank and were paid according to the individual contracts that they worked out with the army Medical Department.

The surgical staff members of the Medical Department were primarily general practitioners from all over the South. Before the war, however, such physicians had little, if any experience with surgeries, even more rarely experience treating gunshot wounds. They gained more than their share of experience with such wounds—and much worse—during the war.

Like the Confederacy generally, the medical service was plagued by shortages of every imaginable medically necessary supply from medicines to instruments and tools. Because of these shortages, the medical personnel had to improvise by seeking their pharmaceutical supplies in "the fields and forests" of the South and by adapting common instruments of everyday life to make their surgical instruments. Their primary job was to relieve suffering, preserve the life of the wounded, heal the sick and diseased, and repair soldiers' "mangled bodies and limbs" as best they could with what they had available.[33]

Although exact and accurate statistics for the number of sick and wounded who were treated by the Medical Department personnel are hard to come by, Jones estimated after the war that the total was "more than three million."[34] The typical soldier could figure on being treated, for wounds and sickness, an average of six times during the course of the war. Jones further estimated that one-third of all Confederate soldiers involved "were either killed outright on the field or died of disease and wounds."[35] Almost all were treated at least once for some sickness. In fact, more Confederate soldiers (some estimates say more than twice as many) died from disease than died from combat wounds.

At least on paper at the start of the war, every Confederate regiment—whether infantry, cavalry, or artillery—was to have one surgeon, and he was to have one or two assistant surgeons and a medical officer to help him. Had this been reality, nearly 2,000 surgeons and nearly 4,000 assistant surgeons would have served in the Confederate military service. But this "paper requirement" did not exist in reality any more than companies and regiments were always at full capacity. Many regiments were short of medical officers. By 1864, "six medical officers ... were on duty in the Surgeon General's office. Eighteen surgeons were serving as medical directors in the field and supervising the work of medical officers there. There were also eight medical directors of hospitals, six field medical inspectors, and seven medical inspectors of hospitals. Five army medical boards were engaged in the examination of applicants for appointment as assistant surgeons and of assistant surgeons for promotion."[36] There were also 154 principal hospitals. But the demand for medical personnel became so great during the war that the Medical College of Virginia (the only medical school to survive the war) began graduating two classes a year to meet the demand.

Jones suggested that it was more likely that, combined, no more than 673 surgeons and assistant surgeons served in the Confederate army.[37] The navy had an additional 73 medical officers. Adding to these army and navy medical personnel who served in all of the general hospitals and the various recruitment and conscription camps, the South still had no more than 3,000 medical personnel.

The common solution for large numbers of gunshot wounds to limbs was amputation. The greatest cause of death during and after amputations was infection. As many people as died from resulting gangrene and infection, however, an estimated 75 percent of amputees managed to survive. Contrary to popular misconception, the surgical patients generally did not bite bullets or drink themselves into a mind-numbing, pain-killing stupor for surgeries. Ether and chloroform were both readily available as anesthetics. By one estimate, about 76 percent of all amputations were performed using chloroform as the anesthetic, 15 percent used ether, and 9 percent used a mixture of chloroform and ether, leaving less than 1 percent to be performed without formal anesthesia.[38] Given the widespread general shortages, especially toward the end of the war, however, there were, no doubt, some incidents when other desperate measures had to be taken.

The South started out the war without a manufacturing base for pharmaceuticals just as it did for industrial products. The blockade made it increasingly harder to obtain medical supplies and drugs from foreign suppliers, although the Medical Department did have an agency in Bermuda that traded cotton and other Confederate goods in return for drugs and medicines and then transferred those goods to smaller, faster blockade runners. Only weapons and clothing were in greater demand than drugs and medicine during the war.[39]

Surgeon General Moore did much to help the Confederate armies during his time in service. He organized the Confederate Medical Department; established examining boards for surgeons and assistant surgeons; oversaw the construction of numerous military hospitals across the South; established review boards and administered exams to weed out untrained and inexperienced doctors; improved the ambulance corps; raised recruiting standards; improved treatment protocols; developed factories to make drugs, surgical instruments, and hospital supplies; and directed the recruitment of surgeons for the Confederate army. The Medical Examining Boards scrutinized applicants' "moral habits, professional acquirements, and physical qualifications" to ensure that the service hired or enlisted only well-qualified and professionally competent personnel.[40]

Another of Moore's major achievements was his influence in getting Congress to pass the Matron Law of 1862. That law allowed non-physicians—notably women—to have administrative control of military hospitals. Many of the women who worked in the hospitals as a result of the law's passage were free blacks. Under his leadership, Moore "transformed the medical corps into one of the most effective departments of the Confederate military."[41]

Always eager to advance the profession through continuing education, Moore founded the Association of Army and Navy Surgeons of the Confederate States and served as its first president. The association members met regularly to hear reports on medical advances and new treatments. Moore also encouraged exemplars to publish the findings of their research and first-hand experience in medicine when he founded the *Confederate States Medical and Surgical Journal*, which was edited by James Brown McCaw. Although the journal lasted only a little more than a year, it demonstrated Moore's commitment to continuous improvement and advancement of the medical profession. As the war progressed and Confederate supplies dwindled, Moore experimented with numerous ways to make essential medicines from the South's native plants. Further promoting continuing education of his staff, Moore wrote and published two books, *Resources of the Southern Fields and Forests, Medical, Economical, and Agricultural* and *A Manual of Military Surgery*.

Congress appropriated only $50,000 for the establishment of military hospitals in 1861.[42] But Congress generally agreed to appropriate more and more funds as the war progressed, indicating that they realized the critical importance of the medical department to the war effort and the general well-being of the troops. The following tables show the increases in the annual appropriations for both the Army Medical Department and the Navy Medical Services.

Table 7. Congressional Appropriations for the Army Medical Department

| YEAR | AMOUNT APPROPRIATED |
|---|---|
| 1861[a] | $ 905,000 |
| 1862 | 5,145,000 |
| 1863 | 14,479,800 |
| 1864 | 33,140,000 |
| 1865[b] | 20,300,000 |

Table 8. Congressional Appropriations for the Navy Medical Services[43]

| YEAR | AMOUNT APPROPRIATED |
|---|---|
| 1861[a] | $ 20,000 |
| 1862 | 61,500 |
| 1863 | 250,000 |
| 1864 | 1,010,000 |
| 1865[b] | 375,000 |

[a] Represents approximately nine months
[b] Represents approximately four months

The two largest hospitals in the Confederacy were both in Richmond. The largest was Chimborazo with more than 12,999 beds. (The second largest was Winder Hospital, with more than 5,000 beds.) Chimborazo had five separate hospitals, each with 30 buildings, or wards (150 total), and each ward accommodated 40 to 60 patients. Each hospital building was 100 × 30 feet and had one story. They were designed with many doors and windows to ensure adequate ventilation. Chimborazo had many rows of many tents separated by wide lanes. It also had its own cemetery, five soup houses, five ice houses, a high-capacity (about 10,000 loaves a day[44]) bakery, and bathhouses. In addition, it included a large farm that raised 200 cows and 300 to 500 goats for provisions. Chimborazo was headed by James Brown McCaw.

Moore was instrumental in developing the forerunner of the modern general hospital.[45] The wounded were not housed with the sick, and efforts were made to house men from the same geographic region together for increased morale. Moore oversaw the general operations of numerous general hospitals. In all, there were 154 general hospitals throughout the Confederacy that were used during the war. There were 50 in Georgia, 39 in Virginia, 23 in Alabama, 21 in North Carolina, 12 in South Carolina, 4 in Florida, 3 in Mississippi, and 2 in Tennessee. These hospitals were carefully and thoughtfully situated to ensure proper sanitation, access to clean water, and adequate transportation facilities and access. Sometimes the armies had to impress buildings to serve as temporary hospitals.

In addition, field hospitals were set up just behind front lines during battles. Although efforts were made to locate these in safe areas, they were still often within sound of the fighting and frequently had to be moved hurriedly as the fortunes of war ebbed and flowed. The Confederacy got a large amount of its medical supplies and medicines from Union field hospitals that the Confederates overran before the Union medical personnel could evacuate their supplies. (One Union soldier reported, "'Our chief distributor [of drugs] in the South was General [Nathaniel] Banks. The Johnnies always managed to capture his well-equipped trains. Our goods went all through the Confederacy and were appreciated.'"[46])

The wounded were carried off the battlefield by comrades or members of the Ambulance Corps or Invalid Corps (wounded men who were recuperating but were not deemed physically capable of returning to combat duty) and treated in these field hospitals. The Invalid Corps numbered 1,063 officers and 5,139 enlisted men by the end of the war. They were then transferred to the closest general hospital. Seriously injured soldiers who were furloughed from these hospitals and sent home to complete their recuperation were aided along the way by several "way hospitals" that were scattered up and down major railroads to provide rations and lodging for sick and wounded soldiers as they returned home to convalesce.[47]

Moore standardized medical care as much as he could given the inevitable shortages that occurred in drugs and medical supplies and equipment. Although he was personally stiff, formal, and somewhat brusque, and although he did everything strictly according to regulations, thereby often offending some people, he was respected for his knowledge and administrative abilities.[48]

Civil War-era medicine has often been portrayed as being just about as primitive as the medical profession of the Middle Ages, but that is totally incorrect. Although American doctors of the mid-19th century—both Northern and Southern—were not as advanced as medical personnel of today, they were comparatively well-educated and practiced well given their amount of knowledge. We cannot judge them for what they could not have known.

For example, when field surgeons used the same unsterilized tools to operate on every patient, wiped the blood on aprons that they wore in surgery all day, and operated with unwashed hands, they were not doing so without regard for their patients' well-being; they were merely ignorant of germ theory. Nonetheless, medical personnel generally did much to ensure as clean, as safe, and as comfortable an environment for the patients as they could under the circumstances. They understood the need for quarantine with certain illnesses and the importance of fresh, clean air and ventilation.

When Civil War-era medical professionals are compared with what was considered the medically best militaries of mid-century—the British in the Crimean War (1854–56) and the French during the Franco-Prussian War (1870–71)—the Americans were favorable. When America's Civil War-era surgical results are compared with the Russians and the Turks of that time, the Americans are far superior.[49]

The war experience produced many improvements in medical care, including hospital administrative system and construction, a heightened awareness of the need for medical mobility (what later became known as mobile army surgical hospitals, or MASH units), and separate wards for different types of wounds and illnesses. It also opened the doors to women to work as trained nursing professionals. Women were instrumental in improving and maintaining soldiers' morale, and medical professionals were realizing the fact that the mental outlook of the patient is a legitimate responsibility that often determined the success or failure of medical procedures.[50]

As medicines became scarcer, Surgeon General Moore encouraged the use of alternative sources, most notably plant derivatives indigenous to the local areas where the hospitals were located. He also encouraged the establishing of pharmaceutical laboratories throughout the South. For example, a navy laboratory operated in Richmond, and "at least eight Army laboratories—in Montgomery and Mobile, Alabama; Macon and Atlanta (later Augusta), Georgia; Lincolnton and Charlotte, North Carolina; Columbia, South Carolina; and Arkadelphia, Arkansas (later Tyler, Texas)."[51] Yet it was all done according to scientific standards; it was not merely "folk remedies" and "old wives' tales." In fact, the war practices did much to turn people, including many in the medical profession, from such quackery and toward more truly scientific medicine.

Food in period hospitals was never totally satisfactory, but medical personnel were keenly aware of its importance to patients' recovery and morale. Medical personnel sought to provide the best possible and most nourishing food considering the local circumstances and supply.

Cunningham concludes that undoubtedly what the surgeon general's corps learned greatly increased the value of medical professionals' services after the war.[52] Much of the training and experience that medical personnel gained during the war allowed them to be better doctors, surgeons, and nurses after the war. And the South, physically and economically broken in the wake of the war, sorely needed those vital services in the post-war world.[53] These lessons were then applied to public health, particularly in the emphasis on sanitation and hospital construction and administration. They especially learned that decentralizing the supply system worked much more effectively and efficiently than one in which all supplies were sent to and then distributed from a single depot.[54] The war also underscored the importance of volunteer assistance societies, such as the Red Cross, and the importance of dental care. Several dentists were assigned at key points throughout the Southern armies.

Moore clearly got along well with both Davis and Congress because money kept coming in increasing amounts to the Army Medical Department every succeeding year throughout the war. (See tables 7 and 8.)

## *Chief of the Ordnance Bureau*

The Ordnance Bureau was technically part of the Corps of Artillery, but in practical terms it was a distinct entity. The one chief of ordnance was Major Josiah Gorgas, who had been the first chief of the Engineer Bureau. He served over Ordnance from April 8, 1861, until April 26, 1865. McPherson posits that the appointment of Gorgas was one of Davis's best choices, calling Gorgas "a master of organization and improvisation."[55]

Gorgas was not Davis's first choice for the position. Davis had wanted Major Alfred Mordecai, commander of the Watervliet Arsenal in Troy, New York, with whom he had had a long prewar connection. Davis, through Colonel

William Hardee, told Mordecai that the Confederacy was going to "'raise a Corps of Engineers and a Corps of Artillery, and the Prest [sic] would be pleased to place you at the head of either as you may elect. The Corps of Artillery will be charged with ordnance duties.'"[56]

Mordecai elected neither. Upon his declining the offers, Davis turned to Gorgas, a Pennsylvania native whom General P.G.T. Beauregard had repeatedly recommended to Davis. Gorgas accepted the offer without delay and resigned his commission in the Union army on March 21, 1861. He was assigned to his duties by Special Order No. 17 on April 8, 1861. (Mordecai stayed in the Union army until May, but he could not bring himself to link himself to the Confederacy.) Gorgas was "specifically responsible for the procurement and purchase of arms and ammunition."[57] He did such a good job at that task that during the war he earned the nickname "the Ordnance Wizard."[58]

Gorgas entered West Point in 1837 and graduated in 1841, sixth in a class of 52. He developed a reputation as a "hothead," demanding overseas duty in Europe and writing an angry, offensive letter to then-secretary of war James Buchanan.

Gorgas accompanied General Winfield Scott to Vera Cruz during the Mexican War, serving as a supply officer. While assigned to duty at Hampton Roads, Virginia, he experimented extensively with various big guns and started getting a reputation as an ordnance expert.[59] In all, he spent about 20 years serving in the field of ordnance, including commands of several arsenals in the South. In 1860, Secretary of War John Floyd put him on the Ordnance Board in Washington, D.C., where he soon was perceived as too friendly with Southerners.[60] He resigned from the army on March 21, 1861, a Yankee who chose to cast his lot with the South, his adopted country.

Because the individual states refused to give up the guns they had seized from Federal sources within their borders or had bought for their own defense, Gorgas had to start with almost nothing.[61] His overriding goals were to create that stockpile by buying weapons from abroad (through his agent, Major Caleb Huse) and to centralize all Confederate ordnance operations. He worked hard to overhaul and enlarge existing facilities, purchased new arsenals, and start up powder mills within the Confederacy.[62]

One of Gorgas's strengths was his ability to locate and employ highly skilled subordinates.[63] One such capable man was George W. Rains, whom Gorgas named to head the powder-making works at Augusta, Georgia.

Among Gorgas's other achievements were the following. He used the Bureau of Foreign Supplies to sell cotton for money to be used to buy weapons in Europe. (An estimated two-thirds of Confederate small arms were obtained from overseas.[64]) He also organized the Bureau of Niter and Mining for the home manufacture of powder and metals and formed the Artillery Bureau. He trained the factory workers at Confederate manufacturing facilities as a home guard to protect their own works, knowing that regular troops could not be spared to protect all of the manufactories throughout the South.

The Confederate war industries never had enough workers, but Gorgas was careful and considerate in how he treated subordinates, giving them wide latitude to conduct experiments and somehow getting the most out of limited numbers of people.[65] He knew as early as 1863 that shortages of both personnel and raw materials would eventually destroy the South's ability to continue waging war effectively. As a last, reluctant resort, he finally supported the impressments of the needed resources, but both private companies and public sentiment resisted those efforts. He never really understood what he perceived to be some Southerners' lack of love for their country.[66]

Having worked so hard to centralize the South's war industries, Gorgas eventually realized that with the South's loss of territory during the war, his focus would have to change. In 1863, he began to advocate *less* centralization of manufacturing operations and to promote "localism," home manufacture of necessary armaments and supplies. The biggest problem he faced in this effort was not in the actual manufacture of the needed goods but in the transportation of raw materials to the manufacturers and of the finished products to the frontline soldiers.

Near the end of 1864, Gorgas was rewarded for his diligence and successful efforts to organize and adapt limited resources when he was promoted to brigadier general.[67] He was hailed as a "miracle worker."[68]

As the Confederacy's armies retreated in defeat, manufacturing facilities closed, the Union forces captured and/or destroyed facilities and equipment, and the workers and raw materials needed for manufacturing continued to dwindle. Gorgas eventually found himself an officer with no subordinates.

Vandiver declared Gorgas to be "one of the ablest officers in the Confederate service."[69] His first action as chief of ordnance was to conduct an inventory to determine just how well the Confederate military was equipped with arms: muskets, rifles and carbines, pistols, artillery of various types, including naval guns, and the types and amounts of powder available. Before the end of his first month, he had reported the results to the secretary of war, Leroy P. Walker. Gorgas discovered from his inventory just how limited the South was in firepower (only 159,010 small arms of various sorts and calibers).[70] The inventory also showed "about 3,200,000 cartridges" in the Southern arsenals and "about 168,000 pounds of musket and rifle powder—potentially another 1,500,000 bullets," and "some two million percussion caps."[71] He also counted 429 heavy guns, but 375 of them were located in one place—Charleston, South Carolina.[72]

On the surface, the results might have sounded impressive, but when compared with the recommended amounts of shot and powder per gun, it was decidedly less so. For example, units were armed with an inconsistent variety of weapons, from ancient flintlock muskets to the newer Enfield rifles.[73] Of the available small arms, many of them were old and obsolete. Most of them had smooth-bore rather than rifled barrels and were therefore less accurate and had less range than rifled barrels. Some of them were also in poor condition and needed varying degrees of repairs. The available "small arms powder would have amounted to roughly 30 rounds per available weapon when the ordnance manual called for 200 rounds per man."[74] Volunteers were told that they would be paid for whatever arms and equipment they brought with them.

To make the situation worse, the South had "no adequate production facilities then in place,"[75] although one was under construction at Augusta, Georgia, and was tooled to make ammunition and knapsacks. Only the Richmond arsenal was capable of producing small arms and everything needed for their use. Other facilities existed in Baton Rouge, Charleston, Montgomery, Mount Vernon, Nashville, and Savannah, but they had no powder for any weapons they produced. Besides, the Charleston and Savannah facilities were tasked with attending to the harbor defenses of only those cities. To solve this problem, Gorgas sought to contract with private companies to make the needed items. He pledged to pay the companies half of the cost up front if they would invest 25 percent up front. A more pressing need than the South's manufacturing ability was its need for more raw materials, especially lead, copper, steel, firebrick, gun metal, and gunpowder.

Simultaneously, Gorgas sent agents to Europe with authorization to "contract and ship raw materials and finished goods from foreign sources."[76] He set over this important task Major Caleb Huse. Months later, Huse would ship about 120 tons of powder through the blockade to the Confederate troops. Gorgas became an early advocate of blockade running and bought four ships for the Ordnance Bureau and had them make the trip through the blockade to Bermuda and Nassau. Between September 30, 1862, and September 30, 1863, more than 113,500 weapons got to the South through the blockade. Between November 1, 1863, and December 8, 1864, another 69,000 weapons and more than 1,500,000 pounds of lead got through, along with more than 1,930,000 pounds of saltpeter, enough to make a substantial dent in the lead shortage.[77]

Eventually, Gorgas realized that if the South were to obtain the necessary materials, it would have to mine them itself. From this realization was born the Niter and Mining Bureau in April 1862. The Bureau's duties included mining and producing all minerals needed to make arms and ammunition, although it would also handle foreign procurement as it could obtain them. Gorgas chose Captain Isaac Munroe St. John to run the Niter and Mining Bureau. He selected

George Washington Rains, a fellow West Pointer, to handle manufacturing operations.

Until the facilities got up and running and foreign purchases of arms and ammunition began to arrive, the Confederacy had to depend on what was currently on hand (for better or worse) and what they could capture from the enemy. Beyond that, they would have to "make do" as best they could through "make-shifts."[78] The assortment of different types and calibers of weapons was astounding, and ordnance personnel had a nearly impossible job to supply the variety of types of ammunition needed. One of Gorgas's many priorities became the standardization of ordnance. In charge of this duty, which fell under the larger duty of being superintendent and chemist at the Confederate Ordnance Laboratories, he placed Captain John William Mallet. Mallet made his headquarters in Macon, Georgia, on September 11, 1863. Under Mallet's guidance, the Confederacy moved toward the desired standardization, perhaps the most important development being the adoption of the English Enfield rifle's .577 caliber as the standard issue for the Confederate military.

Even when the raw materials for making the arms and equipment and the weapons and ammunition were available, the Ordnance Bureau faced another problem that would plague it throughout the war, with the situation getting only worse with time. The transportation system was horrendous. Railroads were often unconnected. Even if they were connected, they were often of different gauges. As the traffic on the lines increased and as the wear of war took its toll on rails, motive power (locomotives), and rolling stock, the situation only worsened. When Union forces occupied areas through which the rail lines ran, the supply of arms and ammunition had to be rerouted, creating further delays.

The roads were no better. In fact, they might have been worse than the railroads. Very few were paved. During periods of rain and spring thaws, the roads became a quagmire. Wagons, horses, and mules got stuck in the mud. As the war dragged on, horses were killed or died of disease or fatigue. Horses were used for cavalry and artillery units as well as for transporting supplies, arms, ammunition, food, medicine, and ambulances. The supply of horse and mule flesh quickly reached crisis proportions. Food, which was never really in short supply, often rotted in warehouses or in railcars because the transportation problems prevented its being moved to the troops who needed it.

## *Chief of the Bureau of War*

The Bureau of War was filled by two men, but the office is generally associated with the work of one man, Colonel Robert Garlick Hill Kean. Kean was appointed to lead the bureau on April 2, 1862, replacing Colonel Albert Bledsoe, whom Leroy Pope Walker had disliked and whom Judah Benjamin had given no work.[79] Kean ended up serving under three successive secretaries of war—Randolph, Seddon, and Breckinridge.

Kean was born in Virginia in 1828. He attended Episcopal High School in Alexandria and studied under headmaster William Nelson Pendleton, who later became Lee's chief of artillery. But finances forced the school to close before Kean could graduate. Next, he attended Rappahannock Academy at Port Royal and then Frederick Coleman's Concord Academy. He graduated from the latter school in 1848.

For a while, Kean tutored in a family before enrolling at the University of Virginia to study law, living for two years in the home of one of his professors. He graduated in 1853 and moved to Lynchburg, where he opened his own law office. He avoided politics but was involved in the temperance movement and the Young Men's Christian Association (YMCA).

When John Brown made his unsuccessful raid on Harpers Ferry, Kean joined other volunteers in forming a home guard, which later was engaged in 24 battles and skirmishes during the war.[80] At the First Battle of Manassas, Kean's regiment was assigned to General James Longstreet's brigade. These green troops held off a Yankee charge in a brief battle preliminary to the main battle, which occurred three days later. During that main battle, when Union troops fled in panic, Kean and his comrades collected and guarded the spoils of battle. While occupying hills overlooking Alexandria, Kean made his first entry in his now-famous diary. The date was September 15, 1861.

Early that fall, Kean was assigned to be the quartermaster sergeant. In November, he applied to become assistant quartermaster. He also applied to become a "lieutenant of the line." But before those applications could be processed, he was ordered to the staff of General George Wythe Randolph to become the assistant adjutant general and was promoted to captain. A few weeks later, Randolph was appointed assistant secretary of war, and he took Kean to his new post with him. After a week in the new position, Kean was appointed chief of the Bureau of War.

The office did not have finely defined functions as did other departments. It coordinated with other offices in the War Department.[81] Kean managed the office, specifically supervising clerks, who copied correspondence and other documents by the bushels. He also decided routine matters and signed orders issued by the war secretary.[82] Kean also wrote the reports of investigating committees that had been set up to blame others for military messes.

Another responsibility of Kean's office overseeing the issuance of passports, and he was inundated with requests for them. He had to try to prevent people from fleeing the draft and to prevent people from trying to profit from trade across the borders with the United States while issuing passports to those who had valid, legitimate reasons for international travel. He also screened visitors to the secretary's office.

Younger concludes that Kean "was highly qualified for his ... position and he made it an important one.... [H]e worked hard and expected hard work of those under him."[83]

Perhaps Kean's greatest contribution, however, was not the immediate war effort or the efficient functioning of the War Department but rather to posterity. During the Confederate government's flight from Richmond, some people suggested that Confederate records be destroyed to expedite their escape. "Kean vigorously protested, insisting that they contained matters of history which would be invaluable in vindicating the South against any malignant or untruthful charge which might be trumped up against her."[84] While Davis and the cabinet continued the flight south, Kean, at Secretary of War Breckinridge's command, remained behind in Charlotte and surrendered the records to Federal officers there.

Kean returned home to Virginia to find that his house had been commandeered by a Union commissary captain as his headquarters. Kean continued to record his observations and thoughts for the next seven months, recording the earliest days of Reconstruction in Virginia and offering his assessment of why the South had lost the war. His diary covers the four years before December 1865, beginning when Kean was 33 years old and a private in the Confederate army. Shortly after he began his diary, he was promoted to captain and made chief of the Bureau of War in Richmond. After the war, as he saw Reconstruction get off to an ignominious start, he concluded that "constitutional liberty had perished with the Confederacy" and made plans to emigrate to Mexico.[85] He later changed his mind, however, because he lacked money to sustain himself there. Instead, he developed a successful legal practice in Virginia. He was repeatedly urged to run for political office, but he refused. He advocated temperance but opposed prohibition. He also advocated paying off the state's war debts in full and supported civil service reforms. He died in 1898 at the age of 70.

Although Kean's diary is not as famous as J. B. Jones's *A Rebel War Clerk's Diary* or Mary Chesnut's *Diary from Dixie*, it offers valuable insights into the workings of the Confederate War Department. Kean was much "better informed" than Chesnut, being on the inside and directly involved in events in the government rather than being merely a spectator to it as she was. His observations are also "more reliable, more discerning, and better rounded than" either of the other two diarists.[86]

## Chief of the Engineer Bureau

The Engineer Bureau was not very successful at holding its chiefs, going through eight different changes, although two of the men served multiple stints at the position, three of them in the first nine months of the Confederacy. The first chief of the Engineer Bureau was Major Josiah Gorgas (April 8, 1861–August 3, 1861). He was followed by Major Danville Leadbetter (August 3, 1861–November 10, 1861), Captain Alfred L. Rives (November 13, 1861–September 24, 1862), and Lieutenant Colonel Jeremy Francis Gilmer (September 25, 1862–August 17, 1863). Rives returned to the position as a Lieutenant Colonel, serving from August 18, 1863, to March 9, 1864, during his second stint. Major General Martin Luther Smith took over on March 9, 1864, and served until April 1864, when Rives, now a colonel, took a third shot at the job until June 1864, when he again stepped aside. The final chief of the Engineer Bureau was Gilmer, who returned to the position as a major general and served from June 1864 until the end of the war.

## Chief of the Bureau of Foreign Supplies

The chief of the Bureau of Foreign Supplies was Lieutenant Colonel Thomas L. Bayne. Born August 4, 1824, in Jones City, Georgia, Bayne was reared by his uncle after his father remarried. He was homeschooled before attending Yale University, from which he graduated in 1847. He studied law in the offices of Slidell and Clarke.

When the war broke out, Bayne joined the army, received a commission as a captain of artillery, and fought at the Battle of Shiloh. He was promoted to colonel and ended up working under Josiah Gorgas, his wife's brother-in-law, in the War Department's Bureau of Foreign Supplies. When Richmond fell, he fled the city with Davis.

Shortly after Bayne resumed his practice of law after the war, President Grant offered to make him a U.S. circuit court judge if he would become a Republican, but Bayne refused. He died in 1891.

## Chief of the Bureau of Exchange

Much of this bureau's work involved negotiations behind the scenes and out of the limelight, so it is no wonder that the man who led it is little known today. The chief of the Bureau of Exchange was Colonel Robert Ould. He was born on January 31, 1820. He studied law at William and Mary, graduating in 1842. He practiced law in Washington, D.C., until the outbreak of the war in 1861. In that capacity, he helped codify the laws for D.C. under President Franklin Pierce and was appointed the District's attorney.

Upon Ould's leaving Washington when Lincoln was inaugurated, Ould was appointed assistant secretary of war under Judah Benjamin in the Confederate government. In 1862, he was named the agent of exchange for the Confederacy and worked for the release and exchange of Confederate prisoners of war. He quickly gained a reputation among the enemy exchange agents for his great efforts to negotiate the exchange of prisoners.

When Lee surrendered at Appomattox, Ould tendered his parole to General Grant, but Grant refused to treat him as a prisoner. He did not consider an exchange agent as being liable to capture. Ironically, Union secretary of war Edwin Stanton arrested and imprisoned Ould and made him stand trial for treason. He was, however, acquitted. Ould later returned to the practice of law in Richmond.

## *Chief of the Bureau of Conscription*

Perhaps one of the most detested bureaus in the whole Confederacy was the Bureau of Conscription. Its broad unpopularity might have had something to do with why three different men served as its chief during its comparatively short life after the first conscription act was passed by Congress in December 1862. The first director of the Bureau of Conscription was Brigadier General Gabriel J. Rains (December 16, 1862–May 24, 1863). He was replaced by Brigadier Charles W. Field (May 25, 1863–July 30, 1863). Colonel (later brigadier general) John Smith Preston then took over and served until the Conscription Bureau was abolished (July 30, 1863–March 17, 1865). These men exercised their authority under the adjutant and inspector general within the War Department.

Both North and South began the war relying solely on volunteers to meet their military manpower needs. Such had been sufficient for all of America's previous military necessities from the Revolution through the Mexican War. The president just put out a call for volunteers, and they showed up in sufficient numbers, even when a portion of the nation opposed the particular war, as occurred when the New England states opposed the Mexican War. In the case of the War Between the States, the people generally thought that the war would be over quickly. Initially, the Confederacy actually had to turn down volunteers because the number of men who responded surpassed the government's ability to arm and equip them. In the summer of 1861, Secretary of War Leroy Walker reported to President Davis that about 200,000 volunteers had offered themselves for service but were rejected because the Confederacy lacked weapons for them.[87] Many of them brought their own weapons and horses, but many others came empty handed.

When it became obvious that the war would last much longer than people had expected and the number of volunteers began to lag behind demands, both the North and the South resorted to conscription, or the draft. Southern leaders first began to express concern about a potential manpower shortage late in 1861. The original one-year enlistments were set to expire in the spring of 1862, and the South's stream of volunteers was slowing to a trickle. If something was not done to resolve the issue, the South would be left in a perilous situation.

One of the first suggestions of a solution to the problem was to try to coax the soldiers to reenlist by offering them a bounty as an incentive. But efforts in that direction were unsuccessful, so a second suggestion gained some support: to require the one-year enlistees to serve an additional two years. But Davis was opposed to forcing those who had volunteered for one-year enlistments at the start of the war to serve two additional years. He said that to do so would violate their contractual agreement.[88] (Similarly, Secretary of War George Randolph did not believe that the law forbidding trade with the enemy applied to the government and cited European history as support for his view. He noted that many warring nations traded with the citizens of the enemy nations, but this "everyone else is doing it" approach did not convince Davis.[89])

But Randolph convinced Davis that it *was* legal because it was the only possible way to meet the South's needs for manpower and therefore constituted a military necessity.[90] Some members of Congress, however, called it tyranny. The state governors, especially Brown of Georgia and Vance of North Carolina, strongly opposed it. Nevertheless, Congress on April 16, 1862, passed the first conscription law.

According to the provisions of the conscription act, all white males ages 18 to 35 were subject to the draft, and they would be drafted for three-year stints. In deference to the democratic principles of the electorate, the men in each company would elect their own officers from among their ranks, and their assignments to units would be limited to units of their own states. Potential draftees were given a brief time to volunteer before they were eventually forced into the army. Those who did not want to serve were allowed to hire substitutes.

General Robert E. Lee had wanted Congress to extend the draft to all men between the ages 18 to 45. He was a little ahead of his time in urging that the whole nation "be converted into an army, the producers to feed and the soldiers to fight.'"[91] He had been advocating a full war economy several years before Sherman recognized that total war could be turned against the enemy's civilian population and economy before they turned it against him.

Southerners opposed conscription from the beginning because it was diametrically opposite the principle of states' rights and sovereignty. For that reason, as well as for less ideological but more practical reasons, conscription faced opposition, sometimes fiercely, throughout the war. It was particularly odious in pro–Union areas such as North Alabama, East Tennessee, and Western North Carolina. The first draft law in American history prompted the first draft dodgers. Not only did men not want to join the army, fight fellow Americans, and risk life and limb for a cause in which they felt they had little or no stake but also they feared what would become of their poor families whom they left behind. Many poor whites and yeoman farmers who were drafted had no one at home to keep their farms producing even a subsistence for their family members, let alone extra for the armies. The longer the war lasted and the more aggressively the army sought to enforce the law, the greater became the opposition. Some draft dodgers fled deep into the dark heights of the Appalachian Mountains. Others, aided by guides, fled to Kentucky, where many of them ended up joining the Union forces that were being raised at Camp Robinson.

When the South experienced military successes in 1862, Secretary of War Randolph attributed the success to the draft. "'Now we are advancing,' he state[d], ... upon an enemy defeated, disheartened, and sheltering himself behind defensive works,'" and such a successful army "'should be cherished and perfected.'"[92]

But those fortunes began to dim with the Battle of Antietam. Lee's army had held the field at the end of the battle, and McClellan did not resume the attack, but the Confederates crossed back over the Potomac, returning to the friendly hills and valleys of Virginia, smarting and with fewer men than they had taken into Maryland. The lost men had to be replaced, but volunteers were even less forthcoming than they had been earlier, and conscription was not enough. The conscription law had to be broadened, and Congress set out to work on doing just that.

The result of Congress's work was the Conscription Act of September 27, 1862. It extended the draft to include all white males 18 to 45 years old (but it delayed the call-up of those who were over 40 until July 15, 1863). But then came the crushing losses at Vicksburg and Gettysburg in the summer of 1863. Ultimately, the second conscription act also proved insufficient, and a third conscription act was passed on February 17, 1864. That third act reached down to take 17-year-old boys and up to get those up to 50 years of age (although those aged 45–50 were limited to service in the state reserve). It also reduced the categories of exemptions. Thereafter, soldiers, rather than exempt civilians, were used to fill vital industrial functions. The civilian industrial workers were forced into the military. The third act also incorporated the use of free blacks as laborers and impressed slaves for various noncombat duties.

A separate law, passed the previous December, repealed the provision for substitutes, and another, passed on January 5, 1865, declared that even those who had already hired substitutes were now eligible for the draft. It also ended term enlistments; everyone was in for the duration. Still another law, passed on March 30, 1865, authorized the use of slaves as soldiers, but the war was so far lost that none of the slaves could be trained quickly enough to get into the war.

None of these acts got easier to enforce; opposition to the draft only increased, and until exemptions were ended, many of the men eligible for the draft sought desperately to be hired in jobs that would make them eligible for an exemption. "An exemption was a specific allowance of a nonmilitary status" to someone who had proven his qualification for it.[93] Exemptions had first been defined in the Act of April 16, 1862, listing specific job categories that would not be subject to the draft because they were considered essential to the overall war effort. Those jobs included state and Confederate "legislative, executive and judicial officials and their clerks and employees; ferrymen, pilots and all actually engaged in river and railroad transportation work; employees in iron mines, foundries and furnaces; telegraph operators, ministers; printers, educators; hospital employees; druggists; and certain employees in wool and cotton mills."[94]

The Post Office Department continually complained about its employees' being drafted, leaving only the elderly or the physically unfit to deliver the mail. Postmaster General Reagan demanded that post office workers be exempted from the draft.

Others also sought exemptions. College students and their professors tried to get exemptions for students, but Congress refused to grant them. The secretary of war in 1863, James Seddon, did, however, allow college students to finish out their current academic year but did not exempt them. Journalists claimed exemption based on the principle of freedom of the press.[95] Those who were not in a profession or job that was exempt from the draft were often sorely tempted to dodge the conscription agents by suddenly entering one of the exempt careers—railroads, mines, foundries, blast furnaces, etc.

The Exemption Act was amended in late 1862 to add more exempt job categories. Categories that were added included farmers, railroad workers (but not porters and common laborers), telegraph workers, river and canal workers, blacksmiths, tanners, cobblers, workers in munitions plants, ship builders, salt producers, miners, and others. The key determining factor seems to have been the workers' criticality to the war effort. The 20 Negro Law also exempted one white overseer for every 20 slaves on a plantation. Religious exemptions were also granted to individuals who were members of traditionally pacifist religious groups, such as Quakers, Nazarenes, Mennonites, and Dunkards (also known as Brethren). Some doctors were also exempted because the civilian population would continue to need such medical services as those men could provide.

A law passed in December 1863 ended the practice of hiring a substitute. The Exemption Act of February 17, 1864, tightened exemptions by reducing the number of eligible job categories by more than half.[96] These new categories included preachers, editors, doctors, rail workers, government officials, and others, and the law made the president the final judge as to who would be granted such exemptions. It also declared that once someone who was eligible for the draft was enumerated, he could not switch occupations, closing that loophole. "Based upon incomplete returns, it would seem that the Confederate Government exempted 44.9 percent of the total number of men summoned to the colors through conscription."[97]

The results of these acts broadening conscription and limiting exemptions demoralized the population, increased desertion, and encouraged draft dodging as more men hid in the mountains or stole away to the North, notably Kentucky.

Generals, including Braxton Bragg and his general staff, complained about the number of people who were somehow able to evade the draft. To Bragg, it seemed as though "'the whole system of exemption'" was determined that "'none of the machinery of society, necessary for its comfort and convenience in a state of peace, is to be disturbed amidst the mighty upheaval of a revolution.'"[98]

Oddly, the Conscription Bureau operated east of the Mississippi River but not west of the Mississippi. The bureau operated under the sole authority of the War Department. The government assigned quotas to enrollment districts, not directly to the states. Draftees could appeal the decisions of the surgeons who determined the physical fitness of men who reported for the draft, but the appeals process was burdensome. When a draftee who was declared physically fit for service appealed, he did so to the district enrolling officer. During the appeal process, he could remain at his normal occupation until his appeal was decided. If he lost his appeal, he could further appeal to the Bureau of Conscription, but he had to report to his assigned camp of instruction during the appeal process. That process, especially the first stage, was notoriously slow, so many (some people said "almost every man") appealed as soon as they were enrolled and were thereby able to stay out of the army for a long period of time.

Dealing with deserters was also the responsibility of the Conscription Bureau, and desertion was a major problem. One estimate placed the number of deserters as of March 1865 at more than 100,000. Many deserters who fled into the rugged mountains of western North Carolina and East Tennessee often banded together in their own makeshift armies to defend themselves from the troops and conscription agents of both North and South and against roving bands of outlaws. Sometimes the bands of outlaws *were* the deserters. The problem became so great that Congress authorized Davis to suspend *habeas corpus* three times during the war to better deal with it (February 27–October 13, 1862, about eight months; October 13, 1862–February 13, 1863, about four months; and February 15, 1864–August 1, 1864, about six months, for a total of about a year and a half.) Vice President Stephens argued that the suspension of *habeas corpus* was unconstitutional. These two issues—conscription and suspension of *habeas corpus*—only increased the disaffection between Davis and Stephens.

The Confederate attorneys general ruled that the conscription acts were constitutional. The first such ruling came only a month after the first conscription act was passed, and it was made by Attorney General Thomas Watts. Because the Confederacy never organized a supreme court, the rulings of the attorneys general were considered final. Vice President Alexander Stephens argued, however, that both conscription and the suspension of *habeas corpus* violated the Constitution. According to his view, the Confederate government could requisition (request) troops from the States only when there were not enough volunteers. But the conscription acts were repeatedly upheld by various states' supreme courts. Texas (*Ex parte Copeland*), Georgia (*Jeffers v. Fair* and *Barber v. Irwin*), Virginia (*Burroughs v. Peyton*), Alabama (*Ex parte Hill in re Willis v. Confederate States, Ex parte Hill in re Armistead,* and *State ex rel. Graham in re Pille*), and Mississippi (*Simmons v. Miller, Enrolling Officer*) all ruled that the conscription laws were constitutional.[99]

Another form of conscription was the impressment of property. The central government gave itself authority to force the sale of horses, crops, cattle, hogs, and any other property that the government thought it needed for the armies in the field. Ideally, the government was supposed to pay fair market value for any impressed property, and the government determined what that fair value was. But it took time to determine those prices, and in a time of such rampant inflation as occurred in the Confederacy, real prices surpassed "book prices" almost as quickly as the government determined the prices the impressment agents were to use. Impressment led to resentment, and farmers began hiding their property and crops whenever government agents or armies were rumored to be in the area. Many farmers cut back on how much they grew, sowing only what their immediate families needed. As wives whose husbands were in the army struggled to survive alone, stories of depredations by government agents' actions putting families in dire straits caused soldiers to desert.

By the time of Appomattox, desertion was epidemic, and it was a major factor in Lee's decision to surrender.

Conscription, then, a law designed to increase the manpower of the Confederate armies, actually ended up reducing those numbers. It seemed to be expedient and helped, perhaps, in the short run, but it ended up hurting in the long run.

## *Chief of the Niter and Mining Bureau*

Originally a division of the Ordnance Bureau, the Niter and Mining Bureau became its own bureau-level organization with its own chief, Colonel Isaac M. St. John, who made it one of the most effective bureaus in the Confederate government.[100] The purpose of the Niter and Mining Bureau was to supply the Confederacy with all the minerals and metals it needed to wage war. This was primarily, but certainly not limited to, niter (also known as saltpeter), the main ingredient in the manufacture of gunpowder and explosives. It was usually found in caves in the South. St. John was fortunate to discover large supplies of saltpeter in the mountains of southeastern East Tennessee. On January 31, 1864, diarist Kean reported that St. John began with practically nothing but had amassed a nearly complete supply of niter.[101]

The Niter and Mining Bureau had two chiefs, the first of which was Lieutenant Colonel Isaac Munroe St. John, who in the last months of the war would become the commissary general, and he served from May 28, 1863, until February 16, 1865. He was followed by Colonel Richard Morton (February 22, 1865–April 1865).

St. John, a native of Georgia, was born on November 19, 1827. He graduated from Yale in 1845. Between graduation and the outbreak of the War Between the States, St. John worked as a lawyer, the editor of the Baltimore *Patriot* newspaper, and a civil engineer for the Baltimore and Ohio Railroad (1848–55) and the Blue Ridge Railroad Company in South Carolina (1855–61).

With the coming of hostilities, St. John volunteered as a private in the Fort Hill Guards of South Carolina. Within six months, his skills became apparent, however, and he was made an engineer assigned to the Army of the Peninsula. By the following April, he was chief engineer under Brigadier General John B. Magruder at Yorktown, Virginia. Shortly thereafter, on April 18, 1862, he was appointed chief of the Bureau of Niter and Mining. He remained in that position until February 16, 1865, when he was reassigned by a special act of Congress to be the commissary general of subsistence.

## 12. Overview

The Bureau also oversaw the mining of coal, copper, iron, lead, zinc, and other minerals required in making ordnance and ammunition.

### Chief of the Bureau of Indian Affairs

Perhaps the bureau of the Confederate government that is the least well known is the Bureau of Indian Affairs. It was established in March 1861 and was headed by three commissioners at different times. The first commissioner of the Bureau of Indian Affairs was David Hubbard (March 15, 1861–April 7, 1862, and 1863–February 21, 1865). The others were Sutton Scott (April 8, 1862–1863) and Brigadier General Douglas Cooper (February 21, 1865–April 1865).

David Hubbard (1792–1874) was a two-term congressman from Alabama. He had supported Breckinridge for president in 1860 and favored secession. He accepted appointment to the post of the chief of the Bureau of Indian Affairs, which included dealing with the Indians and keeping them from helping the Union.[102] He had mixed success in that effort. After the war, he moved to Tennessee, where he ran a tannery.

Douglas Cooper (1815–1879) was a Mississippian and a veteran of the Mexican War. In 1853, he had been appointed the U.S. commissioner to the Choctaws. Because of this experience in dealing with the Indians, he was appointed to deal with the Five Civilized Tribes during the War Between the States. In that capacity, he was able to convince parts of all five tribes to join the Confederate cause.[103] He was well liked and respected by the Indians. In fact, the Chickasaw tribe adopted him as one of its own on May 25, 1861. He not only kept the Indians from joining the Union cause but also raised an all-Indian unit and rose to become a major general. By war's end, he commanded all the Indians in the Trans-Mississippi theater.[104] After the war, he continued working to win for the Indians by pressing their claims against the Union for losses suffered during the conflict.

### Command Structure

The command structure of the Confederate military machine during much of the war put the Confederacy at a decided but unnecessary and avoidable disadvantage, and if it had been changed earlier in the war rather than in the waning months of the war, the war's outcome might have been far different. Although as president Jefferson Davis was constitutionally the Confederate commander in chief, he did not have to try to be president, secretary of war, and general in chief all at the same time. He not only set the broad strategy for the war but also sought to engage in tactical decisions, micromanaging every detail, engaging in disputes between generals, and trying to tell everyone what to do, how to do it, and when to do it.

At the beginning of the war, the Confederate War Department had no single overall commander over the military. Davis acted as not only president but also commander in chief of all military forces. His main military advisor was Robert E. Lee, who exercised broad control similar to a chief of staff. Fortunately for the Confederacy, Lee knew how to get along with Davis, and Davis trusted Lee's advice better than that of anyone else in the Confederate military. On June 1, 1862, Lee was given command of the Army of Northern Virginia, the largest and arguably the most important of the Southern armies. On February 24, 1864, in the wake of a near-mutiny by generals serving in the Army of Tennessee under General Braxton Bragg, Davis named Bragg to fill the position of chief advisor that Lee had formerly held. (Bragg held that position until January 31, 1865.) But Bragg was no Robert E. Lee.

On January 3, 1865, Congress named Lee general in chief. But it was too late. By that point, no Confederate army could take the offensive in any theater of operations, let alone coordinate with other armies across theaters. Every Southern army was fighting for its very life. Lee maintained that essentially symbolic titled until he surrendered the Army of Northern Virginia to Grant at Appomattox on April 9, 1865.

The biggest consequence of the South's lack of a unified central command was that it prevented the Confederacy from launching effective simultaneous and coordinated attacks on multiple fronts. It prevented the Southern forces from acting in unison toward a unified mutually supportive role. It worked against the concentration of forces where they could do the most good. Instead, each theater was left to itself in trying to achieve victories without coordinated command and control, with the frustrations of trying to coordinate multiple, often independent, commands, and with confusion concerning who was really in charge and to whom each command was responsible.

## *Personnel Organization*

Such as it was, without a true central command structure, the Confederate military did have some organization, as the following sections show. In contrast to its command structure, the Confederate military was well organized in its personnel, thanks in large part to the large number of government and military officials who had had formal military experience, including in combat situations. (The Mexican War had been an excellent proving ground for future Confederate commanders. The Confederacy was significantly blessed with many graduates of West Point, especially from the graduating class of 1846, including such future household names as Thomas "Stonewall" Jackson, A.P. Hill, George Pickett, and others.[105])

The Confederate military personnel were grouped according to their function, or the role they would play in combat: infantry, designated by blue; cavalry, designated by yellow; and artillery, designated by red. These colors were displayed prominently on the men's uniforms and head coverings.

The smallest infantry unit, comprising 100 men, was the company. It was led by a captain assisted by two or more lieutenants. Ten companies, 1,000 men, made up a regiment. Each regiment was led by a colonel, lieutenant colonels, and a major. The regiment was the basic organizational unit of the Confederate army. (The term *battalion* was seldom used, but when it was used, it referred essentially to a regiment.)

Four regiments, 4,000 men, made up a brigade, and each brigade was led by a brigadier general. (Sometimes more than four regiments were included in a brigade.) Two to four brigades made a division, headed by a major general. Two to four divisions made a corps, led by a lieutenant general. And two to four corps made up an army, which was commanded by a full general.

In the artillery, there was no organizational structure above the regimental level. There were usually four artillery batteries per infantry division, four to five batteries per brigade, and two or more batteries per regiment. One artillery battery, or company, was made up of two or three sections with a total of 40 to 100 men. Each section had two platoons, led by a lieutenant. Each platoon had one gun and its limber, one caisson, 12 horses, and nine men commanded by a sergeant.

The smallest unit of cavalry was the platoon, led by a lieutenant. Two platoons, 40 to 100 men and their horses, made up a troop, or company. Of the number of men, 25 percent of them were assigned to hold the horses while the other 75 percent were engaged in combat operations. Two troops made up a squadron, 60 to 200 men and their horses and commanded by either a major or a lieutenant colonel. Squadrons were used for operating on detached, somewhat independent service. Two squadrons, 90 to 400 men and their horses, made up a battalion. Two or more battalions, 1,200 men and their horses, made a regiment, which was led by a colonel. Two or more battalions, or regiments, made a brigade under a brigadier general or a colonel. Two or more brigades produced a division, which was led by a major general. And two or more divisions made a corps, which was commanded by a lieutenant general.

## *Acquiring Recruits for the Army*

The personnel needed to create the Confederate army were acquired in one of two ways: volunteers or conscripts. On March 6, 1861, Congress issued a call for 100,000 volunteers and state militia to be ready for an expected invasion by the North. On January 23, 1862, a second call for volunteers was issued, that call being for an additional 400,000 recruits. The results were quite satisfactory. In fact, more people volunteered than the Confederacy had guns and equipment to outfit. As the war dragged on, and especially as it began to turn against the South, voluntary recruitment lagged behind necessity, and the Confederate government felt constrained to turn to conscription.

The First Conscription Act was passed on April 16, 1862, and called for all white males ages 18 to 35 to report for military service for the duration of the war. A Second Conscription Act was passed on September 27, 1862, and it called for the drafting of all white males ages 18 to 45. Finally, a Third Conscription Act passed on February 17, 1864, and it lowered the age to 17 and raised it to 50. Although several prominent officials, both congressmen and generals, called for the arming of slaves to increase the size of the Confederate forces, the Confederate Congress did not pass such a law until March 13, 1865. By that time, it was too little too late. There was not enough time to give the blacks even basic training before the war ended.

## *Field Organization*

In the field, the Confederacy was divided into military departments and districts over which generals were given direct command responsibility. At once both a strength and a weakness of this command structure was the fact that these district commanders operated almost independently of each other, making any sort of coordination of simultaneous operations against the enemy almost impossible.

The departmental system was designed as a way to organize all Confederate forces to protect all the South. Each department had the responsibility of defending a specific, designated geographic area.[106] In keeping with his belief in decentralization, Davis gave each regional commander wide latitude and autonomy.[107]

In theory, each department was supposed to be self-sustaining and purely defensive in nature. In practice, they probably could have been, but the changing realities of war made that practically impossible, especially by 1863, when the South was steadily losing territory in the West. As is discussed in the section dealing with the Subsistence Bureau, as Union forces occupied or destroyed some of the best food-producing areas, the Southern armies suffered and depended heavily on the resources of other departments. And the armies in the departments from which the suffering armies had to get supplies resented giving up their own local resources for armies elsewhere.

At the heart of the Confederate defensive strategy seemed to be the belief that "all objective points were equal."[108] This led to the development of a "cordon defense," the dispersing of troops along long, thin lines all around the perimeters of the Confederacy in a static defense. This arrangement, however, was impractical because some areas were strategically more important than others. It left the central heartland of the South totally unprotected while assigning troops to places that were not of strategic importance. It also led to conflict within the ranks of the army commanders. General P.G.T. Beauregard and other generals, for example, advocated the concentration of troops at strategic locations to be engaged in offensive actions against the enemy. They repeatedly advised dividing the enemy's forces while uniting their own, but it was never done because they did not have adequate unity of command,[109] and the cordon defense made it virtually impossible to concentrate large numbers of troops anywhere quickly. The Confederacy had no shortage of men in the Western Theater, but the troops they had were so scattered among the various departmental commands that it was impossible to effect a concentration of forces.[110]

Another problem with the departmental system was that Davis began tampering with it, trying to micromanage the various departments and districts. The South tried out more than 35 different departmental schemes involving more than 85 different command structures during the war.[111] In July 1861, Davis began reorganization and modification of the departmental system, effecting a degree of concentration in Virginia, the Carolinas, Georgia, and Florida, and he created the Trans-Mississippi Department. He established five large commands: Northern Virginia; South Carolina, Georgia, and Florida; the Trans-Mississippi; and the Second, or Western, Department, which constituted the Army of Tennessee.

Davis again messed with the system when he added a new department, the Department of East Tennessee under General Kirby Smith. He then urged it to undertake a coordinated attack with General Braxton Bragg. But "Bragg's execution was not equal to his conception," and despite his tendency to micromanage everything that was going on in the War Department, Davis was totally clueless about the concentration of the forces of Bragg and Kirby Smith.[112] The result was a dismal failure.

The Confederate government also was always readjusting the boundaries of the various departments. The department commanders were seldom willing to work together to coordinate plans and actions. And even if they did, the commanders were too independent to make effective the unified actions that they did attempt. Finally, in November 1862, Davis united the several Western commands into the Department of the West under the command of General Joe Johnston. And yet, true to the Davis track record throughout the war, Johnston's command was plagued by interference from the capital. Davis's constant butting in on department commanders only made things worse.

As if the situation were not complicated and confusing enough, Davis had another great vice: he never issued direct and unmistakable orders to any commander; instead, he only suggested or asked, thereby leaving his desires open to interpretation.[113] So commanders obeyed if they felt like it and disregarded his requests if they did not feel like it or disagreed with his proposed action. This problem was especially critical in attempts to coordinate the actions of more than one army. As easy as this made it for commanders in the field to assume that his "orders" were merely suggestions, it was complicated by Davis's propensity to be inflexible when it came to military matters and his seeming inability to admit that he had made a mistake.[114] The situation was even further muddled because he refused to allow his secretaries of war to order anything, either; they could only suggest or recommend or strongly urge. Field commanders added their own haze to the mix whenever the secretary of war strongly urged an action on them and they appealed over his head directly to Davis.

Add to this mess the political infighting between the generals and the administration, between Congress and the War Department, and among the generals themselves. A major source of conflict among the generals was disagreements over strategy. Some generals advocated a Napoleonic concentration and offensive in the West. This bloc was dominated by Beauregard and his supporters, but it also included Generals Bragg, Johnston, and James Longstreet. Another bloc advocated that first priority be given to the Eastern theater of operations. The Virginia generals, not surprisingly, led this bloc.

As each of these blocs vied for control over parts of Confederate strategic actions, personality clashes occurred, and even past romantic conflicts resurfaced. (Davis and Johnston, for example, had both once tried to woo the same girl, and one of them lost out to the other, but neither forgot the conflict.)

Beauregard was a great strategist but was often overruled or even ignored by Davis and the War Department. Beauregard had published during the war a book titled *Principles and Maxims of the Art of War* and distributed copies to his officers. He especially believed strongly in the following three principles.

Principle No. 1—Concentrate masses of your army against fractions of your enemy's army.

Principle No. 2—Attack as much as possible the communications of your enemy without exposing your own to attack.

Principle No. 3—Operate always on interior lines.[115]

Unfortunately, Davis did not practice Principle No. 1, concentration of forces, but instead dispersed the southern forces all around the nation's borders. Neither did he set broad strategy and then allow his generals to carry it out, leaving details of tactics to their better discretion. His secretaries of war were, therefore, put in an unenviable position guaranteed to fail. The following five chapters explain how each successive secretary of war had to deal with this set of circumstances.

CHAPTER 13

# Leroy Pope Walker

President Davis's initial nominee for the position of secretary of war was Leroy P. Walker. Although Walker had no formal military training or experience, he held a commission as a brigadier general in the Alabama militia. More important to Davis, Walker was a political operative, having been chairman of the Alabama delegation to the Charleston Democratic convention. He was also a secessionist and was popular with the people of Alabama. Davis needed someone in his cabinet to represent Alabama. Perhaps most important of all, Walker seemed to be someone who would merely do what Davis told him to do without trying to take initiatives of his own.

Leroy Pope Walker came from a long line of historic leaders, so one might have expected him to follow in his forebears' footsteps. His maternal grandfather was one of the founders of the town of Huntsville, Alabama, and Walker was named after him—Leroy Pope. His father and grandfather were two of the members of the Broad River Groups, the earliest settlers of Alabama.

Walker was born on February 7, 1817, in Huntsville in Madison County, Alabama. He grew up in that town until he left in 1833 to attend the University of

Leroy Pope Walker, Secretary of War (Alabama Department of Archives and History).

Alabama. After studying there for three years, he transferred to the University of Virginia to study law. He was admitted to the bar and began practicing law in 1837. He was soon acclaimed as "the foremost attorney in Huntsville and … North Alabama."[1]

Married twice, Walker had two sons from the first marriage. Following his first wife's death, he had two daughters and a son from a second marriage.

One of Walker's notable habits was chewing tobacco. He was always seen with a quid of tobacco in his mouth, so he was forever spitting. He was quiet and mild-mannered and often perceived as being distant and detached.[2] He was not really a politician as one generally thinks of a politician, but he was a good public speaker. While pursing his legal career, Walker became involved in politics. In 1843, he was elected to the Alabama House of Representatives as the representative of Lawrence County. He was elected again in 1847 as the representative of Lauderdale County, and the other House members twice (in 1847 and 1849) elected him their Speaker.

The Alabama Democratic Convention elected him their president in 1848. Walker was a delegate to the Nashville Convention in 1850–51 and in 1850 was elected judge of the Fourth Judicial Circuit, a position he held for three years. In 1853, he returned to the state legislature and was assigned to the Committee on Internal Improvements. In that role, he led efforts to acquire state monies for internal improvements, especially railroads and road construction. In 1856, he supported the successful presidential campaign of James Buchanan.

As the tensions over slavery intensified, Walker became increasingly more pro-slavery and pro-secession in his views. He became a leading advocate of states' rights and was called "'[William Lowndes] Yancey's best aide.'"[3] At the 1860 Democratic National Convention (DNC) at Institute Hall in Charleston, Walker sided with the radical wing of the party. When the DNC refused to include support in its platform for the demand that slavery be allowed in the new territories, Walker led the Alabama delegation and a total of 50 delegates from the hall in protest. They met at nearby Military Hall, declaring themselves to be the real DNC. The convention met again two months later at the Front Street Theater in Baltimore and nominated Stephen Douglas of Illinois to be the party's candidate for president. The delegates who had bolted the Charleston convention then reconvened at the Maryland Institute and named their own candidate, John C. Breckinridge of Kentucky. In all of these internal party squabbles, Walker sided with the radicals, and he supported Breckinridge during the ensuing campaign. He did not waste time attacking Lincoln or Bell, focusing his full attention instead against Douglas. But then, with only two weeks remaining before the election, Walker began attacking Lincoln and the Black Republicans. As he began to recognize the likelihood of Lincoln's winning the election, he talked about the desirability—even the necessity—of secession if Lincoln won.

In taking these positions, Walker was taking a calculated political risk because the voters of North Alabama were divided on these issues. Many North Alabamians were Unionists who opposed the idea of secession and supported the moderate position of Douglas. In fact, his own county—Madison—was "predominantly Unionist or Cooperationist in sentiment,"[4] this in spite of the fact that the county was 55 percent slave. When Lincoln won and Alabama held an election of delegates to the Alabama secessionist convention, Walker pressed for immediate secession but refused to run to become a delegate to the secession convention, and the county elected Cooperationist candidates. Walker, however, attended as a "special commissioner."[5]

Alabama seceded on January 11, 1861. Governor Andrew Moore appointed Walker to be a commissioner to Tennessee's legislature to urge that state's cooperation in secession. There, he read Alabama's secession ordinance to the assembled legislators but failed to convince them to secede. The Confederacy was founded on February 4, the new nation's constitution was written a few days later, and on February 21, the Confederate Congress voted to authorize a War Department to be headed by a secretary of war. The responsibilities of the person chosen for that position would include "'the army and the Indian tribes within the boundaries of the newly-created [Confederate States of America], subject to the general direction and supervision of the President.'"[6] The position was considered to be the most important job in the new government, second only to the president. Davis nominated Leroy Pope Walker to be the first secretary of war.

Why did Jefferson Davis select Walker? After all, Walker had no military training or background, although he did hold a commission as a brigadier general in the Alabama militia. But he had had no combat experience. Dowdey stated that Walker was "unfitted in all ways for the office."[7] The only qualifications that made Walker halfway suitable for the position, Davis seemed to think, were that he came from Alabama, that Davis needed an Alabamian in his cabinet to guarantee representation for every state, and that he would do pretty much only what Davis told him to do, thereby giving Davis the opportunity to be not only president but also, simultaneously, the *de facto* secretary of war. Davis gave no authority to Walker, and Walker did not seem to want any. Some people believed that Walker was Davis's "straw man," a mere figurehead who permitted Davis to run the War Office himself.[8]

Walker actually was not Davis's first choice for the post. Davis's logical choice was another Alabamian, Clement Clay. But Clay turned him down, preferring to run for the Confederate Senate. Walker, too, wanted to run for the

Senate, but he conceded that contest to Clay and worked instead to gain a cabinet position. He enlisted friends to write letters and telegrams promoting his name. Davis offered Yancey a position in the cabinet, but Yancey turned it down, suggesting instead Walker's name. Walker would have preferred to be attorney general, but he would not turn down any position that was offered. Davis did not know Walker personally, but he sent his nomination for secretary of war to Congress based on the recommendations he had received for Walker.

Walker's nomination met with widespread acclaim throughout the South, but it was not without opposition. Although he was well known in Alabama, he was not as well known outside the state. Most of the criticism, however, did not surface until after he was confirmed and assumed office.

When Walker entered office, he immediately began trying to convince Davis and others in the Confederate government that they should avoid any direct clash with the Union. He also focused his attention on arming and mobilizing the border states because if an attack from the North came, those states would be the South's first line of defense, and Walker wanted them to be prepared.

But some early critics accused Walker of being lethargic and apathetic in his new position. He either did not believe that there would be a war, or, if a war did occur, he thought it would be a short one. In one speech, he offered to wipe up all the blood that would be spilled with his handkerchief, implying that it would be a small amount. By the time he finally accepted the fact that war was coming, he energetically sprang into action, but he still was not up to the job.[9]

Leroy Walker had a long, thin, and pale face. Although he had a heavy beard, he had no moustache. His forehead was long, broad, and receding. His eyes gave him an inquisitive appearance, and he had a thin, almost lipless mouth.

Although Walker was "an intelligent man, astute lawyer, and dauntless patriot, [he] was simply not cast by nature for the role of titular head of a department ... over which he had little control and no credit for the real accomplishment he made through thankless detail work."[10] McPherson called him "hapless."[11] His department was understaffed, unorganized, and led by a man who was not gifted with organizational efficiency.[12] Like his president, he micromanaged, trying to do everything himself and working himself sick.[13] In addition, much of what he did was misdirected and wasted, especially time spent handling details that subordinates should have been doing.[14] All of this was proof of Walker's poor administration and a guarantee that the job would soon swallow him up.[15]

February and March 1861 were for Walker months spent in "organization" and "the garrisoning of key fortifications."[16] On March 1, he assigned General P.G.T. Beauregard to command the defenses of Charleston with authority higher than South Carolina's state troops. Beauregard's orders included the integration of South Carolina troops into the Confederate army. He was to focus on fortifying access to Charleston Harbor, but his orders said nothing about fortifying the barrier islands and inlets around the Charleston area. Beauregard advised authorities not to try to defend everything but to concentrate Confederate forces and resources on defending a few strategic locations. They ignored him and did the opposite, trying to defend everything. Only later, when Robert E. Lee was put in command of coastal defenses, did they refocus on key coastal forces and defenses.

Walker ordered Beauregard not to allow any reinforcement of Fort Sumter. He was to treat the fort "as a hostile force within the Confederacy."[17] The plan was to force Major Anderson and his Union troops to leave Sumter because of lack of supplies. Under no circumstances was Sumter to be allowed to be resupplied. He directed the demand that Sumter be surrendered or reduced.

After the Confederate peace commission failed to convince Lincoln to negotiate and in preparation for possible conflict over the fort, Walker called on each of the seven states that made up the original Confederacy to supply 3,000 volunteers to meet any military necessity, for a total of 21,000. (This was a far cry from Lincoln's call for 75,000 volunteers to subdue the "rebellion.") Walker immediately ran up against the doctrine of states' rights. Each state wanted its troops to defend their own state. The Gulf States were concerned about Fort Pickens. Georgia was concerned about defending Fort Pulaski. South Carolina was worried about Fort Sumter. North Carolina's concerns were Forts Hatteras and Clark. Those states did not like the idea of having their troops sent to defend other states. And they insisted that their troops, not Confederate troops, defend their own coasts. This proved to be a fatal attitude: the states' "insistence ... upon their own prerogatives rather than an interest in a national plan of defense."[18] Walker butted heads with several governors over his refusal to accept for Confederate service companies that were under strength. His policy stated that if troops came equipped with their own accouterments, they would be enlisted for 12 months. If the troops came expecting the Confederate government to equip them, they were to serve for the duration of the war. Governors did not like that deal.

Superseding Walker (as he would do time and again with not only Walker but also every other secretary of war), Davis put General Braxton Bragg in command of all Gulf troops. But those troops were undermanned, unprepared, and ill-trained. They were especially unskilled in the use of artillery. Walker's main concern in the Gulf was New Orleans, the key to the Mississippi River and the largest city of the Confederacy.

Walker issued a second call for troops, this one for 20,000 men. He had revised his initial estimate for how many men he thought would be necessary for the coming war—at least 100,000. Congress authorized the raising of those troops through the states' governors. Recruitment fell short of expectations.

The realities of the South's weaknesses slowly began to dawn upon Walker. It lacked training camps. It lacked a sufficient number of qualified people to train recruits. Communications between the War Department and state officials was agonizingly slow. And the south lacked a sufficient number of technically skilled officers (e.g., engineers, telegraphers, quartermasters, and artillerists).

However, "by the time Walker resigned … in September, 1861, the War Department had managed to assemble … an army of 200,000 men … despite the impediments."[19] At that point, his biggest problem was supplying those troops with arms. That was the subject for which he was most fiercely criticized. Until arms could be acquired from other countries, the South's sources of weapons were captured Union forts and arsenals and guns purchased by the states' respective governments. None of these were to be obtained without going through the states, and the states were reluctant to let go of whatever arms they had. Arguments erupted over even the arms that might be captured from the enemy.

Walker was slow to contract with potential foreign arms suppliers. Davis had taken steps in that direction even before Walker's nomination when he commissioned Raphael Semmes to travel overseas in search of arms deals. Walker encountered objections about how the South would pay for any arms that were made available. Arms dealers insisted on payment in gold; the Treasury Department wanted to pay in paper money or government bonds.

Complicating the supply problems was the fact that Walker did not have the help of a quartermaster general until March 25, 1861, when he named Lieutenant Colonel Abraham Myers to that position. Once Myers was in place, however, Walker gave him great freedom. Walker also convinced the railroads to accept only two cents a mile for moving troops and half the going rate to move war materiel. Priority for government transportation was never a sure thing.

Walker did make some progress in organizing his department. He divided it into the following bureaus, each of which was headed by a supervisory chief: Engineering; Ordnance; Quartermaster; and Commissary.

But Walker faced a problem that every Confederate secretary of war would face: Davis's tendency to micromanage everything. Davis insisted on keeping a close, tight hand on the reins of all tactical operations. He left only administrative details to Walker. Granted, whenever he intervened, he consulted Walker, but it was he, not Walker, who made the decisions. Because of Davis's habit of doing things himself, Walker's job was "somewhat perfunctory."[20] Whenever he faced nonoperational matters, he forwarded them to Walker for disposition. Davis, however, allowed Walker "almost complete authority" in one area: Indian affairs.[21] Walker even admitted that as secretary he had no input in determining strategy and could only follow what Congress and the president had already determined the strategy to be.[22]

One of the biggest headaches the president and each of the initial department secretaries, including Walker, faced was office-seekers. Hundreds of letters of application poured in every week. Those applicants who were rejected (i.e., most) became critics of the secretary and the President. Even fellow cabinet members pressured him for favors for their friends and relatives. Walker had to be kind and courteous and reply to each applicant because he did not have the staff necessary to screen them for him. Yet, no one ever accused Walker of "corruption or favoritism."[23]

Walker did have persistent problems in the form of complaints from disgruntled officers. Many of them thought that they had been overlooked or ignored for promotion (always much deserved). They had been unjustly demoted. Several officers threatened to resign over these and other disagreements. Officers complained to the Secretary about each other. He surely felt like a teacher who had a classroom filled with juvenile tattletales.

As all of these problems swirled about him, Walker proved incapable of managing routine business, he procrastinated, and Congress was unable—or unwilling—to give him sufficient clerical help. His office was messy. Instead of neatly filing departmental papers, he tossed them into a chair, and they accumulated in a chaotic pile.[24] Because he procrastinated, work was always behind. He did not answer letters promptly. His office was disheveled. He had no system to his work. He was often indecisive.[25] Eventually, it began to affect his health. He was out sick a lot. Unfinished or untouched work piled up, increasing his stress.[26] His staff thought he was working himself to an early grave, but, like his boss, he could not bring himself to delegate.[27] By the time the capital of the Confederacy was moved from Montgomery to Richmond, his health was nearly broken. His doctor advised him to rest in the country. He did—for two days—and then he was back in his office, resuming his 16-hour days.

With his increasing pressures and declining health, Walker became more conscious of the social and political courtesies due him in his position.[28] He also became more susceptible to criticism aimed at him from all directions. Davis made no effort to defend Walker.[29] In addition, Walker and Davis argued over the Confederate invasion of Kentucky and how that violated the state's proclaimed neutrality.[30] Walker resigned on September 10, 1861, and his successor, Judah Benjamin, took over the office on September 16, 1861.

But more than the stress and his health might have been behind Walker's resignation. Patrick suggests that Davis might have been subtly pushing Walker out the door. After the First Battle of Manassas (Bull Run), Walker became the lightning rod for criticism of the administration, especially for those who thought that the Confederate troops should have pursued the routed Union troops more vigorously. With the passage of time, even congressional criticism of Walker increased, and many people openly doubted his fitness for the job. Navy Secretary Stephen Mallory, Attorney General Judah Benjamin, and Treasury Secretary Christopher Memminger questioned Walker's fitness to run his department. Davis wondered the same thing but tempered his opinion by saying that he doubted if *any* civilian could do that job. Congress investigated the department. Patrick concludes that Davis "gently" forced Walker from the cabinet.[31] While Walker was away from the office caring for a wounded friend, Davis appointed an acting secretary. That and the building criticism, Patrick avers, led to Walker's resignation.

Overall, Walker's time as secretary of war was anything but successful.[32] Yet, considering what he had to work with and the conditions under which he had to do it, Walker was not a complete failure either. He had fewer clerks than did any of the men who followed him in office.[33] George Fitzhugh asserted that never in history had such a large army been raised, concentrated, fed, outfitted, and trained so quickly. Starting from scratch, without even a fully organized government, the South created a quarter-million-man army.[34] And it had happened with Walker as secretary of war.

The day after Walker resigned, Davis commissioned him a brigadier general and ordered him to command an "untrained and unequipped brigade" serving under Braxton Bragg in Mobile, Alabama, a post of the Department of Alabama and Western Florida.[35] The two generals, however, did not get along. Walker became miffed because he did not get "a more active command."[36] Bragg relieved Walker of command on January 27, 1862, and reassigned him to a training position in Montgomery because he would "'be of less harm there.'"[37] About two weeks later, Bragg reassigned him again, this time to protect the railroads in North Alabama. Thoroughly disgruntled, Walker resigned his commission on March 31, 1862, and returned to private civilian life.

By 1863, Walker had concluded that the war was lost. He drafted a resolution for Alabama to reenter the Union, but friends convinced him not to submit it. He focused then on his legal practice. Ironically, many of his cases involved the defense of his fellow North Alabamians who were Unionists and had been charged with treason. Although he had been a committed and outspoken secessionist, he "believed that North Alabama Unionists deserved their day in court."[38] In 1864, he accepted a military commission as a colonel and served on a military court until the end of the war.

After the war, Walker had a hard time convincing President Andrew Johnson to grant him a pardon. He finally was granted one on September 28, 1865.

In the subsequent years of Reconstruction, Walker sought to use his influence to end Republican rule. He campaigned for Conservative Democrats throughout the Tennessee Valley. He was president of the 1875 Alabama constitutional convention, following which Reconstruction ended in Alabama. He campaigned for Samuel Tilden in the presidential election of 1876. He served on the Democrats' 1884 DNC platform committee at the convention where Grover Cleveland was nominated for president. He also defended Frank James, brother of Jesse James, in his trial for committing a robbery in Muscle Shoals, Alabama.

Walker died of peritonitis, an abdominal ailment, on August 23, 1884.

What were the keys to Walker's ineffectiveness as secretary of war? One factor, already mentioned, was Davis's unwillingness to let him be the secretary and do his job as secretary of war. Another was his failure to develop a working relationship with the state governors. A third was the absence of a grand strategy for waging the war, which led to indecisiveness, controversies between individual states and the Confederate government, confusion and disorganization, and frustration.

But none of these factors was unique to Walker; every Confederate secretary of war faced the same problems—and generally with the same results. But Walker was the first man to serve for Davis as war secretary, and the lesson that Davis might have learned from Walker's example was wasted. Despite the significance of the post, Davis again nominated "an accomplished but unqualified subordinate," and that man did nothing to "broaden the scope of responsibility in the office."[39]

CHAPTER 14

# Judah P. Benjamin

Leroy Pope Walker, despite having organized the Confederate military from scratch, is not considered to have been a very successful secretary of war. His successor did not fare much better. In fact, he generated arguably even more criticism than had Walker.

When Walker resigned as secretary of war, Davis named Judah P. Benjamin secretary *ad interim* until he could find a suitable replacement. Benjamin did such a good job in the temporary role that Davis concluded that he was the logical choice to be the full secretary. But Benjamin ruffled too many politicians' feathers, and criticism came cascading down on him. And he also upset too many important generals, including Joe Johnston and Thomas "Stonewall" Jackson, leading many of them to threaten to resign. He became a lightning rod for every complaint and gripe against not only the War Department but also the entire Davis administration.

It soon became apparent even to Davis that Congress would no longer endure Benjamin as head of the War Department. Davis began to look for a way to replace him without offending or hurting his trusted friend and counselor. When Robert M. T. Hunter resigned as secretary of state, Davis had his answer. At the urging of the Louisiana delegation, Davis nominated Benjamin to take Hunter's place at State. The Senate confirmed him. (Interestingly and ironically, one of Louisiana's senators voted *against* Benjamin's confirmation.)

Because Benjamin's biographical information has already been discussed in Chapter 3, we will not belabor those facts again but will simply move on to discuss his performance as secretary of war. Suffice it to say that many of the problems he encountered as secretary of state because of his personality and religious or cultural heritage followed him to his new position. Neither those factors nor his personality changed, so why should anything be any different in a new position?

Because Congress was not in session when Walker resigned, Davis appointed Benjamin secretary *ad interim* on September 17, 1861. Benjamin also served simultaneously as attorney general until he could be confirmed as the secretary of war. Several names were discussed as possible nominees for the full-time position at the War Department, including John C. Breckinridge, Robert E. Lee, Leonidas Polk, and Felix Zollicoffer, all of whom were active generals. But Benjamin seemed to do such a good job as secretary ad interim that Davis decided to nominate him for the position.

As secretary of war, Benjamin set out to correct the many problems of the War Department. Whereas Walker had tried to do everything for himself— from answering every letter personally to meeting every visitor who called— Benjamin systematized the operations of the department. He delegated, assigned specific tasks to others, and ensured that other people handled the routine matters; he himself dealt with only the bigger, more important, and more urgent matters.

Benjamin was almost immediately tested by a crisis that demanded decisiveness. In the fall of 1861, the Lincoln administration led many Unionist citizens in East Tennessee to believe that if they rose up against their Confederate occupiers, a Union army in Kentucky would sweep down across the Cumberland Mountains and capture the region, pushing Confederate oppressors out and securing it for the Union. Secret plans were laid for the simultaneous burning of nine key railroad bridges between Bristol, Tennessee, on the northeastern border of Virginia, and Bridgeport, Alabama, nearly 300 miles to the southwest, on the night of November 8. The bridge burners put their plan into action but were only partially successful, and the promised Union invasion never materialized. Rather, the bridge burning produced a Confederate backlash that led to ill-will among the people of the region that lasted long after the war ended.

One of Benjamin's first acts as secretary of war was to order the court martial of the Unionist bridge burners who were captured after the incident. If they were found guilty, he ordered, they were to be "executed on the spot by hanging" and their bodies left "hanging in the vicinity of the burned bridges."[1] Yet, Benjamin let one of the defendants off because the man had been given safe conduct through Confederates lines, and Benjamin thought that the Confederacy's good-faith reputation was worth more than "the most dangerous enemy."[2] This action was popularly acclaimed in the South.

But Benjamin also early on clashed with numerous Confederate generals and quickly became unpopular with them. As the war turned against the South and as battle casualties mounted, criticism of Benjamin also mounted. Intermixed with dissatisfaction with Benjamin's departmental decisions was a degree of anti–Semitism.

Benjamin was "smart, capable and hard working," and he approached every challenge wholeheartedly, but he lacked any military experience or training and failed to develop any friendships that might have helped him grow into the job.[3] He seemed in all ways to be ill suited to run the War Department. He was "ignorant of military affairs," Mapp quipped.[4] Robert Kean, the chief of the Bureau of War, said that Benjamin was smart and could draw up papers but was "'the least wise of our public men.'"[5]

In his first report to Davis after becoming secretary of war, Benjamin addressed his fear of the 12-month enlistments, which, he warned, were apt to expire just when those soldiers were needed most. He urged only long-term enlistments, three years at the least. But as he was pushing for longer enlistments, the states began raising their own armies, keeping the arms and ammunition they accumulated, and allowing even shorter-term enlistments (three to six months).

The next quarter, Benjamin reported on his emphasis on developing domestic sources of supplies and equipment. He called for more men, more arms, and more money. (Davis actually tripled Benjamin's number and amounts when he placed the report before Congress.)

As secretary of war, Benjamin was, in Bradford's estimation, "a failure. He had no special knowledge, and this made him obnoxious to soldiers."[6] For all of Benjamin's talents, he "lacked sufficient tact and knowledge of military procedure to deal with sensitive generals."[7] While heading the War Department, Benjamin "alienated everybody, and quarreled with so many that his stay there is but a record of harsh words and recrimination."[8] Many of the most outstanding generals thoroughly disliked him. He was ignorant of military protocol, and that led to his offending some generals. For example, early in the war, he overruled the venerable "Stonewall" Jackson on a matter, leading Jackson to complain that, with such interference in his command, he could not be expected to be of much use in combat. He asked to be reassigned to the Virginia Military Institute or allowed to resign.[9]

Benjamin's unpopularity that resulted from his conflicts with Johnston and Jackson really came because he had only carried out Davis's directives. He took the heat that should have been aimed at Davis without a word of explanation or self-justification. That might have been one reason he and Davis got along so well.

Fortunately for the Confederacy, Davis was able to convince Jackson to get along with Benjamin. But when people began to realize that Benjamin's interference had nearly caused Jackson, a hugely popular hero, to resign, they began to vent their anger against Benjamin.[10]

General P.G.T. Beauregard also had highly publicized disagreements with

Benjamin. And, like Jackson, Beauregard was pushed to the point of threatening to resign. Increasingly, the average soldier regarded Benjamin as the epitome of everything that was wrong with the Davis administration.[11] As the war began to go against the South, even members of the military who had not turned against Benjamin now turned on him as a scapegoat. They could not directly attack President Davis, their commander in chief, so they aimed their criticisms at Benjamin, a convenient target. Although the orders for the armies came from Davis in his numerous consultations with Benjamin, the generals perceived them to be from Benjamin himself, and they resented, criticized, and second guessed those orders. The worse the armies fared in battle and the greater their problems from lack of supplies, the greater became the generals' criticism. Benjamin's weaknesses cost him credibility and the ability to build consensus, both of which were necessary for his (or any other secretary's) success.[12]

Yet, the cabinet member in whom Davis confided most was Judah Benjamin. It all came to a climax after the fall of Roanoke Island in February 1862. For a long time, General Henry Wise and North Carolina governor Henry Clark had been pleading with Benjamin to reinforce the troops there, but Benjamin had resisted. When the Confederate forces were defeated at Roanoke Island, Benjamin took the full brunt of the blame. He suffered it in silence. The generals accused him of influencing Davis against them even after he left the War Department.

Benjamin was definitely inexperienced in military matters. But perhaps an inexperienced secretary of war was exactly what Davis wanted. That way, Davis could be his own secretary of war, and the nominee was merely his clerk. As Meade points out, Benjamin "never dominated Davis. But by adapting himself to Davis's character and making himself extremely useful," he became Davis's "most influential advisor."[13] He worked long hours and "devoted all his great talents to securing enough men, ammunition, and supplies to prepare for the expected Northern offensive" and he thereby "put his department on an efficient basis from which all his successors benefited."[14] He especially tried to see the big picture of the military's task and "made a strenuous effort to prevent dispersion of men and materials to nonessential places."[15]

Benjamin was also unpopular with congressmen, and they, too, directed a good amount of criticism against him. Amid these assaults against his secretary of war, Davis moved Benjamin to the newly vacated office of secretary of state, thereby diffusing the criticism against him—for the moment.

CHAPTER 15

# George Randolph

George Wythe Randolph, who followed Judah Benjamin as secretary of war, was well connected. He was the grandson of Thomas Jefferson and was actually born in Monticello, Jefferson's fabled home, on March 10, 1818. Another of Randolph's famous relatives was Edmund Randolph, George Washington's attorney general and the seventh governor of Virginia. In fact, Randolph could trace his lineage back to John Rolfe and Pocahontas.

Randolph attended prep schools in Cambridge, Massachusetts, and Washington, D. C., before becoming a midshipman and serving at sea for six years. He attended the University of Virginia and spent a lot of spare time studying military topics.[1] Although he married widow Mary Elizabeth Adams Pope in 1852, they had no children.

After leaving the University of Virginia, Randolph studied law informally and was admitted to the bar in 1840 and opened his own law practice in Charlottesville. He moved to Richmond, where he was

**George Randolph, Secretary of War (Library of Congress).**

involved in community affairs and founded both the Richmond Mechanics' Institute and the local chapter of the state historical society.

When Southern states began to secede from the Union, Randolph strongly supported the secession of Virginia. He was a member of a special delegation of Southern statesmen (the other delegates being William Preston and Alexander Stuart) who traveled to Washington, D.C., to meet on April 12, 1861, with president-elect Abraham Lincoln in an attempt to work out a deal whereby the South could secede amicably and continue friendly relations with the United States. The delegation found Lincoln to be uncooperative, resolved to hold onto all forts in the South, and determined to use force to return the "rebel" states to the Union. The delegation returned to Richmond three days later without success in their mission.

Randolph accepted a major's commission in the Confederate army and organized an artillery company (Jones called it a "howitzer company," and its name was the Richmond Howitzers) in which he served.[2] Following the Battle of Big Bethel, in which he was chief of artillery, General D. H. Hill richly praised Randolph. Later, Randolph was promoted to colonel and reassigned to Richmond to be in charge of ordnance and supply matters. He was subsequently promoted to brigadier general and assigned the responsibility of defending the Atlantic coast from Virginia to Georgia. He ran for Congress but lost, coming in last in a field of three. President Davis nominated him to be the secretary of war on March 18, 1862, to replace Benjamin. He formally took office on March 24.

People responded favorably to Randolph's nomination to be secretary of war.[3] More than any other war secretary, Randolph sent a lot of correspondence directly to Davis to keep him informed and to solicit his instructions. As Randolph became more comfortable with his position, he corresponded somewhat less with Davis but still did so frequently. He made few decisions himself but simply passed along Davis's decisions to the generals. Although he began favorably, that, as happened with so many of Davis's other nominees, was not to remain the case.

As secretary of war, Randolph was a meticulous organizer and a hard worker, and he greatly improved the department's efficiency. He restructured the department, improved the procurement system, and helped write a conscription bill. As the one-year enlistments of the earliest volunteers approached the expiration of their enlistment periods in the spring of 1862, Randolph, like others before him, became concerned that the South would soon not have enough troops to defend the nation from Northern troops. His proposed solution was to institute a draft. He introduced a bill for conscription, and it passed on November 19, 1861. It provided for an active militia of 21- to 32-year-olds; an active reserve of those too old to serve in the militia; and three years of

## 15. George Randolph

mandatory service for all men under 26 years of age, and after they had served the initial three-year period, they would be eligible to transfer to the reserve.

After Randolph became secretary of war, he pushed for a new conscription bill that made every male between 18 and 35 eligible for the draft. The bill passed the House 53 to 26 and the Senate 19 to 5. Although Davis did not like the bill, saying that it kept one-year enlistments in the military for three more years when they had volunteered to serve only one, he eventually approved it as it was.

Randolph also proposed basic training for Confederate draftees and volunteers. But perhaps his greatest contribution to the Southern government was his emphasis on the western theater of the war, especially strengthening the western and southern defenses and improving the command structure. But that achievement led not to praise, as one might suppose, but to conflicts with Davis, who tended to emphasize the Eastern Theater to the detriment and neglect of all other theaters of operation.

Randolph had quickly seen the need for a unified command in the West. He noted that the situation in the West had developed into three distinct theaters: East Tennessee, northern Mississippi, and the Trans-Mississippi. Across those three areas were "at least six major commands, all operating independently of each other."[4] None of them was strong enough to help either of the others, and transferring of troops would require great amounts of time. Davis was warned of this repeatedly but did not heed the warnings. Randolph concluded that the unique situation of "the West demanded control from a point less remote than Richmond."[5] In October 1862, Randolph ordered Lieutenant General Theophilus Holmes to cross from the western side of the Mississippi River to the eastern side and merge his army with the armies of generals Braxton Bragg and John C. Pemberton. Together, they were to work to regain Tennessee and the Mississippi River Valley.

Davis, learning of the order after the fact, objected strongly on November 12 and countermanded Randolph's order. Davis sent Randolph a memo on November 13, 1862, ordering that from that point (a) every message from Randolph to a general had to go through the adjutant general's office; (b) Randolph had to consult with Davis on all instructions about appointments of *every commanding officer*; and (c) Randolph must consult Davis about all troop movements and officer assignments.[6] Randolph asked if Davis's instructions were to be taken literally, and Davis modified his order in some minor details, but Randolph still could not accept the restrictions and resigned on November 15.

Kean, who worked under the last three secretaries of war, beginning with Randolph, thought highly of Randolph. Kean's sharp criticism of Davis undoubtedly stemmed in part from Davis's treatment of Randolph in countermanding the secretary's orders to the generals. When Randolph resigned, his stated reason for his departure was Davis's "arrogance."[7]

Another possible factor in Randolph's resignation was Davis's resistance to considering any trade with the enemy. (Davis did once approve a trade agreement between the governor of Mississippi and the North for salt in return for cotton but only because it was "made legal" by the fact that a French merchant acted as a go-between and provided transportation for the goods. Davis refused, however, to use such transactions as a policy.) Northrop had told Davis in October 1862 that subsistence was impossible without some trade through Confederate ports that had been captured by the enemy. Northrop and Randolph had recommended to Davis a much larger deal than that of the Mississippi governor, a deal to trade cotton for commissary goods, but it fell through because of Davis's opposition. Randolph and Northrop both knew that without such commerce the South could not survive. Davis did not get it.

Kean believed that Davis's actions were to be explained by the view that he was jealous of Randolph's "independent character."[8] Randolph simply did not like the idea of being merely an assistant or an advisor and not having any authority whatsoever.[9] Whatever the true cause for Randolph's resignation, Seddon, Randolph's successor, greatly appreciated the foundation that Randolph had laid for him in the department.

Randolph quickly saw the futility and weakness of the South's inelastic and inflexible defense of all points along the borders of the South. Some Confederate military leaders mildly proposed switching the military emphasis to the West as the primary theater of operations, having the bulk of the troops with the most important commanders serving there instead of around Richmond and Washington, D.C. The most outspoken proponent of this elastic defense was General Joseph Johnston, and his importunate insistence on it was the major source of his ongoing feud with Davis throughout the war.

Like many of Davis's other war secretaries, Randolph was little more than an administrator. As far as policy, particularly military policy, goes, Randolph was a nobody. He was not even invited to Davis's military conferences or told about major decisions and changes in command. Although he was full of innovative ideas, he was not given latitude to incorporate them. Every time he tried to do so, he ran up against someone who was responsible to Davis and who prevented his acting on his ideas. Some people think that Davis wanted it this way so that the secretary of war could accept blame if things went wrong, but he did not want them to initiate decision-making. He gave them responsibility for what happened in the department but no real authority. Patrick concluded that although every war secretary influenced Davis to one degree or another, Randolph's influence was almost nonexistent.[10]

## 15. George Randolph

But Randolph suffered from tuberculosis, and his ill health soon limited any possibility of his exerting any effectiveness in office. He served less than eight months as secretary of war. He resigned abruptly on November 15, 1862, citing health as the reason, but the more likely reason was his conflicts with Davis. Within the first year and a half of the life of the War Department, Davis already had gone through three war secretaries.

After leaving the cabinet, Randolph resumed a field command, but his failing health forced his retirement in late 1864. Randolph then returned to the practice of law, ironically defending those who tried to evade the draft. In 1864, he went with his family into exile in England and France, not returning to Virginia until 1866. He died at his plantation less than a year later, on April 3, 1867, and he was buried at Monticello.

CHAPTER 16

# James Seddon

The longest-serving Confederate secretary of war was James A. Seddon of Virginia. Nominated by Davis to replace George Randolph on November 20, 1862, Seddon served until February 16, 1865.

James Alexander Seddon was born on July 13, 1815, in Falmouth, Virginia. During his childhood, he was frail, so his family provided him with private tutors, and he received much of his education at home. He also attended for a time Fredericksburg Grammar School.[1] He enrolled at age 21 in the University of Virginia in Chancellorsville, where he studied law. He became the head of his family soon after arriving at college when both his father and his older brother died. He used the family finances wisely, investing in a Louisiana plantation. He thought for a while about moving there, but he studied law instead. In particular, he "studied the works of states' righter John Taylor of Caroline, read the fiery antigovernment speeches of John Randolph, and became fast friends with his classmates Louis Wigfall ... and William J. Robertson."[2]

James Seddon, Secretary of War (National Archives and Records Administration).

## 16. James Seddon

Seddon graduated from the law school at the University of Virginia in 1835 as first orator of the class. He was admitted to the bar in 1838. He again thought about moving to Louisiana because his land in Virginia was not as fertile as it had been. But he followed the advice of John C. Calhoun and settled in Richmond to practice law and get involved in politics. Among his early political connections was Robert M. T. Hunter, who would later become secretary of state in the Confederacy.

Seddon began his spasmodic political career in 1844, when he was elected to the U.S. House of Representatives as a Democrat, defeating John Minor Botts with 52.8 percent of the vote. During his freshman year in the House, he first met Jefferson Davis, and the two found that they had much in common; they both supported a low tariff and agricultural exports and opposed the Wilmot Proviso. Although Seddon could have been reelected in 1846, he declined the nomination because he disagreed with certain planks in the party platform. He did, however, run for the same seat and against the same opponent in 1848 and again won, that time with 53.64 percent of the vote. He declined the nomination again in 1850, citing poor health.

Seddon was selected to attend the Washington Peace Convention in 1861 in an unsuccessful search of a peaceful resolution of the conflict between North and South. He then became a radical secessionist and broke with his friend Robert M. T. Hunter, who was merely a moderate secessionist. In July 1861, when Virginia seceded, Seddon was elected a delegate to the Provisional Confederate Congress in Montgomery. When his term expired, Davis named him a prisoner exchange commissioner, but he soon got sick and resigned.

On November 20, 1862, Davis nominated Seddon to be secretary of war, although he had neither military nor administrative experience. As has been mentioned already so often as to be a recurring theme of this work, some critics suggested that that was how Davis wanted it, so that Seddon would do only what Davis told him to, having no experience on which to base any other actions. Others who were less skeptical said that it was purely political in that Davis wanted another Virginian to replace Randolph, thereby keeping the states equally represented in the cabinet.[3] Seddon also was someone with whom Davis was already familiar since he and Davis had been acquainted since their days together in Congress.

Seddon had deep-set, penetrating eyes that were shadowed by heavy brows and a broad forehead. He had little hair on top of his head but ample amounts on the sides, and it effectively covered his ears. He sported a hint of a beard with a full moustache. He was "gaunt and sallow,"[4] "a quiet, unassuming gentleman" who always wore a black skullcap, "a man of rare intelligence and decision-making capacity."[5] Patrick concluded that Seddon was a somewhat "neurotic … semi-invalid."[6]

Once Seddon took office, he immediately began to develop the Department of the West more fully, building on the work that Randolph had initiated. He tried but failed to coordinate the logistics in the Confederate supply system. Most importantly, he failed, like so many other cabinet members did, to gain Davis's full and consistent cooperation.

Kean quickly sized up the new secretary and noted how he handled his new responsibilities. Kean seemed to perceive that Seddon "staggers under his load," "is physically weak," and is lacking "in readiness in dispatching business."[7] The clerk reported shortly after Seddon became secretary that about 1,500 papers, *all* involving officer appointments, had accumulated on Seddon's desk since he became secretary. Seddon did not bother looking at the papers because he knew that he could not make decisions on them, that privilege being reserved for the president himself.[8] That was yet another evidence of Davis's micromanaging of his cabinet officers' affairs. Kean quickly concluded that Seddon, like all of the other secretaries of war, had little real power or influence over Davis.

Nonetheless, Seddon was a hard worker despite both Davis's restrictions on him and his chronically poor health. Like Alexander Stephens, Seddon acted vigorously in contrast to the striking frailty of his body. He was a naturally talented administrator, and he was a planner with ability to come up with "original schemes."[9] But he could not translate his plans into concrete actions and results. He was, however, good at delegating.

Seddon's first crisis as secretary was the aftermath of the Battle of Sharpsburg (Antietam). He helped Lee reorganize the Army of Northern Virginia. At first, he had some influence with Davis because he acted tactfully and deferentially toward Davis.[10] As an administrator, he seemed to be in charge, but by the summer of 1863 he had begun to lose power and, consequently, influence where it counted.[11] This political reality put Seddon between the proverbial rock and a hard place, between Davis and political lobbyists, such as his friend Congressman Wigfall. As frustrating as he found his job, he held on longer than any of the other secretaries of war, primarily because he had diplomatic skills that allowed him, for a time, to deal with Davis personally while also handling complaining military commanders and anti–Davis congressmen and bureaucrats.

Despite Davis's continual interference with and micromanagement of the War Department, Seddon was able to accomplish something in his capacity as secretary. Patrick believed that Seddon influenced Southern military strategy more than any other secretary of war.[12] Seddon created the Department of the West, something that many of the generals had been calling for since the war began. Lee had basically fought to a draw the Union generals in the Eastern theater, but in the West, the Union was slicing through the Confederacy like a hot knife through butter. Seddon had great confidence in General Joseph E. Johnston and wanted to put him in command of the entire Western theater. But Davis and Benjamin did not like Johnston, and they at first refused to allow it. But Seddon finally convinced them to accept Johnston in the West. Then he had to work to convince Johnston that he had full authority in the West. Seddon did not, however, like General Braxton Bragg or think much of his abilities and wanted him removed from command. Johnston, however, opposed Bragg's removal, as did military leaders in the East. When Seddon tried to move General George Pickett to the West as a reinforcing influence, Lee opposed it, as did Davis. Even when Bragg was finally removed from command in the West, however, it did no good because Davis made him his military advisor. From that point, Seddon's influence on military strategy declined.[13]

Confederate military power reached its peak while Seddon was Secretary, but so did desertions because of the conscription laws, inflation, and general economic conditions on the home front, which wives, mothers, and sweethearts continually complained of in their letters to the soldiers. Seddon also refused to consider the proposal, made by numerous officials, to arm blacks. He resigned about a month before a new law doing just that was passed, but even if he had stayed in office until it became reality, it was, again, too little too late.

Seddon failed, however, in his efforts to create and coordinate the logistical support system that the armies required to effectively conduct the war. Perhaps his most important failure, however, was his failure to gain Davis's cooperation.

Kean detected early signs that Seddon was tiring of being in such a position where so much was expected of him but without having any real influence or power. On August 23, 1863, Kean noted that both Randolph and Seddon had complained to their close friends about Davis's endless meetings with Davis that produced no results. That led to lack of "vigor" and "*policy.*"[14] Less than a year later, in May 1864, Kean wrote about how disgusted Seddon seemed to be with his job and the difficulty Seddon had getting along with Davis.[15] He added, "If the President cannot get on with a man as smooth and yielding as Mr. Seddon, nobody can please him."[16]

One decision came back to haunt Seddon at the end of the war. As secretary of war, he had ordered Captain W. Sidney Winder to help Georgia governor Joseph Brown choose the location for a prisoner of war camp near Americus, Georgia. That camp became the infamous Andersonville Prison, housing some 18,000 Union prisoners. After the war, some people, including Edwin Stanton, wanted to charge Lee, Seddon, and other Confederate leaders with conspiracy to commit war crimes because of the deaths of soldiers at

Andersonville. Ultimately, only two people were tried and convicted in connection with alleged war crimes there. Henry Wirz, the commandant of the prison, was captured in May 1865; tried by a military tribunal between August 23 and October 18, 1865; found guilty of 11 of 13 charges of murder and conspiracy; and executed by hanging on November 10, 1865. James Duncan, who worked in the quartermaster general's office at Andersonville, was found guilty and sentenced to hard labor at Fort Pulaski, but he escaped after serving about a year of his sentence.

Wirz was one of only two people executed for war crimes committed during the war, the other being Confederate guerrilla Champ Ferguson, who committed atrocities (many people say he was merely taking personal revenge against his enemies, not fighting the war) in north central Tennessee and south central Kentucky. Seddon might easily have been tried in connection with the Andersonville prison, but cooler heads prevailed.

As if Seddon's frustrations with the president were not enough, he also chaffed at the attitudes and actions of many of his generals. Exasperated by Joseph Johnston's apparent reluctance to do combat with Sherman's troops in northern Georgia, Seddon declared that Johnston's policy was "'never to fight unless strong enough ... to overwhelm your enemy, and ... merely to continue to elude him.'"[17] Johnston seemed to do nothing but dig in, retreat, and dig in again, but never engaged the enemy in a great battle. Finally, Davis replaced him with General John B. Hood, who was known for his hard-hitting attacks against the enemy. Hood, understanding that Davis and Seddon wanted the Confederate army to attack, launched a series of brutal but futile, desperate, and, some might say, foolhardy attacks. They all failed, and Atlanta fell in July. Now it was Hood who was retreating.

By June, however, the situation had gotten so bad for Seddon that Seddon did not even bother making appointments, instead referring callers to the president through the Adjutant and Inspector General. Kean's intense disappointment with and disdain for Seddon has already been noted,[18] yet even he acknowledged that much of Seddon's failures were the result of Davis's own weaknesses.

Davis seemed to want to get Seddon out of the way in the War Department and in the summer of 1864 suggested that he take over the Treasury Department. But Seddon did not want to leave the War Department. He remained there but against Davis's wishes. Finally, however, Seddon had had enough, and he resigned in January 1865, citing health reasons. John C. Breckinridge took over as secretary of war on February 7, 1865.

James Seddon endured longer than any other Confederate secretary of war. Many people attribute his feat to his malleability. He was willing to do

## 16. James Seddon

what Davis told or allowed him to do, did not oppose or contradict Davis's policies, and tolerated Davis's micromanagement within the department. But Seddon had an even harder time getting along with the states' governors and with Congress. Perhaps his greatest conflict with Congress resulted from his concurrence with Davis on the removal of General Joe Johnston as the commander of the Army of Tennessee. Eventually, the criticism became too much even for Seddon, and he resigned just months before the war was over.

After Richmond fell, Seddon was arrested on May 7, 1865, and imprisoned, along with George Trenholm, secretary of the treasury, at Fort Pulaski, Georgia.

Cooper concluded, "In a demanding job and under difficult circumstances, Seddon for more than two years had ably served his president."[19] Others said that he had done the best he could under the circumstances but thought that he might have been too much controlled by Davis—a common opinion.[20]

Seddon died at his home, "Sabot Hill," in Goochland County, Virginia, on August 19, 1880.

CHAPTER 17

# John C. Breckinridge

He came from a distinguished political family that reached back to the Puritans. He studied law at Princeton. He served as a state representative, a U.S. representative, a U.S. senator, U.S. vice president, and secretary of war in the Confederacy. He was a combat veteran and rose to the rank of major general.

What a resume!

This is the career summary of John C. Breckinridge, perhaps the best—and the last—secretary of war. Probably no one else in the cabinet had such a breadth of credentials and experience as he had. But he was too little too late for the Confederacy.

John Cabell Breckinridge was born January 16, 1821, at Thorn Hill, the family estate, outside of Lexington, Kentucky. He was from a family of devout Presbyterians, the only son among five sisters. He attended Pisgah Academy, a religious boarding school in Lexington. His father died in 1823, so John was reared by his mother and influenced by male relatives, including an uncle who taught at Centre College in Danville, Kentucky. The uncle convinced him to enroll in the college, which he did

**John C. Breckinridge, Secretary of War (Library of Congress).**

in November 1834, graduating four years later. He then spent six months studying law at the College of New Jersey (now known as Princeton). He returned to Kentucky to read law with Judge William Owsley. He spent all day reading law and then three hours at night studying history and English literature. In 1840, he began the second year of law at Lexington's Transylvania University. He received his law degree in 1841 and was admitted to the bar.

Breckinridge practiced law briefly and then, on September 6, 1847, was commissioned as a major in the Third Kentucky Regiment for service in the Mexican War. By the time the regiment arrived in Mexico, however, most of the fighting was over, and they did not get involved in any combat. Rather, they were an army of occupation in Mexico City, and Breckinridge was more in demand for his legal skills than for his military prowess. His status as a war veteran, however, helped him when he returned to Kentucky and sought involvement in politics.

Breckinridge's appetite for politics was whetted during the 1844 presidential contest, when he campaigned for Democrat James K. Polk, and four years later when he supported the ticket of Lewis Cass. Supporters encouraged him to run for the Kentucky legislature in 1849. He did so and won. Although he himself owned five slaves and opposed any measure that threatened the institution, he had defended free blacks in court, favored voluntary emancipation, and supported the Kentucky Colonization Society. He eventually sold his slaves and got out of the slave-owning business.

In 1851, Breckinridge ran for a seat in the U.S. House of Representatives as the underdog and won. He was then reelected for a second term. As a U.S. representative, he made clear that he was a strict constructionist regarding the Constitution. He opposed the protective tariff. He spoke with a clear, strong voice and was passionate and winsome in debate. He was even mentioned by his colleagues as a possible candidate for the speakership, but he declined to run for the position.

Whenever he was home in his Kentucky district, Breckinridge tried to visit Henry Clay, and he visited him daily as the Great Compromiser neared death. He was widely considered to be the heir to Clay's political position. He also campaigned for the election of Franklin Pierce, who, following his inauguration, offered to make Breckinridge territorial governor of Washington. But Breckinridge declined, preferring to run for reelection to the U.S. House. Pierce also nominated him to be ambassador to Spain, but he declined that, too.

In 1854, however, reapportionment changed the political demographics of the district in which Breckinridge had to campaign, and he chose not to run rather than to lose the race, as he was likely to do in those circumstances.

Breckinridge was a delegate to the Democratic Convention in 1856, where he supported Stephen Douglas. Douglas lost the nomination, however, to James Buchanan. Politicos suggested the wisdom of balancing the ticket of Pennsylvanian Buchanan and pacifying disgruntled Douglas supporters by choosing Breckinridge for the second spot. They did so, and Breckinridge proceeded to break tradition by actively and tirelessly campaigning for the ticket of "Buck and Breck." They were opposed by the candidates of the fledgling Republican Party, John C. Fremont and William Dayton. The Buchanan-Breckinridge ticket tallied 174 electoral votes to 114 electoral votes for the Fremont-Dayton ticket. Breckinridge became the youngest vice president in American history when he was inaugurated at the age of 36 on March 4, 1857.

Oddly, Buchanan and Breckinridge were never close, neither as running mates nor as executive department colleagues. Buchanan never seemed able to forgive Breckinridge for having supported Douglas over him for the presidential nomination. He seldom consulted Breckinridge on anything, and he met with him infrequently. Breckinridge consoled himself by presiding diligently and fairly over the Senate during the most divisive era of the institution. But, as president of the Senate, he could not enter into the debates, and he chafed at the restriction. Before his term as vice president ended, the Kentucky legislature elected him to the Senate for a term that would begin on March 4, 1861.

When the 1860 Democratic presidential convention was held in Charleston, South Carolina, Breckinridge was absent, but his name was clearly present as a possible nominee. The convention was unable to choose an acceptable candidate, and several Southern state delegations walked out, paving the way for the nomination of Douglas. The protesting delegates later met in Baltimore, where they nominated their own candidate, Breckinridge. Sensing the splits in the party (John Bell of Tennessee was also running as a third-party candidate on the Constitutional Union ticket), Jefferson Davis sought to work out a deal that would unify the party and prevent a Republican victory by default. All of the candidates would withdraw, and the Party would then choose a compromise candidate. Bell and Breckinridge were in agreement, ready to drop out of the contest, but Douglas would not. The party remained split.

With the Democrats split so many different ways, Lincoln's election seemed a foregone conclusion. Some people, however, believed that Breckinridge still had a chance if the election could be thrown into the House of Representatives, where they thought that Breckinridge could garner more support and Lincoln's radical views stood less of a chance. In the end, it did not work out that way. Although Breckinridge came in third in the tally of popular votes and second in electoral votes, he was still well behind Lincoln. The Republican got 180 electoral votes, Breckinridge carried 11 of the 15 slave states and got

72, Bell got 39, and Douglas got only 12. Breckinridge carried all of the Southern states, except Tennessee, Kentucky, and Virginia, all of which Bell captured.

As the sitting vice president and the president of the Senate, Breckinridge was responsible to announce Lincoln as the winner in the Electoral College (similarly to what happened in 2000 when Vice President Al Gore had to announce that his Republican opponent, George W. Bush, had won the presidency in the Electoral College). That must have been a bittersweet responsibility for him, but he did so on February 13, 1861. On February 24, he met with the president-elect. He also swore in Hannibal Hamlin as his successor, then switched places with him, and Hamlin swore Breckinridge in as a U.S. senator.

Breckinridge wished to the end that a compromise could be worked out between the North and the South. He supported compromises between the sections and determined to use his presence in the Senate to oppose Lincoln's radicalism. He wasted no time in assailing his victorious opponent's initial actions as president. He argued that Lincoln's call for and arming of 75,000 troops for a war against the seceding states that Congress had not declared was a violation of the Constitution. He condemned Lincoln's suspension of *habeas corpus*. Breckinridge had always been a strong Unionist, but he declared that if his state, Kentucky, ever sided against the Southern states, he would leave the Senate. He did his best, however, to ensure the neutrality of Kentucky.

In September 1861, both Southern and Northern troops violated Kentucky's self-declared neutrality. Shortly thereafter, Breckinridge received a report that Union generals intended to arrest him, so he fled South, where he offered his services to the Confederacy. In November, he was indicted in federal court for treason. In December, the Senate declared him a traitor by a vote of 36–0 and expelled him from the Senate.

Based on the recommendation of General Simon Bolivar Buckner, Breckinridge was commissioned as a brigadier general in the Confederate army, although he had relatively little military experience and had seen no combat to that point in his career. He was placed in command of the 1st Kentucky Brigade, which was nicknamed the "Orphan Brigade" because its men felt abandoned by their state. Breckinridge and the brigade served under General Buckner within the army of General Albert Sidney Johnston.

Patrick revealed that Breckinridge decorated his military career with exemplary "courage and bravery."[1] But his leadership style was one of extremes of "energy and indolence"; he performed vigorously when he got fired up but had to be prodded to reach that point.[2]

As a general, he shared every danger and deprivation his men faced. Breckinridge subsequently gained vast experience leading troops in combat in both theaters of the war but mainly in the West. He saw action in the battles of Shiloh (during which Johnston was fatally wounded), Vicksburg, Baton Rouge, and Port Hudson. He and the brigade were later reassigned to service under General Braxton Bragg as he prepared for a proposed invasion of Kentucky. Bragg, however, got along with Breckinridge no better than he did with most other fellow generals. Bragg seemed to resent Breckinridge's good relations with many of the generals with whom Bragg did not get along, such as Joe Johnston and Wade Hampton. Over time, the animosity became mutual as Breckinridge concluded that Bragg was incompetent and undependable.

Bragg reassigned Breckinridge and the 1st Kentucky Brigade to serve under General William Hardee's corps near Stone's River. When Union forces under Rosecrans attacked during the Battle of Stone's River, Bragg ordered Breckinridge to reinforce him on the opposite side of the river. Breckinridge was slow to obey the order because of a rumor that General Pegram had heard to the effect that a large Union force was about to attack where Breckinridge currently was. During the ensuing engagement, nearly one-third of Breckinridge's troops were cut down, causing him to refer to them as his orphans. Bragg criticized Breckinridge's performance in his after-battle action report. Breckinridge demanded a court of inquiry, but he was denied.

In mid–May 1863, after again being reassigned to a command under Joe Johnston, Breckinridge was engaged in combat at Jackson in an unsuccessful attempt to relieve Vicksburg. When Vicksburg fell on July 4, however, he was again returned to Bragg as Bragg moved the Army of Tennessee south of Chattanooga. On September 20, 1863, the second day of the Battle of Chickamauga, he was engaged in a successful attack against the Yankees by a division of General D. H. Hill's troops. In late November, Breckinridge was involved in Bragg's unsuccessful defense of Missionary Ridge south of Chattanooga when Generals Joe Hooker and George Thomas, the "Rock of Chickamauga," launched the Union's breakout from Chattanooga. Following this defeat, Bragg accused Breckinridge of being unfit to command and of being drunk not only during the Battle of Missionary Ridge but also earlier at the Battle of Stone's River. He then removed Breckinridge from command. Although Bragg's charge probably was untrue (Breckinridge was admittedly a heavy drinker, but many people noted that he was able to withstand the normal consequence of such drinking, that is, drunkenness), its result was the same as if it had been true: he lost his command.

Attesting to the doubts surrounding Bragg's accusations and demonstrating his confidence in Breckinridge, Davis personally ordered Breckinridge to take command of the Department of East Tennessee and Western Virginia, where he had to start over building his command. Later, General Lee ordered Breckinridge to lead a scouting mission to shadow Union forces commanded by Franz Sigel. The two forces clashed in the Battle of New Market, and Breckinridge's troops, including notably more than 250 cadets from the Virginia Military Institute, gained the victory.

Breckinridge next reinforced Lee and the Army of Northern Virginia just in time to get involved in the Battle of Cold Harbor, where Breckinridge's horse was shot from under him and he was pinned beneath the unfortunate animal. He later participated in General Jubal Early's celebrated raid into the defenses outside of Washington, D.C., throwing the government there into a panic. For a while, he was thought to be the replacement for the dead Stonewall Jackson in the Shenandoah Valley.

Returning to command the Department of East Tennessee and Western Virginia, Breckinridge protected the important salt works at Saltville, Virginia (October 2, 1864) and drove Union General Alvin Gillem's Yankees back into Knoxville in November before driving—not without difficulty—Union cavalry led by George Stoneman from the area in December. Shortly after the turn of the New Year, James Seddon resigned as secretary of war, and Davis named Breckinridge to take his place. That would be his final position in the Confederate government, and he would be the Confederacy's last secretary of war.

Patrick states that Breckinridge ran the War Department with a tight rein, immediately improving its organization and the movement of food and supplies.[3] He also strove to end the war with honor, meaning that he rejected the possibility of continuing the war through guerrilla warfare.[4]

Kean quickly recognized that his new boss was evidently not "a man of papers" because he seldom read or wrote anything. Kean feared that his work will be get behind as a result.[5] Rather, Breckinridge was a man of action. Kean declared that Breckinridge was one "to dare and do almost anything."[6]

Breckinridge was confirmed as secretary of war on January 29, 1865, but he was not sworn in until February 7. From the start, he "infused new energy into the War Department."[7] His first act as secretary was to order an inventory of the South's war-waging resources, and he discovered that they were penniless; credit depleted; short of food, clothing, ammunition, horses and mules, forage or those animals, and men; and they could get no more foreign imports because Wilmington had fallen.[8]

Some people think that Breckinridge was a more efficient administrator than all of the Confederacy's previous secretaries of war. But one must consider that he had less to administer—in numbers of troops and in territory under his control. Yet, he had to administer a dying department in a dying government, squeezing from it the last it had to offer in a by-then-inevitably defeated cause. He was, however, able to escape at least some of Davis's notorious micromanagement and actually offer substantive strategic advice to generals in the field, make assignments, and recommend promotions. And the generals and Davis generally acquiesced because they knew that Breckinridge was speaking from the knowledge of actual field experience. His first actions, however, which also no doubt further enhanced his reputation among the troops and their commanders, were to promote Robert E. Lee to general in chief of all Confederate troops and to recommend the replacement of Lucius Northrop as commissary general for subsistence by Isaac St. John.

Perhaps the most important suggestion that Breckinridge made affecting military strategy was his belief that the South's only hope at that point was to annihilate Sherman, and he proposed to concentrate Confederate forces, pulling troops from areas of minor or peripheral importance to the primary force of the enemy, Sherman's army in the Carolinas. This would give Lee an army that had a real chance against Sherman. A quick, sharp attack might succeed. Lee agreed, but no troops were available.[9]

As secretary of war, Breckinridge essentially presided over the death throes of the Confederacy. It took less than a month in his new position for him to conclude that the cause of the South was lost. But he was determined to give it his best efforts while the Confederacy remained alive. His leadership of the department produced improvements in supply and strategy, but they were too little too late. With the help of Joe Johnston and P.G.T. Beauregard, he convinced Davis that the end was approaching quickly. He then took part in Johnston's negotiations with Sherman for the surrender of Johnston's army, but he negotiated as a general, not as the secretary of war of a civilian government.

The Union army ordered that Davis, Breckinridge, and Benjamin were to be arrested and executed upon capture. When Davis and the rest of the cabinet fled Richmond, Breckinridge sent his assistant secretary of war, Campbell, to ensure the destruction of facilities and supplies. When the fall of Richmond proved imminent, Breckinridge gave his last order: that the bridges over the James River be burned, then he, too, fled, riding to join the president and the rest of the cabinet. But at that point, he stopped being secretary of war and became instead "a general in the saddle."[10]

Breckinridge stopped en route to visit General Lee in Farmville from the evening of April 5 until departing on April 7. He then went to Danville, arriving on April 11, and learning then both of Lee's surrender on April 9 and that Davis and the cabinet had left Danville and were in Greensboro. He proceeded to Greensboro, arriving on April 13. That is when he advised Davis that all of the other armies should be surrendered. Davis and Secretary of State Judah Benjamin disagreed with him, and only Johnston's army surrendered.

Perhaps Breckinridge's greatest achievement as secretary of war was convincing Davis not to follow the advice and desire of several generals, who

## 17. John C. Breckinridge

wanted to continue the effort as a guerrilla war. Such efforts would be futile and lead only to more death and destruction and harsher measures against the South once the guerrilla warfare finally ended in defeat, as it inevitably would. Breckinridge's sane reasoning on this issue allowed calmer thinking to prevail. Only when they arrived in Abbeville, South Carolina, was Breckinridge, with help from Basil Duke, finally able to persuade Davis that it was over.

Davis entrusted $150,000 in specie from the Confederate Treasury to Breckinridge, and the entourage proceeded south by train to Washington, Georgia. Breckinridge used the treasury funds to pay the soldiers in his escort, then he deposited the rest in the banks of Washington, Georgia. He discharged the soldiers who were with him and wrote a letter declaring the War Department disbanded. With this final act by the Secretary, the War Department ceased to exist, and the Confederacy died.

Breckinridge then traveled south to Milltown, arriving on May 11. Congress had charged him with treason, and he was not about to get captured and subjected to who knew what fate at the hands of the Radical Republicans. He would flee the country. He, his son Cabell, and a servant left Milltown and journeyed to Madison, Florida, where John Taylor Wood joined them briefly. When Wood learned that they intended to go to the Bahamas, he separate from them, stating that he had reactions to mosquito bites. Breckinridge then advised him to turn himself in to the first Union officer he encountered.

Breckinridge, Cabell, and the servant proceeded to Gainesville, Florida, where they obtained a lifeboat and used it to float down the St. Johns River to Fort Butler. From there, they hauled the boat overland for more than 25 miles to the Indian River, reaching it on May 31. They reached the Atlantic and skirted the coast southward. On June 7, they spotted a Union steamer, convinced the crew that they were hunters, and then, after boarding, disarmed the crew and took over the boat. They then struck out for Cuba, arriving on June 11, and traveled by train to Havana. From there, they boarded a ship to Great Britain, arriving in late July.

In Europe, Breckinridge lived in Great Britain and France and traveled extensively throughout Europe. Eventually, however, he returned to North America, settling in Niagara, Canada. Even after going to Canada, Breckinridge refused to seek a pardon. He waited until President Johnson issued a general pardon for former Confederates on December 25, 1868. He returned to the United States on March 9, 1869, when he determined that it was finally safe to do so.

Back in Kentucky, where he made his home for the rest of his life, Breckinridge resumed his law practice and became involved with the administration of railroads and insurance companies (to varying degrees of success). But he steadfastly refused to get back into politics. He did, however, publicly denounce the activities of the Ku Klux Klan.

Breckinridge suffered from steadily deteriorating health. Following a second surgery to treat him for fluid buildup in his lungs, he died at 5:45 p.m. on May 17, 1875. He was buried in Lexington, his birthplace.

Assessing Breckinridge in retrospect, Patrick concurred with Breckinridge's self-assessment: he was not really a war secretary but rather a military commander while he headed the War Department. He never issued reports. He wrote very few letters. Although he was undoubtedly loyal to the president and did his duty to the very end, he actually thought that a Confederate surrender in February 1865 was the better option.[11]

## Part IV

# Navy Department

Chapter 18

# Overview

So important was the naval defense of the new nation that the Confederate Provisional Congress authorized a Committee on Naval Affairs even before it authorized any of the cabinet departments. At the first meeting of the committee—at which Commander Raphael Semmes, who would later play such a key role in Confederate naval affairs, was in attendance—the members discussed the military and naval resources available in the South and how best to defend the fledgling nation. On February 21, 1861, three days before Jefferson Davis was inaugurated president, Davis sent Semmes to the North to procure ships and arms. At the same time, he sent Caleb Huse to Europe with the same mission. On the same day, Congress passed an act establishing the Navy Department and providing for a secretary of the navy.

Until secession and the founding of the Confederacy, the South had relied on the North to provide ships and sailors for its commerce and defense. The South focused on agricultural concerns and allowed others to provide the transportation for all commerce and protection on the high seas. Suddenly, the South found itself with neither and a treasury that was empty. It faced the real possibility of attack upon not only its commerce but also its geographic territory. In the early months of the fledgling Confederacy's life, some of the individual states had small navies but few ships and sailors. They later turned those navies over to the Confederate Navy Department, not that their contributions added much of value to the national navy.

Congress authorized the president to buy or construct "ten steam gunboats for coast defences."[1] Commander L. Rousseau was appointed to command at the New Orleans naval station. Captain Duncan Ingraham was put in charge of the coastal and river waters of Alabama. He was also ordered to find ways to obtain wrought iron plates two to three inches thick. He later was reassigned to Charleston, South Carolina, to prepare the defenses of that city.

To make a bad situation worse, the South was limited as to how and where it might obtain the necessary protection for its coasts and rivers. The United States operated ten navy yards in 1860, two of them in the South at Norfolk and Pensacola. Furthermore, most of the few private shipyards in the South were "rather simple affairs."[2] Even if the South had had the necessary ships and facilities, it had almost no domestic capabilities to make or supply the steam engines, parts, weapons, and ammunition required for them. Although it had a couple of small powder mills, it lacked the facilities to make balls, shells, or other ordnance materials. But "there was a complete absence of certain essential facilities for the outfitting of warships such as ordnance and ropewalks."[3]

At the start of the war, the South had a severe shortage of all of the necessary ingredients for waging war, but the North had (or could develop) them in abundance: navy yards, shipyards/shipbuilding facilities, foundries for making marine machinery and ordnance (especially facilities that could produce two-inch plate), engine manufactories, powder mills, outfitters for rigging and ropewalks, iron ore and other raw materials, and transportation infrastructure for movement of raw materials and finished products.[4]

As for the facilities capable of producing two-inch plate, only three were developed during the course of the war: Tredegar Iron Works (Richmond, Virginia), the largest; Scofield & Markham Iron Works (also known as the Atlanta Rolling Mill), the second largest; and Shelby Iron Company (Columbiana, Alabama), the third largest.[5] Other smaller facilities included Shockoe Foundry (Richmond, Virginia), Columbus Iron Works (Columbus, Georgia), Bellona Iron Works (Richmond, Virginia), and Mecklenburg Iron Works (Charlotte, North Carolina).[6]

The only naval powder factory of significance was in Petersburg, Virginia. It was forced by the vicissitudes of war to move to Columbia, South Carolina, in 1862. In fact, many such facilities were forced to move as the enemy armies approached and the battlefield extended too close for comfort. For example, the Atlanta Ordnance Works started out in Atlanta, moved first to Augusta, Georgia, and then moved to Fayetteville, North Carolina. The Atlanta Rolling Mill moved to Columbia, South Carolina.

The South eventually developed a few plants to cast guns, make rolling plate for armor, and manufacture machinery, but without a supply of iron they were useless. Furthermore, the army, the navy, and numerous industries competed among themselves throughout the war for not only raw materials but also logistical equipment and labor. The South did have plenty of lumber, but it was in standing timber and, even when it was cut, it was green and unusable until it could be dried and cured. That process took time, which was in short supply for the Confederacy. The South had iron, but it was in the ground and had to be mined. And both timber and iron ore had to be transported to the iron-making and ship-building facilities, and the South's transportation system was abysmal.

In 1860, the Union navy had approximately 1,000 officers and 7,500 seamen of various ranks and responsibilities.[7] At the time of the founding of the Confederacy, by contrast, the South had only approximately 300 officers, most of whom had resigned their commissions in the U.S. navy and offered their services to their states or, eventually, the Confederacy. But the South had no institution for training either officers or seamen in seamanship and naval command so they could replace the first volunteers when they might retire or be put out of action by death, injury, or capture.

Such were the problems facing the first—and only—secretary of the navy, Stephen Mallory. President Davis's first assignment for Mallory was broad and foundational: "to prepare and publish regulations for the general government of the navy."[8] On March 16, 1861, Congress passed an act authorizing Davis to appoint "four captains, four commanders, thirty lieutenants, five surgeons, five assistant surgeons, six paymasters, and two chief engineers, and to employ as many [other naval employees] as [the Secretary] deemed necessary," not to exceed 3,000.[9] Mallory immediately set out to fulfill that mission and to address the glaring weaknesses such as to develop and build an adequate naval defense of the South. In the process, he initiated or encouraged several scientific and technological developments that would play a key role in not only the War Between the States but also the later military history of the world. To help him in his seemingly impossible task, Mallory had a personal aide (Midshipman Clarence Cary), a chief clerk (E.M. Tidball), two to four junior clerks, and a messenger.

Mallory's work can be categorized into six major tasks as follows: to develop domestic ship-building and ancillary manufacturing facilities, to procure ship-building contracts with foreign companies or countries, to purchase already-constructed ships from foreign companies or countries, to commission official Confederate navy commerce raiders, to develop a Confederate Naval Academy, and to develop a comprehensive naval defense strategy that incorporated both coastal and river factors.

Each of these categories of activity will be discussed in detail in this chapter. But before Mallory could progress with any of these activities, he had to organize his department. He found himself on the eve of a war "the head of a naval department ... without a ship or any of the essentials of a navy."[10] From scratch, he developed the following bureaus within the Navy Department.

## Bureaus Within the Navy Department

Mallory first established a central Controlling Bureau to provide general supervision for the other four operational departments, or bureaus. Then he set up each of those bureaus, defined their areas of responsibility, and appointed an appropriate individual to head each bureau. (In 1862, Mallory added a fifth bureau that worked under the direct supervision of the Controlling Bureau.)

### Office of Orders and Detail

This office prepared and issued all orders and details for service, dealt with all personnel issues, including courts-martial, courts of inquiry, and matters relating to navy personnel at the direction of the Secretary.[11] It was, in a manner of speaking, the Confederate navy's human resources department. Mallory initially chose Captain Samuel Barron to head this bureau.

Turnover in the Office of Orders and Detail was high because each officer in charge seemed focused on securing himself an operational command.[12] After Barron, the following men led the office: Captain Lawrence Rousseau, Captain William Lynch, Captain Franklin Buchanan (who would later command the famed ironclad CSS *Virginia*), Captain French Forrest, Commander John Mitchell, and Captain Sidney Smith Lee (older brother of Robert E. Lee).

According to the rules laid down by Mallory in the navy's organizational structure, officers were classified and employed as follows:

Table 9. Classification of Officers in the Confederate Navy

| CLASSIFICATION | HOW HE ATTAINED THE RANK |
|---|---|
| **Commissioned officers:** admirals, vice admirals, captains, commanders, lieutenants | Nominated by president, confirmed by Senate |
| **Warrant officers:** masters, midshipmen, boatswains, gunners, master's mates | Approved by secretary of the navy |
| **Appointed officers:** secretaries to flag officers, captains' clerks, paymasters' clerks | Approved by a senior officer authorized by secretary of the navy |

Minimum requirements to join the Confederate navy were as follows: at least 14 years of age; at least four feet, eight inches tall; if under 21, parental consent; if a "free man of color," special permission from the Navy Department or the local squadron commander[13]; and "slaves could be enlisted with their owners' approval."[14]

## Office of Ordnance and Hydrography

The Office of Ordnance and Hydrography was organized "to design, develop, purchase, produce, test, distribute, and provide for the maintenance of guns, ammunition, ordnance stores, tools, pyrotechnics, and navigation instruments.... [It also was tasked to] chart production and distribution," collect and distribute "other hydrographic information," maintain "aids to navigation, and ... [train] midshipmen."[15] This office was headed initially by Captain Duncan Ingraham, then Commander George Minor, and finally Commander John Brooke. (Brooke was soon renowned for two famous projects: reconstruction of the *Virginia* into an ironclad and development of the Brooke gun. In the latter project, Brooke rifled old smoothbore cannons and reinforced their breeches by adding multiple layers of bands of wrought iron. The same process was later used in making new guns.)

The summary responsibility of the Office of Ordnance and Hydrography was making navigation charts and instruments as well as ammunition available to the navy.[16] In relation to the responsibility for ordnance, the office contracted with both foreign and domestic companies to produce guns and ammunition. In addition, it was in charge of operating and maintaining navy yards (where they did everything in manufacturing, except make gunpowder), ordnance works (made guns, gun carriages, armor, and solid shot), ordnance laboratories (made fuses, primers, and explosives), and powder mills (made charges).

The Confederate military branches inherited many obsolete guns. The Office of Ordnance and Hydrography, through a process of trial and error, learned how to convert them into more efficient weapons.

The hydrography part of this bureau offered the Confederate navy little help. Because Confederate authorities thought that lighthouses, buoys, and maps were of more use to an invading enemy than they were to the defensive units, lighthouses were darkened, buoys were removed, and lightships were converted to other uses. Safe and efficient navigation were left to each ship's captain, a treacherous prospect at best. Complicating the matter was the fact that just about the time officers began to know the local waters of their assignment, they were transferred elsewhere.

Under this office also fell responsibility for the Confederate Naval Academy. More will be said about the Academy later.

## Office of Provisions and Clothing

Commander John De Bree led this bureau, which dealt with provision of food and clothing for the navy personnel. Officially, it was responsible for everything involved with navy food and uniforms.[17] Procurement meant not only making contracts with various manufacturers or purchasing directly from producers but also organizing factories, bartering, and impressing necessary items.

Navy rations were heavy on "salt pork or beef, rice, and dried peas or beans—items which would keep a long time at sea. Fresh fruit and vegetables were to be furnished in port ... ."[18] Scarcity was a common problem, but "the navy ate better than the army."[19] (This situation seems to have continued in the U.S. military, as the song from the Jerry Lewis–Dean Martin movie *At War with the Army* alludes: "The navy gets the gravy, but the army gets the beans.")

As for clothing, officers had to buy their own uniforms, including the brass buttons with the letters "CSN" on them. To save money, they usually removed the buttons from their old uniforms and transferred them to the new uniforms. As a result, there was a noticeable lack of uniformity in uniforms throughout the navy. Seamen's uniforms were issued to them by the navy upon their enlistment, and they were given new uniforms whenever necessary. Shoes, however, were always in scarce supply.

The Office of Provisions and Clothing also served as the payroll department. Sailors serving abroad were paid more than sailors serving stateside. Sailors at sea were paid in gold, whereas land-based sailors were paid in Confederate paper money. Pay for everyone in the Confederate navy was always "inadequate and frequently in arrears."[20]

## Office of Medicine and Surgery

As the name indicates, this bureau dealt with all of the health care for navy personnel, not only caring for the wounded through first aid and surgery but also ensuring both sanitary conditions and proper dietary provisions. This responsibility included the purchase of medicines, drugs, and all medical supplies for the navy. It was under the leadership of Dr. W.A.W. Spotswood, Surgeon in Charge. C.N. Fennell was his chief clerk, and Robert Lecky was purveyor (supplier). The office included just under 90 medical officers. One thing the navy was never short of, unlike the army, was medicines.[21]

## The Torpedo Bureau

This final bureau was small and very secret.[22] It was the bureau that was responsible for developing and using "torpedoes," or mines, and other weapons for use under water.[23] Captain Matthew Maury of Tennessee had already established a name for himself in the U.S. navy as the "Pathfinder of the Seas" for his description of ocean currents ("the paths of the seas," alluded to by the psalmist David in Psalm 8:8). He gained further renown as the inventor of the electric torpedo.

Mallory was near the cutting edge of naval technology with his focus on ironclads. But he *was* the cutting edge in his use of torpedoes and submersibles. The Confederate torpedo was a crude weapon that came in several varieties, from beer kegs or barrels filled with gunpowder to electrically activated devices. Some of them were floated randomly down a river, perhaps hitting Union vessels that were in the way. Others were attached to the prow of small boats or on the end of spars attached to the bow. The intent was to ram an enemy vessel, imbed the torpedo in the wooden keel, and back away, detonating the torpedo and, hopefully, sinking or heavily damaging the enemy vessel.

The Confederate torpedo might have been the most feared weapon of the war. Estimates of the numbers of Union vessels sunk or damaged varies, depending on who did the estimating, but that number seems to have been between 39 and 58. The total might actually have been even higher. Regardless of the actual total, U.S. navy secretary Gideon Welles declared (perhaps with a more than slight exaggeration) after the war that the North "'lost more vessels by torpedoes than from all other causes whatever.'"[24]

The Torpedo Service is perhaps the least discussed but most quietly effective division of the Confederate navy. It began with experimentation with mechanically and electrically detonated explosives as means to defend against iron-clad gunships and led to experiments with submersible delivery systems.

Many people presented different plans to the Confederate War and Navy Departments for both mechanical and electrical detonation devices. Those that were intended for use on land were turned over to the army; those that were meant for use on or under water went to the navy. Both types were considered by the enemy to be immoral and less than honorable, and the Union military let it be known that anyone caught engaging such weapons would be hung or shot. But after the war, the enemy apparently had a change of moral perspective and sought to employ them for the U.S. military purposes.

The Confederacy sorely needed some means of defending the harbors and navigable rivers that led to the South's interior regions, especially Charleston Harbor and Richmond, the nation's capital. The idea for using mines—or torpedoes, as they were called at the time—in the first place is generally attributed to Secretary of the Navy Stephen Mallory. Early in his administration of the department, Mallory ordered Captain Maury to conduct experiments with torpedoes for such defensive purposes. Maury wasted no time but began those experiments in the spring of 1862.

Maury's experiments "consisted of placing a series of hollow spherical shells of iron, containing about fifty pounds of powder, and extending across the bottom of the river, and connecting them electrically by insulated copper wires leading to galvanic batteries on shore. Inside these shells fuses were placed, which were to be ignited by the passage of an electric current through a fine platinum wire."[25] These experiments proved that more than 50 pounds of explosives had to be used in torpedoes under ten to 15 feet of water if their explosion was to produce enough force to destroy a ship, especially an ironclad.

Maury was later replaced as head of the Torpedo Division by Lieutenant Hunter Davidson. Davidson's subsequent experiments faced numerous obstacles, including shortages of the following five key components: cannon powders, insulated copper wire, fine-gauge platinum wire, acids, and materials for making batteries.

The division's first laying of defensive torpedoes occurred on the James River about six miles below Richmond. Two iron torpedoes, each loaded with a thousand pounds of powder, were submerged in 12 feet of water and connected by wires to the shore, where they were connected to a battery. The locations of the torpedoes were noted by a crude sighting system, and a man was ordered to contact the wires when an enemy boat got to the spot where the torpedoes were hidden. When the first Union boat came upriver, the man prematurely detonated the first torpedo when the boat was 20 to 30 yards from it. The explosion swamped the boat with water, washed some crewmen overboard, and caused minor structural damage, but the boat turned around and made no other attempt to go beyond that point.

Another attempt at employing torpedoes was made at Drewry's Bluff, where the river was deep and narrow. And other torpedoes were set up at several other points farther down the river, each torpedo being loaded with 2,000-pound charges of powder. The army made other attempts to use mechanical torpedoes, but those were dangerous for friend and foe alike. Besides, the army and the navy were not able to coordinate their efforts for maximum advantage.

Operations were next moved to the area around Wilmington, North Carolina. The purpose was the defense of Forts Fisher and Caswell at the mouth of the Cape Fear River. That presented the personnel of the Torpedo Division with the challenge of securing torpedoes in the ocean. They set seven 2,000-pound-charged torpedoes in the main channel and connected them by wires to a battery on shore. Such was the Union navy's respect for or fear of Confederate torpedoes that they dared make no effort to ascend the river until after they captured Fort Fisher. During a thunder storm, lightning struck two of the torpedoes, setting off premature explosions. And Union forces discovered that the old inlet at Fort Caswell was undefended by torpedoes, thereby allowing them to use that alternate route around the underwater dangers.

Efforts to use torpedoes on the Mississippi River failed because the river was too deep; the silt deposits built up around torpedoes, muffling the impact of explosions; and the swift current made it impossible to keep torpedoes in one place for long and often disconnected the wires.

Charleston Harbor, however, was a perfect place for using torpedoes. The mutually supporting points at Morris Island, Sullivan's Island, and Fort Sumter between the first two locations, and the relative shallowness of the channels made the harbor nearly ideal for their use. But the South lacked the necessary components to build the torpedoes needed. In all, the Confederates placed 123 torpedoes in Charleston Harbor and in the Stono River. The Federal forces, however, *believed* that the harbor was heavily defended by torpedoes, and perception is often as effective as if it had been reality.

Perhaps the area most notably defended by torpedoes was Mobile Bay, where a variety of types of torpedoes, both mechanical and electrical, were used. Some were iron; others were merely wooden kegs or barrels. During the Union attack on Mobile led by Admiral David Farragut on August 5, 1864, the Union ironclad *Tecumseh* struck a mechanical torpedo and sank almost immediately with her commander and crew of more than 100 men. Thereafter, the commanders of the other Union gunships were reluctant to press the attack. In frustration, Farragut uttered his famous command, "Damn the torpedoes! Full speed ahead!" His confidence helped the Union seamen overcome their fears of the Confederate torpedoes and won the day and the battle.

Other torpedoes were arranged on the Yazoo River, and one Union gunboat, the *DeKalb*, struck one of them. The captain, however, immediately aimed the damaged vessel toward shore, and it sank in only 12 feet of water near the river bank.

All of the uses of torpedoes in our discussion to this point were defensive in nature. Mallory and Rains were eager to put them to use offensively. Only in that way could they ever hope to assist in breaking the blockade. And the only way to get close enough to a Union warship undetected long enough to set off a torpedo was to use a submersible vessel. Originally, the idea was for the submersible to approach the intended victim, power under the enemy vessel while towing the torpedo, and then detonate the explosive when it was beneath the ship. But there were technical problems with this approach, so the method was changed to that of attaching the torpedo to a long, bow-mounted spar, ramming it into the enemy vessel below the water line, putting the submersible in reverse, and then, when the submersible was a safe distance away, detonating the explosive.

The first experimental submersible designed for military uses had been David Bushnell's egg-shaped *Turtle* during the American Revolution. Although that craft was unsuccessful, the idea of a submersible warship had not died. Robert Fulton had also experimented with and developed such a weapon, which he named the *Nautilus*. He had offered it to first France and then Great Britain, but neither country was interested. Then came the War Between the States, and the Confederate navy revived the idea yet again. In February 1862, James McClintock and Baxter Watson developed the *Pioneer*. That three-man submersible actually sank a barge during trials on Lake Pontchartrain in Louisiana. It ran under the barge, towing behind it an explosive charge, and the charge detonated when it made contact with the keel of the barge. But before it could be used in actual combat, Union armies captured New Orleans, and the *Pioneer* had to be scuttled lest it fall into enemy hands.

But McClintock and Watson moved their operations to Mobile, where they were joined by a third partner, Horace L. Hunley. Together, they built *Pioneer II*, also known as the *American Diver*. But that vessel met a sad fate when it sank during a trial run. Undeterred, the men got other men to invest in their efforts to build a successful submersible that could be used as a naval weapon. The result was the *Hunley*, which was completed in July 1863.

Horace Hunley had made several successful trial runs in the submersible named for him. On August 12, 1863, the *Hunley* arrived by train in Charleston, where the team hoped to interest the Confederate government in their invention. Hunley invited General P.G.T. Beauregard and other Confederate military leaders to examine it. They called it the "torpedo fish."[26] Some of the examiners did not have much confidence in Hunley the man or *Hunley* the invention simply because the man lacked military experience. Fearing what might happen if they turned him down, however, the Confederate military authorities seized the vessel and gave control of it to the Confederate navy .

The *Hunley* and its all-volunteer, eight-man crew set off on August 29 for yet another test run. But the sub went under the water before the hatches could be closed, drowning five crewmen. The vessel was salvaged, however, and Hunley convinced the naval officials to let him get a crew from Mobile, men who knew how the vessel worked because they had built her. On October 15, 1863, that all-volunteer, eight-man crew, with Hunley himself serving as captain, also went down. All eight men perished.

Again the *Hunley* was raised, and a third all-volunteer crew was recruited under Lieutenant George Dixon's command. On the night of February 17, 1864, the *Hunley* set out once more, this time with a target: the Union's largest blockade ship, the U.S.S. *Housatonic*. About four miles outside of Charleston Harbor, the eight Confederate crewmen powered the *Hunley* through the water. A lookout aboard the *Housatonic* saw a shape approaching beneath the water but at first thought it was one of the numerous porpoises in the area. But as the shape got closer, he realized that it was not a porpoise, and he sang out an alarm. Union crewmen began firing into the water with rifles and pistols. The *Hunley* powered into the Union vessel near the stern, embedding the 135-pound torpedo into its victim. Then the Confederate submariners reversed their sub, quickly retreating the length of their 150-foot tether. Then the torpedo exploded.

The *Housatonic* burned and sank quickly with the loss of five crewmen. The *Hunley* surfaced and sent to shore a quick message of a mission accomplished. That was the last anyone saw of her for more than 150 years. She sank, with the loss of all her crew. It was a pyrrhic victory for the South.

In addition to the 123 torpedoes placed in Charleston Harbor, the Torpedo Division planted 101 torpedoes in the Roanoke River in North Carolina, sinking six of 12 Union vessels (one other being sunk by land-based fire).[27] At Mobile Bay, three ironclads were sunk, according to Rains, but Major General Dabney Maury contended that it was 12. The *Hunley* sank the *Housatonic* using a torpedo. Whether the total number of enemy vessels sunk was 39 or 58 or a number somewhere in between those two estimates, the Confederate Torpedo Service did an amazing job with what it had to work with and was on the cutting edge of military technology for the time. J.R. Soley assessed the value of the Confederate navy's Torpedo Division, saying that it "probably contributed more to the defense of the Confederacy than all the vessels of its navy."[28]

## Domestic Shipbuilding and Ancillary Manufacturing

To obtain the ships the Confederate navy needed, Mallory tried several different methods. He first tried to buy already-built ships in the South. He authorized the purchase of 30 such ships, 22 of them by the end of 1861.[29] It soon became obvious, however, that ships of the kind Mallory needed for warships were generally unavailable in the South. The ships that were available were in bad condition, unequipped, slow, or incapable of being refurbished to meet the requirements of warships or gunboats. He then sought to have ships built specifically by his design and to his and the navy's specifications.

The biggest problem with the latter effort, however, was the lack of facilities sufficient to the task. The only shipyards in the South were at Norfolk and Pensacola, and neither shipyard was equipped for constructing warships.

## Foreign Shipbuilding and Purchase of Existing Ships

Next, Mallory turned to foreign markets for ships. "As early as March 1861, Mallory sent agents to the North, and in May 1861, agents were sent to Canada to arrange for the purchase and construction of ships."[30] In April and

May, he sent agents to Europe for the same purpose. He was especially interested in obtaining rams, shallow-draft vessels protected by armor plating that could run into the Union's wooden vessels, shattering them below the waterline and thereby sinking them. European nations had been experimenting with such vessels for years, and Mallory thought that they could break the Union's blockade of the South almost singlehandedly.

The agents that Mallory sent to the Northern states and Canada were generally unsuccessful. That put even more pressure on the agents that he had sent to Europe. President Davis had sent the first commission to Europe, appointing A. Dudley Mann, Pierre A. Rost, and William Lowden Yancey commissioners to Great Britain and France. The European governments would not even meet with them. Opposition to slavery and the desire to avoid offense to the United States prevented it.

On May 8, 1861, Mallory sent James Dunwoody Bulloch to England to obtain both ships and supplies for the Confederacy from private citizens or companies. Mallory's instructions were for Bulloch to act independently of Confederate diplomats, to become thoroughly familiar with legal issues of building and equipping ships in Great Britain, to obtain the needed ships as quickly as possible, and to obtain naval supplies just as quickly.

Bulloch was a long-time veteran of both the U.S. navy and the merchant marine. He had become a midshipman at the age of 16; spent 14 years at sea; "had served on every class of war vessel"; commanded several merchant ships; and knew ships, the sea, and international law well.[31] Essentially, Mallory ordered Bulloch to buy a whole new navy.[32] He assigned Bulloch "to find ingenious ways of sidestepping the Foreign Enlistment Act and procuring ships for the fledgling Confederate navy."[33] Mallory warned him not to get the Confederate diplomats into embarrassing situations over allegations of violating neutrality laws.[34] Mallory wanted everything to be done according to international law, but he wanted it kept secret from Northern agents. He knew that they would be spying aggressively on the Southern agents and would complain to European officials at the first suspicion that those nations were constructing—or allowing the construction of—warships for the Confederacy. And the Northern agents—led by Charles Francis Adams, grandson of founding father John Adams—were formidable and held in high esteem by the British government.

By the Foreign Enlistment Act, a measure of Parliament, it was illegal for Englishmen to equip ships for any nation that was waging a war in which Britain was a neutral.[35] If they were to build ships for the South, it had to be done in such a way as to seem to comply with the act of Parliament. So Bulloch began his assignment in Europe with three strikes against him: he had to arrange for ships to be built in a foreign country for another country that had neither diplomatic recognition nor credit.[36]

Mallory authorized Bulloch to order the purchase of "several steam-propelled vessels" that they could use as commerce raiders, attacking the U.S. merchant marine.[37] The first priority, of course, would be for ships that were already finished, thereby allowing them to get into action quickly. If that proved unsuccessful, Bulloch was authorized to contract for new construction of the ships needed. He was given "a long list of supplies" that the Confederate navy needed.[38] And he was authorized to meet with the firm of Fraser, Trenholm, and Company, which was acting as the financial repository and resource of the Confederacy. They even provided an office for Bulloch in their own building.

Bulloch's efforts with private shipbuilders seemed to bear the desired fruit. He contracted with Fawcett, Preston, and Company of Liverpool to build one commerce raider. That ship became the first British-built Confederate cruiser. Known in the shipyard as the *Oreto*, it was also known variously as the *Palermo* and the *Manassas*. It was later rechristened with its official name, the C.S.S. *Florida*. The finished ship sailed from Liverpool disguised as a merchant vessel. It sailed to Nassau, where Captain James Maffit came aboard to command it from that point. There it was armed, equipped, and entered Confederate raiding service.

People in the British government began to take notice. Chancellor of the Exchequer William Gladstone said something that showed just how close the Confederacy had come to gaining British diplomatic recognition: "There is no doubt that Jefferson F. Davis and the leaders of the South have made an army; they are making, it appears, a navy; and they have made what is more than either—they have made a nation."[39]

Bulloch also contracted with Laird Brothers in Brinkenham for construction of another raider, but this one was "larger and more heavily armed than the [*Florida*]."[40] Quality was foremost with the Lairds, although the Confederacy needed the ships quickly, and they used only the best materials.[41] Repeatedly but unsuccessfully, Union agents tried to get the British government to seize the ship as a violation of the Enlistment Act. Despite repeated failures, the Union agents continued to press the British government. Finally, the British relented. Learning of the impending seizure of the vessel, Confederate agents convinced the Lairds to release the warship. Under the guise of making a test run, the ship sailed from Brinkenham and never returned. Known in the shipyard as simply "290," or sometimes the *Enrica*, it later was named the C.S.S. *Alabama*. The vessel sailed to the Azores, where she met supply ships, which equipped her with guns, supplies, and a crew. The *Alabama* also got her commander there—Raphael Semmes.

In both instances, Bulloch—to adhere to the spirit, if not the letter, of British law—arranged for the ships to be outfitted with ordnance and supplies outside of Great Britain at a neutral location. There, the ship would obtain its permanent captain and crew and head onto the high seas in search of Northern commerce.

Bulloch also contracted with the Lairds to build two ironclad rams. Mallory admitted from the start that his navy would never match the U.S. navy ship for ship, so he chose to focus his construction efforts on "a few powerful, relatively invulnerable vessels."[42] Although some European nations had been working to develop their own ironclads over the preceding decades, they were still experimental, and Mallory eagerly pushed technological advances, especially if they advanced the development of ironclads. He realized that the future navy would be armored, not wooden, just as they were becoming steam powered rather than wind powered. He had supported and encouraged the development of ironclads while on the U.S. Senate's naval committee.

During Mallory's time as the Confederate secretary of the navy, about 21 ironclads were built or converted domestically by the Confederacy, an amazing accomplishment when one considers the economic condition of the South.[43] Of all the navy's efforts, that program presented the South its best potential for reward.[44] Of the ironclads built in European shipyards, only the *Stonewall* left a port, and she never reached Southern shores or even fought for the Confederacy. But "four out of every five ships built in the Confederacy after the spring of 1862 were ironclads."[45]

Bulloch helped design the rams that the Lairds agree to build, specifying that they be protected with from three to four-and-a-half-inch-thick armor plating. The entire center portion, where the engines and boilers were, was covered by four and a half inches of plating that tapered toward the ends to three inches.[46] They would have sails to back up the steam engines. Each ram was to have three gun turrets and iron armor five and one-half inches thick backed by 12-inch-thick teak.[47]

As quietly as Bulloch tried to have the rams built, prying Union agents' eyes saw what was going on and worked hard to get the British government to seize them. Then, in January 1863, Clarence Younge, who had once been Bulloch's secretary in Liverpool and later the paymaster aboard the *Alabama*, deserted and went straight to the Union authorities with the story of the Laird rams. The game was up. Armed with this first-hand account as proof, the Union agents demanded that the British seize the unfinished ships. Learning of the treachery, Bulloch tried to get the rams transferred to the name of a foreign owner, Bravay and Company of Paris, which posed as agents of the Pasha of Egypt.[48] The Lairds were unaware that the transfer was fictitious, and when construction was nearing completion, they scheduled a trial run. Fearing that the ram would slip through their fingers the way the *Alabama* had, Union authorities demanded action by the British government, and they got it. The ram was seized before it could leave port.

Bulloch tried to get ships built in other countries. Repeated efforts to get contracts in France failed, as did their efforts to woo the French dictator, Napoleon III. Bulloch's assistant, Lieutenant James North, worked to get a frigate built in Glasgow, Scotland, but the British foiled that effort, too. Later, the Confederates were able to get a contract for several ships with Lucien Arman, the biggest shipbuilder of France, but Arman refused to begin the keels until he saw the money.[49] Thanks to money provided from the Erlanger loan (see Chapter 8), arrangements were made for construction of four ships. One-fifth of the cost of construction was to be paid up front, one-fifth when the ships were "in frame," another fifth when the contractor laid the beams, another fifth when the ships hit the water, and the last fifth upon delivery of the ships. So eager was the Confederacy for speedy delivery that it threatened to deduct from the agreed-upon price a thousand francs for each day's delay in delivery.[50] But as the ships neared completion, the French government began to cool on the idea of letting the ships go. The emperor had stipulated that release of the rams depended on their construction remaining secret. But word had leaked out; their existence was now public knowledge. Then, in 1863, as the fortunes of war deserted the Southern armies at Vicksburg and Gettysburg, the French government suddenly ceased being such a friendly country. Napoleon III would not allow the rams to be released.

In desperation, Bulloch told Arman to sell the rams to a legitimate foreign government.[51] Consequently, Arman sold them to Denmark and Prussia. He also sold to Peru four corvettes that were also being built. And then the vicissitudes of history intervened and offered another faint ray of hope. The Danish war ended in October 1864, and since the Danish government no longer needed the ram, it cancelled the sale based on the fact that the ship had never been delivered on time.[52] Arman ignored the notification and sent the ram anyway. When it arrived, the Danes refused to accept it, and a Danish crew agreed to return it. Instead of returning to Bordeaux, however, they took it to Quiebron Bay, Belle Ile, off the coast of France. There, Captain Thomas Jefferson Page of the Confederate navy took over. The ship was named the *Stonewall*. Unfortunately, in the ill-advised attempt to cross the Atlantic in mid-winter, the *Stonewall* was badly damaged and put into port in Spain to be repaired. By the time the *Stonewall* was able to resume the journey, almost all Southern ports had been sealed by the blockade. Page sailed to Cuba, where he learned that generals Lee and Johnston had both surrendered their armies and that, for all practical purposes, the war was over. He sold the *Stonewall* to the Spanish in Cuba and received just enough to pay the crew.

Although the South was not very successful in building or buying a large navy, Mallory must be credited with going farther toward that goal than anyone else in history. Considering how little he had to work with and how short a lifespan the Confederacy had, that was no small accomplishment. Also, he had as his primary foreign agent "the man who singlehandedly created the Confederate navy's blue-water cruiser force."[53]

During the entire war, the Confederacy started construction on 52 ironclads, and they completed almost 30 of them, but those built domestically "were little more than armored, floating artillery batteries, capable of little more than harbor defense."[54] The commerce raiders, or cruisers, were another story.

## *Confederate Commerce Raiders*

Mallory had a fourfold purpose for the commerce raiders:

1. they would attack Northern commerce, thereby hurting economically a lot of politically influential people in the North and increasing their likelihood to oppose a continuation of the war;
2. they hoped to force the U.S. secretary of the navy to weaken the blockade by ordering a lot of his best ships to chase the commerce raiders;
3. they wanted to force the U.S. navy to spend more money on equipping ships to chase the raiders, thereby decreasing the amount that could be spent on the blockade; and
4. they would prevent the likelihood that the North would attack anywhere along the South's coast line.[55]

Both of the first two ships, the light, wooden *Florida* and the *Alabama*, were built for attacking merchant ships but were not strong enough to attack Union blockade vessels.[56] These two ships and the *Shenandoah* were "masterpieces of design and technology," capable of sailing by sale or steam and of staying at sea for extended periods.[57] Mallory wanted "these behemoths [to go] far beyond blockade-running and storming American inland waterways."[58] Their sole role, like that of all other raiders, was to harass and destroy Northern commerce to the point that the losses incurred hurt the Northern economy and their owners and investors demanded protection from the Union government. At that point, the Union navy would be forced to pull warships from the blockade fleets and send them in search of the Confederate raiders. The raiders were not intended to engage in combat with the Union warships, only to bring them away from the Southern coast and onto the high seas in search of the elusive and speedy raiders.

The raiders were, considering their small number and the many limitations and handicaps of their government, quite successful. "During the Civil War, the only force opposing the United States Navy on the high seas was eight Confederate cruisers. Their mission was to dismantle the American carrying trade and force wealthy shippers to press the federal government for a peaceful settlement. Manned by a handful of resolute Confederate officers, they very nearly succeeded."[59] Only eight cruisers wreaked havoc with Northern shipping, and the effects are seen in the number and values of ships and cargoes captured and in the reaction of Northern shippers and the Union government to the raiders' successes.

The eight legendary Confederate cruisers were as follows: *Alabama*, commanded by Raphael Semmes; *Florida*, commanded first by John Maffitt and later by James Iredell Waddell; *Georgia*, which was purchased by Matthew Maury; *Sumter*, Semmes' first command under the Confederate navy; *Nashville*; *Tallahassee*; *Chickamauga*, the last four all armed in the Confederacy; and *Shenandoah*, the "last flag down."

The *Shenandoah* was unique in that she preyed not on Northern shipping in the Atlantic, Caribbean, or Mediterranean but in the Northwest against Northeastern whalers.

Eventually, merchants concluded that no vessel having U.S. registry and flying the U.S. flag was safe in international waters. "More than half the American merchant fleet disappeared during the Civil War. The Confederate cruisers destroyed 110,000 tones of shipping."[60] As a result and in an effort to protect themselves, hundreds of merchant ships were transferred to foreign registries.[61] The following table shows merely the number of ships captured by each of these magnificent vessels and their captains and crews.

**Table 10. Legendary Confederate Cruisers**[62]

| Ship | Number of Enemy Vessels Captured |
|---|---|
| CSS *Alabama* | 66[a] |
| CSS *Chickamauga* | 7 |
| CSS *Florida* | 37 |
| CSS *Georgia* | 9 |
| CSS *Nashville* | 2 |
| CSS *Shenandoah* | 38[b] |
| CSS *Sumter* | 18 |

| Ship | Number of Enemy Vessels Captured |
|---|---|
| CSS *Tallahassee* (earlier named the CSS *Olustee*) | 39 (includes 6 as the CSS *Olustee*) |
| Total | 216 |

[a] Estimated value of vessels burned—$4,613,914; bonded—$562,250
[b] Estimated value of vessels destroyed—$1,172,223; bonded—$118,600

## *The Confederate Naval Academy*

The man-of-war CSS *Patrick Henry* fought in her last combat role on May 15, 1862, at the Battle of Drewry's Bluff on the James River. Her solid-shot eight-inch gun and two of her rifled 30 two-pounders were taken from her and installed on the bluff. Her sacrifice helped defend Richmond from a Union attack. But her contribution to the Confederacy was not finished. She had a potentially much greater role to play in another capacity. She became home and classroom to the Confederate States Naval Academy.

Since becoming the Confederate secretary of the navy, Mallory had been acutely aware of the need for the training of naval officers and seamen for the Confederate navy. At Mallory's urging, Congress passed a bill providing for the founding and establishment of just such a school in the spring of 1862. Lieutenant William Parker was appointed superintendent of the Academy. His first assignment was to come up with rules for running the school. The task of organizing the school, its curriculum, and classes fell to Commander John Brooke. Both Parker and Brooke were graduates of the U.S. Naval Academy. The commandant of midshipmen was Lieutenant Benjamin Loyall (until the fall of 1863) and Lieutenant James Rochell (from that point until the end of the war).

Classes began at the Academy in October 1863. Facilities aboard ship proved inadequate, so cabins were built along Drewry's Bluff. Because Congress refused to appropriate sufficient funds to accommodate all of the allotted students, a system was developed whereby midshipmen on land and midshipmen at sea would be rotated through the Academy for alternating sessions.

Appointees had to be at least 14 but not more than 18 years of age. They were given written exams on "such elementary studies as reading, writing, spelling, and arithmetic."[63] They were also held to fairly strict physical conditions. Fifty-nine midshipmen had resigned from the U.S. Naval Academy upon secession, and those completed their studies at the Confederate States Naval Academy. Midshipmen were assigned to ship or shore duty, and were expected to continue reading and studies during times when they were not on official duty.

The goal of the naval academy was to prepare midshipmen to be promoted to lieutenant.[64] The U.S. Naval Academy was the model for the curriculum of the Confederate Naval Academy.[65] Midshipmen were also drilled in infantry tactics because naval personnel were also expected to be ready to and capable of rendering assistance to land forces as necessary. Many of the midshipmen got true-to-life, on-the-job-training in actual combat while on duty aboard ship or at naval shore installations during the war, especially around Richmond and along the James River. Twice a year, the midshipmen took written exams. They were advanced according to how well they did on those exams. It was not unusual for a student to be advanced more than one class if he did well. "As soon as the midshipmen were deemed proficient, they were ordered to ships, batteries, or other duty."[66]

As critical as Mallory and other Confederate naval officials deemed the Academy, other civilian officials, notably many congressmen, failed to grasp that reality. They rejected two proposals of greater appropriations for more and better facilities at Drewry's Bluff and for the hiring of more instructors. President Davis vetoed a similar bill that managed to pass Congress.

As the war crept ever closer to Richmond and the end looked near, Mallory recommended that the Academy be moved inland, and Congress approved such a move. But the Union army severely limited any possible move to a suitable site. During the evacuation of Richmond, midshipmen from the Academy were assigned to guard the train hauling the government's records and about half a million dollars of its bullion. They "stayed by the stuff" all the way to Washington, Georgia, where "the treasure was deposited with General Basil Duke, commander of the cavalry unit escorting President Jefferson Davis."[67] None of it was lost while it was under guard by the Academy students.

Meanwhile, ten midshipmen had been left behind at the Academy with instructions to scuttle the CSS *Patrick Henry*. That was their last duty to the Confederacy. Nine of the ten were captured.

## *Failures of the Comprehensive Confederate Naval Strategy*

One major criticism of Mallory's Navy Department was that it lacked an overall strategy. Although Mallory worked near-wonders in building a blue-water navy of cruisers and in beginning to address the blockade with his rams and ironclads, he failed strategically in one major respect: he did not establish a way of protecting and controlling the nation's inland waterways. His attempt to justify that omission was the claim that the inland waters were the responsibility of the Confederate army. Apparently, the Confederate army thought differently. Therefore, no one took that responsibility seriously.

Mallory expected the armies in their respective theaters to protect the waterways by building fortifications sufficient to the purpose at strategic locations and to patrol those waterways frequently enough to dissuade any enemy incursions into Confederate territory, to warn of any such attempts, and to repel any invasion. The fact that he was slow to acknowledge the navy's role in protecting these waterways "enabled enemy forces to seize the initiative which they never lost."[68]

The Union understood, as the Confederacy failed to understand, the importance of cooperative efforts by the army and the navy. In fact, General Winfield Scott's Anaconda Plan early in the war established joint operations of the army and navy as a large part of the Union strategy. The first incursions were along the Cumberland and Tennessee rivers, with the resulting loss of Forts Henry and Donelson. That was followed by the eventual loss of control of the Mississippi River when the Union—which did have a river strategy—captured New Orleans and Vicksburg. Whereas Mallory "underestimated the need for a navy on the upper reaches of the Mississippi River," the Union made it a major priority.[69] The results were the only proof they needed for the wisdom of that priority. History might have turned out differently had the Confederacy developed a corresponding defensive river strategy.

General Leonidas Polk, however, did foresee the need for a naval involvement in the Confederates' Western Theater. He repeatedly asked Mallory "for boats on the Mississippi, Tennessee, and Cumberland rivers, calling them 'indispensible to our defenses.'"[70] Likewise, Tennessee Governor Isham Harris pleaded for the navy's involvement in protecting the interior of his state.

Mallory's strategy was at first *active*—trying to break the blockade by crushing Union commercial shipping with his cruisers, thereby pulling the Union navy out to sea away from blockade duty so that blockade runners could slip into Southern ports. But as the war progressed, his strategy became more *reactive*. Mallory became increasingly concerned about the danger posed by an enemy gunboat fleet going *down* the Mississippi to New Orleans. After all, the Union fleet had recently taken Island No. 10. What he failed to see was that the Union naval assault would be *up* the river against New Orleans and then farther up the Mississippi Valley—Vicksburg, Memphis, and who knew where else. "One of the characteristics of the river war was the relative equality of opposing naval forces when the war began. Mallory allowed the enemy to build first and compounded his error by concentrating on boats whose construction period would be lengthy."[71] Meanwhile, Davis was always preoccupied with army matters and scarcely noticed that there even was a navy.

## 18. Overview

What underlay Mallory's omission of a proper emphasis on river defenses? His thinking was occupied primarily with the blockade and how he could break it. The blockade determined Confederate naval policy, meaning that Mallory focused almost exclusively on cruisers and ironclads.[72]

Beyond this, however, was a problem with how the department was organized, failing, as it did, to build and maintain the ships and their mechanical apparatus.[73] Included in this problem was Mallory's failure to make a priority of "obstructing and mining rivers and harbors."[74]

To his credit, however, Mallory initiated a program for building two river fleets, one in Memphis and the other in New Orleans. The vessels were only small rams and gunboats, but they were a beginning. Yet, they were too little too late. Most of them were destroyed in just two confrontations with Union vessels that were larger and more numerous than the Confederate vessels, one when New Orleans was taken in April 1862 and the other when Memphis was captured in June 1862.

On the other hand, Mallory worked with what he had and tried to enhance that little. In addition to the cruisers that raided Union commercial shipping and the ironclads that he had built, Mallory turned to private enterprise to help achieve his goals for the Confederate navy. After May 6, 1861, Davis had congressional approval to grant letters of marquee and reprisal. These were official government incentives for private ship owners to prepare ships that would then attack Northern vessels. From this vote of authorization and September 1864, the Confederate government issued more than 30 such letters.[75] Although opponents of the practice viewed it as "legalized piracy," Mallory favored it because, like successful cruisers, it applied pressure on the North to pull ships from blockade duty and assign them to guard against and chase down privateers.

The success of the combined efforts of the Confederate raiders and the privateers forced Northern merchants to transport their goods on ships other than American-flagged vessels. "In 1860 over two-thirds of the commerce was carried by American ships, but by 1863, three-fourths was carried by ships flying a flag other than American."[76] Insurance rates skyrocketed. These results, and the lack of effectiveness of the blockade, led Great Britain on May 14, 1861, to recognize the Confederate States of America as a belligerent power; therefore, Southern sailors and privateers were not pirates. In that sense, the Navy Department had done what it could and therefore can be said to have been successful, at least to that extent. The State Department, however, failed to "close the deal" by convincing Great Britain—or any other country—to grant the Confederacy diplomatic recognition.

CHAPTER 19

# Stephen Mallory

The first—and only—Confederate secretary of the navy was Stephen Mallory. He is perhaps the "most neglected member of the Confederate Cabinet."[1] Yet, in many ways, he was the most loyal, most consistent, and most successful cabinet member, considering what he had (or rather did not have) to work with.

Stephen Mallory, Secretary of the Navy (**Library of Congress**).

Mallory was born in 1813, on Trinidad in the British West Indies. His father was an American; his mother was an Irishwoman. The family moved a lot but eventually settled in Key West, Florida.

He was enrolled at Blakely, a boarding school near Mobile, Alabama, when he was only nine years old. Being younger than the other students, he tended to be a loner and learned early to entertain himself. He also learned to think for himself and to act on his own.[2] When his father died unexpectedly, his mother brought him back to Key West, where, with his help, she opened a boarding house for sailors. About 1826, after the boarding house got on its feet, his mother enrolled him in a Moravian school near Nazareth, Pennsylvania. Although his parents had reared him as a Roman Catholic, the Moravians introduced him to their form of German pietism and unpretentious spirituality, an experience that colored the rest of his life.

After he had spent three years at the Moravian school, however, his mother could no longer afford to send him there. She had him return to Key West, thus ending his formal schooling. But Mallory had learned perhaps the most important lesson in life—how to learn—and he never ended his informal quest for knowledge.

About 1830 or 1832, Mallory was appointed Inspector of Customs of Key West. This marked the first rung on his self-determined career ladder. He wanted to study law and become a lawyer. But he had an even higher goal: he wanted to be elected to the U.S. Congress. Toward that end, he developed a method of study that involved reading a wide variety of subjects and taking copious notes on everything he read.[3] No doubt from much of that reading, he began to pay close attention to developing moral convictions and conduct. To help himself toward that goal, he wrote out and posted in conspicuous places all over his room pithy, thought-provoking quotations that would direct him in that direction. He never drank or smoked. He kept himself pure, and tried always to be sincere and truthful. He also opened himself to further religious influence by joining as a charter member the first church ever opened in Key West, the Protestant Episcopal Church.

About this time, the Seminole War broke out, and Mallory volunteered for the navy. He was actively involved in two campaigns during that war.

Following that short naval adventure, Mallory returned to Key West to pursue the study of law, reading law in the office of Judge William Marvin of the U.S. District Court. As customs inspector, his job naturally involved a lot of maritime law, so that became his primary focus. As his success as a lawyer increased, so did his political visibility, and he was soon elected judge for Monroe Country. He quickly developed a reputation for honesty.[4]

In 1850, Mallory was chosen to be an alternate delegate representing Florida at the Nashville Convention. He declined, saying that he had other engagements, but he actually was not very positive concerning the potential for success at the convention.

Also in 1850, Mallory agreed to run for the U.S. Senate against the incumbent Democrat David Yulee. Yulee was a fire-eater; Mallory was known as a moderate who had conservative political opinions. Mallory won on the fourth ballot. Off he went to Washington, D.C., but so did Yulee. When it came time to seat Florida's senator, Yulee challenged Mallory's credentials and hired Edwin M. Stanton, future secretary of war under Lincoln, to present his case against

Mallory to the Senate. Henry Clay, in his last speech before the Senate, defended Mallory, however, and swayed his colleagues. Mallory was seated as Florida's duly elected senator. Neither Yulee nor Stanton ever forgave Mallory, as would become evident after the War Between the States, when Stanton exerted his considerable influence to extend Mallory's imprisonment and even sought to have him tried for treason.

Mallory was assigned to the Naval Affairs Committee, and in 1853 he became chairman of that committee. He immediately began reading and studying naval history and talking to naval officers to learn all he could about naval matters. He sought to keep abreast of the latest advances in naval technology, especially those involving ordnance. Finding the navy in deplorable shape, he emphasized the need to ensure that young officers rose through the ranks and achieved positions where their vigorous minds and bodies could be used for the greater benefit of the navy and national security. He also, however, sought to ensure the retirement or removal of older officers who had passed their prime physically and who were stuck in their traditions and were close-minded to new ways of doing things. Technology was changing, and the navy and its leadership had to reflect that change if the navy was to remain competitive among the other navies of the world. He also sought to enforce strict discipline in the navy, including returning to the practice of flogging. He pushed for construction of more and better ships to increase the size and effectiveness of the navy, including experimentation with ironclads. Much of this thinking became incorporated in the Naval Reform Bill, or what was popularly known as "Mr. Mallory's bill."[5]

In 1857, the Whigs and the Know-Nothings in Florida united in an effort to unseat Mallory. They were unsuccessful, and he was reelected by the Florida legislature. In his second term, Mallory continued to press for improvements in the navy. His intense interest in this effort reflected a growing belief that a bigger and better navy would increase U.S. prestige abroad and help improve American commercial relations.[6]

The next year, 1858, President James Buchanan offered to make Mallory the U.S. ambassador to Spain. Mallory declined.

Mallory was not a fervent secessionist. He was a cooperationist, willing for Florida to secede but only if Georgia and Alabama would do so in concert with Florida and, hopefully, other Southern states. Nevertheless, he foresaw the day when secession might become necessary to protect constitutional rights. Apparently, however, he did not really think that that day or crisis would ever occur. Rather, he feared that the Republicans were determined to have a civil war.[7] He thought that the Republican Party would split before that civil war came about. Four weeks later, however, he was standing before the Senate announcing his resignation after Florida had seceded from the Union. They preferred to leave peacefully, he declared, but it was up to the Republicans whether they would be able to do so.

Mallory returned to Florida and was prepared to retreat from public life, perhaps returning to his law practice, when he was contacted by Jefferson Davis, who wanted Mallory to come to Montgomery, where the seceded states were organizing the Confederate government. Davis informed him that he was nominating Mallory to be the secretary of the navy. Mallory headed to Montgomery, as requested, but he intended to talk Davis into withdrawing his name from consideration.

Several factors might have been in Davis's mind when he selected Mallory to head the Navy Department. As former senators, the two men were already familiar with each other. Davis had no doubt seen the work and influence of Mallory on the Naval Committee and had been impressed with Mallory's seriousness about strengthening and improving the U.S. navy. He must have recognized and appreciated the fact that Mallory was conscientious and reliable.[8] Davis also knew that Mallory was from Florida, and Davis needed a representative of Florida on his cabinet to maintain balance and equality among the original seceded states. Davis also surely had seen that Mallory was conservative, nothing like the rash and hasty fire-eaters. Some people who knew another side of Davis wondered if Davis chose Mallory because he did not grumble too loudly when he disagreed with someone.[9]

But not everyone was for Mallory's nomination and actually opposed it, including two of Florida's three representatives. (They contended that he "was not sufficiently sound upon Southern Rights."[10]) Until receiving Davis's summons, Mallory had purposely stayed away from Montgomery to squelch any rumors that he was campaigning for a position in the Davis government. But when he arrived in the city at Davis's request and learned that his name had already been placed before the Senate and was being debated, he decided not to oppose it. A firm believer in Providence, he would let Providence take its course and determine the issue. Providence worked such that Mallory was confirmed by a vote of 36–7.

Mallory had a kind, calm, broad, round, almost cherubic face. His mouth, however, was stern, undergirded by a neatly trimmed beard but no moustache. Generous amounts of hair adorned the sides of his head while the center was neatly parted and almost plastered, albeit neatly, in place. His eyes were serious and intense.

Mallory had a generally cordial association with Davis but thought that not many men could be as cold as Davis.[11] Davis was wrapped up in army matters and therefore gave more operational and administrative freedom to Mallory with naval matters than he did his secretaries of war. Yet, even Mallory complained that Davis tended to muddle in military matters and to try dictating them.[12]

Mallory assessed his new responsibilities and quickly realized that he was being called upon to perform miracles. He found himself the head of a virtually nonexistent navy. He had to build one essentially in nonexistent facilities from insufficient resources. And he had to do so essentially without funding because the Confederate Treasury was virtually penniless. And as if those problems were not enough to discouraged him or drive him to despair, Mallory would soon be faced with a Union-imposed naval blockade that would compound and complicate his myriad problems.

He set about organizing his newly created department. He established the following four bureaus, or offices, to run the operations of the navy (Each of these having been dealt with in detail earlier in this chapter, we will not further belabor them here): Office of Orders and Detail, Office of Ordnance and Hydrography, Office of Provisions and Clothing, and Office of Medicine and Surgery.

Later, Mallory established several other "semiautonomous administrative units" within the Navy Department.[13] These included the Construction Bureau, the Torpedo Bureau, and the Marine Corps.

When Mallory assumed the position of secretary of the navy, the Confederate navy had only 12 ships and about 200 officers.[14] Many of the states had their own navies, all of which were to be turned over to the Confederate government. But those states insisted on retaining some control, even assuming the right to act independently of the central government if they thought the circumstances warranted it.

But Mallory's biggest and immediate problem was procuring ships with which to build his navy. Among his options were these: make them domestically or use foreign shipbuilders; buy them domestically or on the foreign market; and capture them from the Union military or merchant fleets.

Among his first actions as secretary, Mallory commissioned agents to travel the Northern states and Canada in search of ships to purchase, to travel the South in search of shipyards to construct warships, and to travel Europe in search of ships to purchase or contractors to build ships to Confederate specifications. In the last six months of 1861, the Navy Department arranged 32 contracts for "forty gunboats, floating batteries, and vessels of war."[15]

James Bulloch and James North were Mallory's foremost agents in Europe. (For more information on the contributions of Bulloch, see the section titled "Foreign Shipbuilding and Purchases of Existing Ships" in the preceding chapter.) Using the financial services of Trenholm and Company, and relying on Confederate rapport with the British people, especially the Lairds, the Con-

## 19. Stephen Mallory

federate government contracted for the construction of numerous vessels, only a few of which were completed and spirited through Union spies and foreign red tape into Confederate service. Mallory's two primary areas of focus on warship procurement were the cruisers, or raiders, and the ironclads, or Laird rams.

Later, Mallory would focus much of his attention on the development of torpedoes, or mines. Another area of his attention was submersibles, or submarines, most famously the *Hunley*. (For more information on torpedoes and the *Hunley*, see the section titled "Torpedo Bureau" in the preceding chapter.)

In his thankless job, Mallory faced critics and opponents from the very beginning. He "started his Confederate career as an unpopular man and he received little if any credit for the navy's subsequent achievements during its brief moments of glory."[16] Chief among the critics were Edward Pollard, editor of the Richmond *Examiner*, and Matthew Fontaine Maury. Pollard's reporting and editorializing carried a lot of weight all across the country. He was the head of one of the most widely read and quoted newspapers in the Confederacy. The paper certainly was powerful in that it covered first-hand the daily workings of the Davis administration after the capital of the Confederacy was moved from Montgomery to Richmond.

Matthew Maury was an old and highly acclaimed veteran of the navy. He had become known as the "Pathfinder of the Seas" for his discovery and description of the various ocean currents. But Mallory had thought him to be an example of officers who stayed in the service beyond their usefulness and thereby prevented younger officers from advancing to positions in which they could gain experience and offer their best service. Mallory's proposed naval reforms threatened to retire Maury and other similarly elderly officers. That did not sit well with Maury, and he was not silent about it. He seemed to criticize Mallory at every opportunity. When he entered Confederate service, he began immediately to complain about the Navy Department's red tape and Davis's administration generally. His criticisms only increased in vitriol as time passed. Mallory finally assigned him to Europe to purchase supplies for the navy and to continue there the torpedo experiments that he had begun in the South.

Mallory also suffered regular criticism from many other lesser known figures, including several members of the Confederate Congress. His nomination was the only one of Davis's original cabinet appointees to be delayed in the Confederate Congress. Many of the congressmen were like a dog worrying an old bone, never letting go of the old criticisms that Mallory was not loyal and that he was not a strong-enough supporter of secession. The criticism only intensified after the fall of New Orleans.

Mallory even caught criticism from Mary Chesnut, the South's self-appointed diarist and opinion setter. She especially criticized Mallory's slowness to build ships. "And now," she wrote on March 19, 1862, "too late by one year, when all the mechanics are in the army, Mallory begins to telegraph Captain Ingraham to build ships at any expense."[17] In spite of such criticism from all sides, Mallory remained focused on doing his job of establishing and strengthening the Confederate navy. It is a tribute to his patience and tolerance that he remained in the cabinet for the entire life of the Confederacy.

Mallory proved his loyalty to the very end. He was only one of two original cabinet members still in the cabinet when the Confederacy came to an end. On May 2, 1865, only when it became obvious beyond the faintest doubt that the Confederacy was irreversibly doomed to defeat, Mallory tendered his letter of resignation to the president. Soon after Davis's capture, Mallory was arrested in Atlanta, Georgia, where he had gone to reunite with his family. One of his final instructions to his wife before his arrest was that she go through all of his private papers and destroy everything that was political.[18]

After his arrest, Mallory was imprisoned in Fort Lafayette in Connecticut, sharing a cell with Benjamin Hill, Confederate senator from Georgia. He read a great deal, especially from the New Testament, and played chess, often against himself. He prayed a lot but ate little. (His typical breakfast was "a single piece of toast and a cup of tea."[19]) After three weeks, he wrote to President Andrew Johnson, applying for a pardon. He did not receive a reply. His wife visited Washington and met with Johnson, seeking the pardon, but she, too, was unsuccessful. Mallory briefly was hopeful when Union secretary of war Edwin Stanton, during a visit to the prison, spoke with Mallory. But by the time Stanton left, Mallory regretted having had the conversation. The longer he stayed in prison, the more discouraged he became. His primary concerns were for his wife and children, especially after he learned that his wife had been injured in a train wreck. His comfort came from prayer, visits from family members, and the diary he kept during his imprisonment.

But Governor William Marvin, provisional governor of Florida, had been working behind the scenes on Mallory's behalf. And Mallory's wife's visit to Johnson had not been entirely without effect. Consequently, on March 10, 1866, Mallory left the prison with a "partial parole."[20] He was forced to stay in Connecticut until he got permission to return home. In early June, he was allowed to travel to Washington to meet with and thank President Johnson for his pardon. While there, he requested permission to return to his home in Florida. Johnson magnanimously granted his request.

Arriving home, Mallory had to start all over. He repaired his dilapidated house and reopened his law office, working with Judge Augustus Maxwell. Although his former slaves were now free, most of them chose to remain with him, and he kept them on as hired hands, although he could hardly afford to keep himself up, let alone them too. People watched to see what his reaction to the Radical Republicans' reconstruction program would be.

Mallory believed "in a superintending, overruling Providence," so he viewed the South's defeat as God's will.[21] He believed that the Southern states now had to get themselves back into the Union quickly, accept whatever consequences would come, and try their best to recover.[22]

But Mallory was also determined to do what he could to oppose the Radicals. They scared him because "they had 'made voters of the ignorant, the vicious, the brutal.'"[23] "They had given the benighted Negro the right to vote and the power to rule, while at the same time they admit his unfitness for either by directing, controlling, and sustaining him in his new relations by means of the Freedmen's Bureau, the bayonet of the soldier, and the disenfranchisement of the citizen."[24]

Mallory did not feel well and was listless on the morning of November 11, 1873. That night he became very sick. He died early the next morning.

Scharf assessed Mallory's time in the Confederate cabinet thus: "The administration of Mr. Mallory is not to be judged and condemned by its failure, but it will excite surprise and win admiration for what was accomplished with the means and resources at his command."[25]

Part V

# Post Office Department

CHAPTER 20

# Overview

The backbone of the Confederate Post Office Department was made up primarily of individuals whom Davis's choice for postmaster general, John Reagan, had convinced to leave the U.S. Post Office Department to join the Confederate equivalent. He and three assistants awaited replies from the people in Washington, D.C., to whom he had made overtures. "Within two weeks, much of the United States Post Office had moved southward."[1] These men were the discs in the postal backbone:

- Henry St. George Offurt—Chief of the Contract Bureau and Assistant Postmaster General
- Benjamin N. Clements—Chief Clerk to the Postmaster General and Chief of the Bureau of Appointments
- Joseph F. Lewis—head of the bond division
- Gustav A. Schwartzman—head of the Dead Letter Office
- J. L. Harrell—Chief of the Finance Bureau

After Reagan had the main personnel in place, his next step was to hire subordinate personnel and to instruct them in their duties. He established a school for this purpose, and conducted classes from 8:00 to 10:00 every evening. He also prepared a personnel book, which he called the appointment-book, that contained the Confederate postmasters' names and information about their offices, including the names of the Post Office agents and how much each was paid.[2] It also showed the delivery routes that were under Confederate control and the names of the contractors and their prices, including the railroad and steamship companies that were involved in the transportation and delivery of the mail.

While all of this organizing was going on, the Confederate Post Office, such as it was, continued delivering the mail just as it had under the U.S. postal system. It followed the same regulations as it had under the U.S system, charged the same rates that the U.S. system charged, and delivered by the same routes and schedules as the U.S. system did. Many of the delivery personnel were also the same. By agreement with the U.S. Post Office Department, the Confederate Post Office Department was to assume full responsibility for the postal services in the 11 states that made up the Confederacy on June 1, 1861. (One might think that such an arrangement amounted to de facto recognition, that the United States was recognizing the legitimacy of the Confederate States of America by recognizing the existence of the Confederate Post Office Department, but such was not the case.)

On April 29, 1861, more than a month before the stated deadline, Reagan reported to Davis that the Post Office Department was completely organized and ready to begin operating as the postal service of the Confederacy.[3] This rapid organization of the system was a tribute to Reagan's commendable administrative abilities.

On June 1, all postal employees in the Confederacy were supposed to send their names and job titles to the Confederate Post Office Department so that the new government could give them new commissions.[4] The employees would continue doing everything as they had been doing it; they would just have a new boss, so to speak. Contracted service providers were to do the same, sending the department information about their route(s), schedules, etc. These requirements show "Reagan's fine regard for precision and law," and "the tendency of the Confederacy toward strict and literal compliance with the rules of law and justice."[5]

Although some historians (e.g., Garrison) have stated that Reagan made the Confederate Post Office "out of nothing,"[6] that statement is simply not as true as it might be of Stephen Mallory, who truly did start the Confederate navy from nothing. Reagan, however, had something—a fully functioning postal system, in fact—to build upon. Even many of the employees, contractors, railroads, and steamship lines remained the same as they had been before secession. That said, however, it does not mean that Reagan had an easy job to do. He had to work hard, especially in keeping the contractors happy and working out realistic and practical delivery and rate schedules. And he did face a number of problems that the former system had not grappled with.

For example, the Constitution of the Confederate States of America stipulated that by March 1, 1863—roughly two years from the time Reagan reported that his department was fully organized and ready to begin service—the Post Office Department was to be self-sustaining.[7] Although Reagan had inherited a system that was already in the red, he took common-sense steps to put the department on a sound financial footing that would show by the deadline that the department was self-sufficient. He called upon representatives from all railroads involved in delivery of the mail to meet in a special meeting in Montgomery in April 1861. At that meeting, they all readily agreed to the following cost-cutting measures.

- The amount they received for carrying mail was cut in half.
- The rates for delivery of letters, packages, and newspapers were increased.
- Unnecessary routes were discontinued.
- Frequency of delivery on some routes was reduced.
- The weight of the mail to be delivered was reduced by ending the franking privileges for government officials.
- The length of routes was shortened.
- Competition was encouraged.
- Some routes were dropped to prevent duplication.
- Some routes were abandoned altogether.[8]

Furthermore, the attendees agreed to propose to Congress (and Congress passed it a few days later) a measure assigning each railroad to one of three categories, depending on its geographic location, its routes, and the volume of mail it typically delivered. Class One railroads were large lines that connected major cities or points and carried a heavy volume of mail. Class Two railroads connected smaller cities and less important points but still carried a heavy volume of mail. And Class Three railroads included short branch lines and unfinished railroads, and none of them connected important points or carried very much mail.[9] According to the bill that Congress passed based on these definitions of the various railroads, Class One railroads would be paid $150 per mile, Class Two lines got $100 per mile, and Class Three lines got $50 per mile.[10]

But the amity demonstrated at this meeting and the concord evidenced by the agreements made there proved superficial and temporary. Both the railroads and the Post Office Department became disillusioned and "mutually suspicious."[11] The regulations that looked so good on paper proved inconvenient in practice. Although most of the railroads had signed contracts by the end of 1863, some of them refused to sign. Although the railroads were willing to carry the mail, they did not want to be controlled by the government.[12] And even those that signed contracts complained that they were not paid enough.

Whenever one side was blamed for something, it tried to shift blame or responsibility to the other side. For example, erratic railroad schedules angered many people, and they blamed the postmaster general. The Post Office Department tried to shift the blame to the railroads.[13]

Another problem that the department faced was competition from express companies. The Confederate postal service was supposed to be a monopoly, but express companies often violated that "right."[14] Such companies were prohibited by law from delivering mail unless it had been prepaid and was enclosed in a stamped government envelope.[15]

Although much is made of the disparity between the North and the South in railroads, the South actually increased its rail mileage during the first years of the war, and the Confederate Post Office Department took full advantage of this fact. The South experienced an increase of 1,256 miles of trackage in the first two years of its existence. The number of railroads and branch lines increased from 91 to 109. And the number of contracts by railroads to carry mail increased from 19 to 55.[16]

As the war progressed and tracks, motive power, and rail facilities suffered wear and damage, the condition and serviceability of the railroads deteriorated. Also, as Union armies slowly forced their way deeper into the Confederate heartland in the Western Theater, the Post Office Department had less territory to cover in delivering mail. Routes in Union-occupied territory simply ceased to exist, and the personnel servicing those routes lost their jobs. Furthermore, the Constitution stated that after March 1, 1863, the post office had to pay its own expenses from its revenues.[17] With its territory and the amount of population remaining under the authority of the Confederacy dwindling almost daily, the Post Office was hard pressed to take in enough money to sustain itself and pay its bills.

Yet another problem that the Post Office Department encountered throughout the war, and especially after each Conscription Act was passed by the Confederate Congress, was the loss of manpower. Before conscription, many young men and postal workers who were already trained for their jobs volunteered to serve in either the Confederate army or their states' militia or home guard, thereby leaving gaping holes in the ranks of postal employees. The problem only increased with the institution of the draft, which took not only young men but also older men as subsequent conscription acts expanded the age range of eligible draftees. Reagan waged an ongoing battle with the War Department to exempt postal workers from the draft.

To show that he was not being unpatriotic in insisting that the Post Office employees be exempt from the draft, in June 1863 Reagan notified General Elzey that he had organized the Post Office Department employees and the employees of the Richmond post office into a military company and had requested arms for them. The company was made up of 81 officers and privates. He offered them to the War Department to help with the defense of the city if that became necessary.[18] Reagan complained about some employees who had thought that they were exempt but who had been arrested and forced to join the army anyway.

Still another problem that the Post Office Department faced was obtaining and retaining a good printer for stamps, envelopes, stationery, and other printed supplies to be used for mailing letters and running the various post offices across the Confederacy. The first printer put under contract for the department, John H. Seals, of Atlanta, was a major embarrassment to the department because he repeatedly failed to fill orders. His contract was annulled in November 1861. Another contract was then granted to Ritchie and Dunavant of Richmond, and they held the contract to the end of the Confederacy.[19] A related problem was the price of paper, which was ten cents a pound in 1861 but increased to a dollar or more per pound by 1863.[20]

And then there were the problems associated with the supply of stamps, which compounded the problems of the price and availability of paper and the costs of printing. The first stamps were not delivered until October 1861, and when they were finally delivered, they were in short supply. During the course of the war, their scarcity got so bad that local postmasters would accept payment for postage and, having no stamps to apply to the mail, wrote or drew their own designs on the mail to show that postage had, indeed, been paid. The smallest denomination of Confederate paper money was a one-dollar bill. Postmasters could not give out change in specie in such small amounts, and it was inconvenient for people to purchase a dollar's worth of postage stamps at one time. Those facts and the increasing inflation in the Confederacy made pocket change scarce, so postage stamps in smaller denominations became a medium of exchange as a substitute for pocket change.

CHAPTER 21

# John Reagan

John Henninger Reagan was born October 8, 1818, in Sevier County, Tennessee, which is nestled at the base of the Great Smoky Mountains. He came from a hodge-podge of cultural backgrounds. He was "English in his love of order, Irish in his prediction [predilection?] for politics, German in his desire for knowledge, Welsh in his persistence of purpose."[1]

Reagan spent his youth in Tennessee, where he worked with his father on the family farm and in the father's tanyard. He early demonstrated a thirst for knowledge and got what schooling he could in his frontier environment. His first education, of course, was in the use of frontier tools and weapons. But he also learned the qualities and values that distinguished the "gentlemen of the South"—hospitality, simplicity in daily life, respect for females, fervent patriotism, and a sense of personal honor.[2] Other qualities he valued were directness and frankness in conversation while exhibiting tact and patience.[3]

Reagan also had common

John Reagan, Postmaster General (later also Secretary of the Treasury (Library of Congress).

sense, which developed as he attended classes in the school of life. As for formal education, he attended school at Nancy Academy and Boyd's Creek Academy, both in Sevierville. He also studied for two sessions at Maryville Seminary (now Maryville College) in Maryville, Tennessee.

At the age of 19 or 20, Reagan moved to Texas, where he worked at various jobs, including bookkeeping, tutoring, overseeing a plantation, fighting Indians, and surveying. He was also licensed to practice law.[4] Then he expressed an interest in politics. He was a typical Jacksonian Democrat, favoring simplicity in government, faithfulness to the Constitution as literally interpreted, and the primacy of the individual over the state.

Reagan was a self-made man. He was self-taught in the law and was licensed to practice in 1846. Soon thereafter, he began a steady climb up the political ladder when he was elected justice of the peace. In 1846, he was also elected probate judge in Henderson County, Texas. In 1847, he was elected to the state legislature. Although he was defeated in his bid for reelection, he was elected a district judge in Palestine, Texas, in 1852. (The title of "judge" stayed with him for the rest of his life, preempting even all other titles of greater note.) He served as district judge until 1857, when he was elected to the U.S. House of Representatives based on his efforts to defeat the American, or Know-Nothing, Party.

In Congress, he was known as a moderate who supported the Union and opposed reopening the slave trade. Although he supported states' rights, he did not advocate secession. At the same time, however, he was quick to point out that the Founders had recognized slavery in the Constitution, and he thought that the laws made concerning it should be enforced by all regions of the country. Rather than secede, he proposed a convention to obtain guarantees and to reaffirm the constitutional rights of the South. Only when it became clear that there was no support for that measure did he reluctantly accept the idea of secession.

Above all, Reagan was a man of principle. As a candidate for governor, he refused to allow his party to nominate him for political office because he disagreed with parts of his own party's platform.[5] He strongly insisted that the Constitution should be followed faithfully and literally. And he believed that the Constitution gave the state governments primacy over the national government. So when Texas called a convention to discuss secession, he was elected a delegate.

The secessionists were in firm control of the convention, and although he was personally not a strong secessionist, he recognized the right of a state to take that step, and he followed Texas out of the Union. He was also selected to be one of the state's six delegates to the Provisional Congress of the Confederacy. He resigned his seat in the U.S. Congress in January 1861. Within a month of arriving in Montgomery for the Confederate Congress, he was nominated by Jefferson Davis to be the Confederacy's first (and proved to be the only) secretary of the Post Office Department.

John Reagan was one of only two Confederate cabinet members who sported both a beard and a moustache. Both were full, heavy, and dark. His dark, neatly combed hair and dark beard and moustache seemed to accentuate his dark, intense eyes. He was also characterized by his crudeness, rude-spokenness, and constant whittling. At age 42, Reagan was the youngest member of the Davis cabinet.

Reagan was not Davis's first choice for postmaster general. Davis had first nominated Henry T. Ellet, and the nomination was quickly confirmed. But Ellet declined, and Davis nominated Wirt Adams, but Adams also declined. That is when the Texas delegation suggested Reagan. Davis knew him from their years together in Congress. Reagan, with his recognized abilities and reputation for honesty, as well as a broad acquaintance with the territory that the Confederacy encompassed, had been a member of the postal committee when he was in the U.S. House of Representatives.[6]

Although Reagan certainly had experience, his nomination might have been more the result of flattery than of ability. After spending his first day in the Confederate Congress working on the legislation discussed that day, he visited President Davis to offer his congratulations on Davis's election as president. In a surprisingly candid moment, he told Davis that if he had been in town the day the vote for president was held, he would not have voted for Davis. But then he tactfully added, "Not, however, because I distrusted ... your fitness for the high office, but because I wanted ... you at the head of the Army."[7] Davis, who had been both a soldier in the Mexican War and the U.S. secretary of war, considered that statement to be a great compliment. In fact, although Davis was the president of the Confederacy, and not its secretary of war, he would conduct himself as though he were the secretary of war, thereby reducing his numerous secretaries to the status of mere clerks who did his bidding in that department. Perhaps as a reward for such a compliment, Davis nominated Reagan to be one of his cabinet members. And Reagan did not disappoint him.

But Reagan was not easily obtained as a cabinet member. He turned down Davis's offer of the postmaster general's position twice before a delegation of Davis supporters, "prominent cabinet members and congressmen," convince Reagan to accept the nomination.[8] His acceptance, however, was reluctant, and he often asked himself how he could have allowed himself to be roped into such a responsibility.

As he walked home from the conference with Davis and the delegation that had convinced him to accept the post, Reagan mulled the question of where he should begin to put together his department. As he walked and mused, the answer practically bumped into him. He happened to pass on the street a friend, H.P. Brewster, and the answer to his dilemma was looking him in the face. Explaining his new duties to Brewster, Reagan asked him to travel to Washington, D.C., as his personal emissary and to "raid the United States Post Office of its Southern personnel."[9] Brewster was to deliver letters from Reagan to those people, offering them the same or higher positions in the Confederate Post Office if they would join him. He also asked them, if they chose to accept his offer, to bring with them copies of forms, maps, and other documents used in their departments.[10] Reagan did not intend to reinvent the wheel!

Reagan then began to assess the current situation of the postal system as it related to the Southern states to determine what he had inherited. He discovered that the year before the war began government expenditures for the postal service in the South reached $2,879,530, but post office receipts were only $938,105, leaving a deficit of nearly two million dollars.[11]

From that unpromising beginning, Reagan revolutionized Southern postal delivery in monetary terms. His department not only provided the Confederacy with better mail service for less money than it had cost under the Union but also actually increased the net income of the department every year, this in spite of the fact that the Confederacy's financial condition was steadily getting worse.[12] Granted, he was *required* by the Confederate Congress to operate his department in the black; expenditures *could not* exceed receipts. Yet, he continued to deliver the mail and to keep costs down.

But the Confederacy contained more than enough "soil" for abundant growth of criticism, and Reagan's "honeymoon" period was short lived. Soon, he and his department became the target of critics and complainants, just as had every other department and department secretary. People complained about the rates being too high, about mail not being delivered on schedule, and about misdirected or undelivered mail. They demanded stamps, stamped envelopes, and other goods and services that the Post Office either did not provide at all or had trouble getting or maintaining a ready supply. They alleged inefficiency and corruption by post office employees.

Because mail delivery affected practically everyone in the Confederacy to some extent, it seemed that everyone complained and criticized. Newspaper editors and the Confederate Congress were experts at such griping and sniping. But "the bitterest and most militant opposition" came from groups whose business had been hurt most by postal regulation, especially the railroads.[13] Reagan responded to such criticism by working hard to correct abuses whenever and wherever he found them and by ensuring that his department was financially self-sufficient.[14]

Reagan also had to handle problems with other cabinet members. He was considered "the most aggressive member of the Cabinet."[15] He often opposed the majority on the issues being discussed. He threatened to resign if his manner was objectionable to the president, but Davis always backed him, so Reagan never resigned. (He offered to resign in 1862, but Davis refused to accept it and convinced Reagan to stay on.)

Because finances in the Post Office Department were so tight, and because of the constitutional requirement that the department operate within its means, Reagan locked horns in June 1863 with Secretary of the Treasury Christopher Memminger "over the deposit and withdrawal of postal funds from the Treasury."[16] He also had an ongoing dispute with the various secretaries of war "over army impressments of transportation facilities used by the mails, and over military conscription of postal clerks, mail carriers, and contractors."[17] He won many of his arguments with the Treasury Department, but he was at loggerheads with the War Department until the very end of the Confederacy.

Reagan also sometimes disagreed with other cabinet members on nonpostal issues. When he reached a conclusion on something, he held to it tenaciously. He had definite ideas on things, and his expressions of them were conspicuous in cabinet meetings. His views were clear-cut.[18] For example, in his very first cabinet meeting, he openly disagreed with President Davis and several cabinet members over the distribution of troops. He thought that the weakest point in the Confederacy's defenses was Kentucky and that troops should be sent there first. The president and others, however, thought that northern Virginia was the key and that the troops should be sent there.

Perhaps Reagan's most forceful opposition was to Lee's proposed invasion of Pennsylvania. Instead, Reagan argued, Lee should send some 25,000 to 30,000 of his Virginia troops to reinforce Pemberton at Vicksburg. (Generals D.H. Hill, James Longstreet, and P.G.T. Beauregard joined Reagan in this opinion.[19]) Perhaps it would have been better for Lee and Davis to have followed that advice, because the Confederacy lost both the siege of Vicksburg and the Battle of Gettysburg in early July. Reagan was also one of the earliest supporters of the idea of arming slaves to fight, but again he was outvoted. Davis and the Congress eventually agreed that that measure was necessary, but they acted too late to get colored troops into combat.

In the end, Reagan—like Mallory at the Navy Department—accomplished a lot, especially considering how little he had to work with not only at the beginning but also throughout the war.[20] One must remember that as the war progressed and the South lost more and more territory, especially in the West, Reagan had less and less to work with—less geographic territory, less equipment, and less manpower.

In the closing days of the war, Reagan was the one who informed Davis, who was in church at the time, that Lee was abandoning his defenses at Petersburg and that Richmond itself would have to be evacuated. As Davis and the cabinet fled southward from Richmond, Reagan was there with the Administration. During the flight of the administration, George Trenholm resigned as secretary of the treasury because of poor health, and Davis named Reagan acting secretary of that department on April 27, 1865. Reagan held that position for just a couple of weeks, during the death throes of the Confederacy. He also advised Davis on how to obtain the best possible surrender terms for the Confederacy.

Reagan and Davis disguised themselves and continued their flight under assumed names, Davis as a congressman from Texas and Reagan as a Texas state judge, which was true.[21] Reagan was captured along with the president near Irwinville, Georgia, on May 10, 1865. He was one of only two original cabinet members to remain in the cabinet from start to finish (Mallory being the other).

Reagan was sent to Fort Warren, in Boston Harbor, where he was imprisoned just down the hallway from Vice President Alexander Stephens. He spent 22 weeks in solitary confinement. From his prison cell, he penned perhaps his most famous letter. Written to the people of Texas, it urged them to admit that their cause was lost and to accept the consequences of the war so that they would escape even heavier burdens and problems that would undoubtedly come upon them if they continued an attitude of resistance.[22] He also wrote a letter to Andrew Johnson, pleading the case for Jefferson Davis's release from prison and his being given a pardon.

When Reagan was released from prison in December 1865, he returned to his farm in Texas, "defeated and disfranchised."[23] He later resumed the practice of law and was elected to the U.S. House in 1875 and to the Senate in 1887, where he served on the Committee on Commerce. He became famous for sniffing out the least taint of corruption. He helped get the Interstate Commerce Act passed, and he was the first chairman of the Committee on Post Offices and Post Roads. When he was 72, he resigned his Senate seat to become chairman of the Texas Railroad Commission, a position he held for ten years. Then he retired, returned to his home, and began working on his memoirs, which were published shortly before his death. He also helped found the Texas State Historical Association and became a leading spokesman for prohibition. He died on March 6, 1905, the longest-surviving member of the Confederate cabinet.

In his assessment of Reagan, Burton Hendrick pointed out that while Reagan was the head of the Post Office, that department had no deficit. "It not only paid its own way, but yielded a profit," and he did it "by discharging unnecessary clerks, cutting off costly and unneeded routes, and driving hard bargains with contracts, railroads, and the like, and by increasing rates for postage," so, in that sense, "he may be regarded as the most successful member of the Administration; at least he was the only one who actually performed the task assigned to him."[24] Of all the cabinet officers, only Reagan escaped accusations of "indifference or inefficiency."[25]

Part VI

# State Department

Chapter 22

# Overview

Second only to the Treasury Department, the State Department was arguably the most important Confederate cabinet position before the outbreak of the war. Diplomatic recognition of the Confederate States of America by foreign governments was critical to the continued existence of the Southern government and might even forestall war or prevent it altogether. Short of formal diplomatic recognition, the Confederacy desperately needed to foster trade with foreign nations, working out deals whereby the South could exchange her agricultural products, especially cotton, for manufactured goods and weapons. Therefore, the quest for recognition became the primary end of the Confederate State Department, and "King Cotton diplomacy" became the means to that end. To head this important department, Jefferson Davis chose Robert Toombs of Georgia.

Toombs and the State Department began with no official foreign policy; he had to develop it as he went and as needs arose or became obvious. The process was disorganized and ugly. When one citizen bumped into Toombs on the street and asked where the State Department was, Toombs reportedly replied, "In my hat," where he kept his important papers.

Davis early showed his tendency to micromanage his cabinet members' departments by naming, apparently with no input from Toombs, three men to be major State Department diplomats: former senators William Lowndes Yancey of Alabama, James Mason of Virginia, and John Slidell of Louisiana. Although the latter two had some diplomatic ability and experience, Yancey had none whatsoever. The quality of the Confederacy's diplomatic corps was never as good as its military leadership. The South's diplomatic ineptitude was in stark contrast to the professional skills of their counterparts in the U.S. State Department, led by William Seward and Charles Francis Adams, the U.S. envoy to London.

The Confederate State Department was supported by the fewest civilian personnel of any cabinet department with a high of 29, not counting any foreigners whom Confederate commissioners abroad might have hired. It had seven departmental officers and staff members and 22 commissioners, agents, and secretaries in foreign missions.[1]

In addition to the primary goal of gaining formal diplomatic recognition of the Confederacy, the State Department had three other sub-goals to work on: to obtain credit, to find buyers for Southern cotton (and other agricultural products), and to obtain "munitions, machinery, and ... manufactured goods."[2]

These tasks were assigned to the various agents and commissioners. They worked not only in England and France but also extensively in Mexico and Canada. They were only partially successful in their efforts. Although they did not gain formal recognition for the Confederacy, they did get several countries—including Brazil, France, Great Britain, the Netherlands, and Spain—to recognize the South as a belligerent.

Conflicting accounts and opinions exist concerning whether Duke Ernst II of Saxe-Coburg and Gotha actually formally recognized the Confederacy. The duke was the brother-in-law of Queen Victoria of Great Britain, who was the brother of Prince Albert. Duke Ernst was a strong supporter of the United States, but he was the only European ruler to appoint a consul to the Confederacy. He appointed Ernst Raven, who lived in Texas, to that post on July 30, 1861. Whether that action constituted formal diplomatic recognition might be debatable, but if—for the sake of argument—that recognition was granted, Saxe-Coburg and Gotha surely did not constitute a formidable or impressive vote of confidence for the Confederacy.

The whole idea behind the State Department's quest for recognition lay in the hope that it would shatter all resolve by the North to try forcing the South back into the Union. That would ensure Southern independence because the North dared not risk war with either Great Britain or France and certainly not with both nations.

According to William C. Davis, the South's diplomatic corps faced several problems, the first of which was to overcome the influence of the blockade in preventing foreign recognition of the Confederacy. The South had to persuade Great Britain to help the Confederacy reduce the effectiveness of the blockade by declaring it illegal and then demonstrating that fact by consistently getting goods through the Union blockaders. At first, Confederate blockade runners were fairly successful in demonstrating the blockade's ineffectiveness. But as the Union's naval war machine gathered steam, the blockade got progressively stronger and less porous, thereby nullifying that argument of the South.

## The Union's Blockade

On April 19, 1861, Lincoln issued a proclamation by which he unilaterally and without congressional approval (because Congress had not yet begun its session) imposed a naval blockade of the South's coastline and ports, thereby cutting off international trade for the infant nation. Following is the full text of that proclamation.

*Proclamation of Blockade against Southern Ports*

BY THE PRESIDENT OF THE UNITED STATES OF AMERICA.

A PROCLAMATION.

Whereas an insurrection against the Government of the United States has broken out in the States of South Carolina, Georgia, Alabama, Florida, Mississippi, Louisiana, and Texas, and the laws of the United States for the collection of the revenue cannot be effectually executed therein conformably to that provision of the Constitution which requires duties to be uniform throughout the United States:

And whereas a combination of persons engaged in such insurrection, have threatened to grant pretended letters of marquee to authorize the bearers thereof to commit assaults on the lives, vessels, and property of good citizens of the country lawfully engaged in commerce on the high seas, and in waters of the United States;

And whereas an Executive Proclamation has been already issued, requiring the persons engaged in these disorderly proceedings to desist therefrom, calling out a militia force for the purpose of repressing the same, and convening Congress in extraordinary session, to deliberate and determine thereon:

Now, therefore, I, Abraham Lincoln, President of the United States, with a view to the same purposes before mentioned, and to the protection of the public peace, and the lives and property of quiet and orderly citizens pursuing their lawful occupations, until Congress shall have assembled and deliberated on the said unlawful proceedings, or until the same shall cease, have further deemed it advisable to set on foot a blockade of the ports within the States aforesaid, in pursuance of the laws of the United States, and of the law of Nations, in such case provided. For this purpose a competent force will be posted so as to prevent entrance and exit of vessels from the ports aforesaid. If, therefore, with a view to violate such blockade, a vessel shall approach, or shall attempt to leave either of the said ports, she will be duly warned by the Commander of one of the blockading vessels, who will endorse on her register the fact and date of such warning, and if the same vessel shall again attempt to enter or leave the blockaded port, she will be captured and sent to the nearest convenient port, for such proceedings against her and her cargo as prize, as may be deemed advisable.

And I hereby proclaim and declare that if any person, under the pretended authority of the said States, or under any other pretense, shall molest a vessel of the United States, or the persons or cargo on board of her, such person will be held amenable to the laws of the United States for the prevention and punishment of piracy.

In witness whereof, I have hereunto set my hand, and caused the seal of the United States to be affixed.

Done at the City of Washington, this nineteenth day of April, in the year of our Lord one thousand eight hundred and sixty-one, and of the independence of the United States the eighty-fifth.

ABRAHAM LINCOLN

By the President:
WILLIAM H. SEWARD, Secretary of State

Several items in this proclamation were noteworthy for the Confederate State Department and foreign nations. First, Lincoln had used the term *insurrection* to identify the secession of the Southern states. This was a rhetorical ploy to discourage foreign recognition of the Confederacy by implying that the secessionist actions of the states were a mere domestic problem within the United States and not an actual war. But in a slip of contradiction, Lincoln's proclamation specifically called his action a *blockade*, which made it an act of war. Lincoln's actions spoke louder to foreign nations than did his words, and his proclamation thereby showed the truth of the situation.

Second, the wording of the proclamation showed that the real motive was revenue collection, not preservation of the Union. Third, the proclamation also alleged that the Confederacy condoned and promoted piracy ("pretended letters of marquee"). In fact, Lincoln defined any opposition to the blockade to be piracy. Finally, the term *competent force* put the onus of effective enforcement on the shoulders of the United States. International law required that the nation imposing the blockade had to demonstrate that its blockade was being effectively enforced. According to the 1856 Declaration of Paris, "'blockades to be binding must be effective—that is, maintained by a force really sufficient to prevent access to the enemy's coast."[3] Based on this international agreement, Confederate officials built a definition that proved the Union blockade's ineffectiveness. They then used that definition to coax European intervention on behalf of the Confederacy.[4]

In other matters, Lincoln bent over backward to avoid doing anything that would lend credence to the South's claims to be a legitimate sovereign government. But in the eyes of international law at the time, the imposition of a blockade of one belligerent's ports by another nation is an act of war. This was certainly how the Confederate government saw it (and hoped that foreign powers also saw it). The blockade was *de facto* recognition that the Confederacy was a belligerent; therefore, the blockade was an act of war.

Confederate naval commander Raphael Semmes related,

> When, at last, it became necessary to declare the Confederate ports in a state of blockade, and to send ships of war thither, to enforce the declaration, the sly little game which they had been playing was all up with them. A blockade was an act of war, which came under the cognizance of the laws of nations. It concerned neutrals, as well as belligerents, and foreign nations were bound to take notice of it. It followed that there could not be a blockade without a war; and it equally followed, that there could not be a war without at least two belligerent parties to it. It will thus be seen, that the declaration of neutrality of Great Britain was a logical sequence of Mr. Lincoln's and Mr. Seward's own act.... So much was this act considered, as a matter of course, at the time, that all the other powers of the earth, of sufficient dignity to act in the premises, at all followed the example set them by Great Britain, and issued similar declarations; and the four years of bloody war that followed justified the wisdom of their acts.[5]

A country does not *blockade* its own ports, even in a time of insurrection; it closes them, as Britain closed the port of Boston following the famous Tea Party. Lincoln's proclamation, therefore, made the Southern government eligible for diplomatic recognition by the nations of the world. This became the primary goal of the Confederate State Department. It also gave the South the right to seek loans and obtain arms from foreign nations. Ultimately, as Semmes related, Great Britain—and, following Britain's lead, France—recognized both the United States and the Confederacy as *belligerents* but did not proffer full diplomatic recognition.

Another ramification of the blockade was that, according to international law, the nation that initiates a blockade has to announce it and then enforce it. That means that the blockading nation at least has to keep a permanent naval force patrolling the enemy's coasts and ports. "The Confederacy vigorously argued that the blockade was not effective and that Lincoln's proclamation violated neutral rights of their primary trading partners, but that argument failed to persuade Great Britain, which officially recognized the blockade in February 1862."[6]

## The Blockade's Effectiveness

Although the blockade sounded formidable, the actual enforcement presented a major challenge to the U.S. navy. It was a huge undertaking, and the Union simply did not have sufficient equipment or personnel to enforce it at the time Lincoln issued the proclamation. To cover the South's 3,549 miles of coastline, with its numerous rivers, bays, inlets, and harbors, and especially the broad areas essential for blocking the 12 major ports, the Union navy had about 9,000 men and 42 warships.[7] Of those, only three were deemed fit and available domestically for blockade duty. The navy also had 48 other ships in port, but those vessels had no crews. The situation improved, however, during the rest of 1861 and progressively throughout the war. By the end of 1861, the Union navy had about 24,000 men and 160 ships. By the end of the war, it had about 500 ships of war. But initially, the Union had no practical means of enforcing the blockade, so it was a paper blockade. As James McPherson said, "In 1861 the blockade was a leaky sieve indeed."[8]

Just how effective was the Union blockade of the South? The answer to that question depends on how one measures "effectiveness." Several historians have studied the issue from many different angles and using different criteria. The most prominent criteria are those posited by Bonner and McCord.

1. *Psychological effectiveness*, which is based on anecdotal comments of the blockade's effects on individuals and their opinions of those effects, such

as one finds in Mary Chesnut's diary entries that mention conditions that resulted from (or at least were popularly attributed to) the blockade.

2. *Deterrent effectiveness*, which tries to show how and to what extent the blockade discouraged continued trade efforts by individual ships, captains, or nations, and tries to estimate how many ships might have decided not to attempt running the blockade because of the presence of Union ships. (McPherson took this position.[9])

3. *Contributory effectiveness*, which focuses on how the blockade might have contributed to the crippling of the Southern war efforts through the shortages and increased prices it helped produce.

4. *Cost/benefit effectiveness*, which tries to answer the question of whether the degree of the Union blockade's effectiveness was sufficient to justify how much the North was spending on the task.[10]

One oft-cited "proof" of the blockade's effectiveness involves the decline in cotton exports. In 1860, the South had exported 3.8 million bales of cotton, but by 1862, the South exported "virtually nothing."[11] But that "proof" is misleading because it does not consider the fact that the Confederacy had placed a *self-imposed embargo* on all cotton exports in the hope that European demand for Southern cotton would force England, France, and other countries to recognize the Confederacy. Although that strategy backfired, it cannot be discounted as the primary reason for the drop in cotton exports. The Confederacy itself, not the Union blockade, was the cause for that decline. Ekelund and Thornton state as the thesis of their essay "The 'Confederate' Blockade of the South" that the South was hurt more by Confederate government policies than by the blockade.[12]

The only legitimate measure of the blockade's effectiveness, then, is the percentage of ships that successfully ran the blockade versus the number that attempted to run it or the kind, amount, and value of goods that eluded the blockade enforcers. Ekelund and Thornton estimate that the chance of *capture* in trying to run the blockade was 16 percent,[13] meaning that the chance of *successfully* running the blockade was 84 percent!

Some Union naval officers as well as modern historians—including Frank Owsley (*King Cotton Diplomacy*, 1931), Stephen Wise (*Lifeline of the Confederacy: Blockade Running during the Civil War*, 1988), and Robert Browning, Jr. (*From Cape Charles to Cape Fear: The North Atlantic Blockading Squadron during the Civil War*, 1993) questioned the effectiveness of the blockade. Admittedly, then, the effectiveness of the blockade was debatable at best, especially in the first part of the war; its effectiveness increased somewhat throughout the war.

But did it ever reach the degree of effectiveness that justified foreign governments' conclusion that it was sufficiently enforced to meet the demands of international law?

Owsley concluded that in 1861, one in every 14 vessels was captured (i.e., 13 of 14 successfully ran the blockade). In the spring of 1864, one in every three vessels was captured (i.e., two of three successfully ran the blockade). Owsley estimates the upper limit of blockade runners captured as stated in Table 10.

Table 10. Estimated Effectiveness of the Union Blockade[14]

| Year | Estimated Number of Blockade Runners Caught |
|---|---|
| 1861 | 1 in 10 |
| 1862 | 1 in 8 |
| 1863 | 1 in 4 |
| 1864 | 1 in 3 |
| 1865 | 1 in 2 |
| Average | 1 in 6 |

Some blockade runners made up to 20 successful trips through the blockade and were never captured. Probably at least 150 blockade-runners were still operating when the war ended.[15] And as for contributory effectiveness, Owsley estimated that approximately 370 attempts were made to bring arms shipments through the blockade and, using the 1-in-6-captured average, more than 300 of those attempts were successful. These data hardly seem to demonstrate that the blockade was effective.

## The Union Blockade Strategy Board

After Lincoln's proclamation, one of the first things Union secretary of the navy Gideon Welles did was to recall all ships on overseas assignment that could be spared for blockade duty. He also tried to obtain ships by leasing them so he could further increase the number of ships for enforcement duty.

After the need for personnel and equipment for the blockade, the Union navy's most pressing needs involved developing a working knowledge of the local coastlines and providing for its forces logistically.[16] Acting on an idea suggested by Alexander D. Bache, the superintendent of the Coastal Survey, Welles proposed to Lincoln and had accepted the establishment of a Blockade Board (sometimes referred to by historians as the Blockade Strategy Board). Welles named Captain Samuel F. DuPont to be the chairman of the new board. Secretary of War Simon Cameron nominated Major John G. Barnard of the Army Corps of Engineers to represent that branch of the military on the board. Welles made Commander Charles H. Davis the board's secretary. And Bache, the brainchild of the board, was named to finish out the board's membership. Bache knew personally or professionally every member on the board.

The board determined in its first meeting what its priorities must be, and then they acted on them methodically. First, they had to organize the available forces into manageable areas of responsibility. The entire southern coast was just too much for one commander. Then they had to establish a clear-cut command-and-control system for each of those sectors. Next, they had to establish supply bases for each sector. Finally, they had to determine the best places along the coast of each sector from which to launch amphibious assaults to capture permanent bases for their blockading fleet and from which the Union armies could initiate land campaigns into the Southern heartland.

The first of these goals the board achieved by dividing the blockading forces into two squadrons. The Atlantic Squadron would operate from Alexandria, Virginia, to Key West, Florida, and would be commanded by Flag Officer Horton Stringham and based out of Hampton Roads, Virginia. The Gulf Squadron would be responsible for enforcing the blockade from Key West to the U.S.-Mexican border at Matamoros, Mexico/Brownsville, Texas, at the mouth of the Rio Grande. It would be commanded by Captain William Mervine and based out of Key West. Later, the northern portion of the Atlantic Squadron would be further subdivided into two independent commands. One would extend from Cape Henry to Cape Romain (~370 miles), the other would stretch from Cape Romain to St. Augustine (~220 miles).[17] The Gulf Squadron was similarly subdivided. This split arrangement of the blockading forces "ease[d] the burden of the commanders while increasing the blockade's efficiency."[18]

Another priority of the board was to conduct a survey of the coast to gather intelligence and draw all of the maps and navigational charts the naval officers would need to enforce the blockade. Using the information gathered, the board would select the best locations to use as coaling and supplying stations that the blockading ships would need and the most strategically advantageous locations for making the joint navy-army amphibious landings.

## *King Cotton Diplomacy*

A second problem for the Confederate State Department was one of its government's own making. Davis insisted on using cotton as a diplomatic weapon, but that tactic backfired. He based his insistence on the belief that if the South withheld cotton—which was in high demand in Britain and France—

from the market, those countries would complain to the North about the blockade and even threaten war to keep Southern cotton flowing to European textile mills.

On the surface, this argument seemed justified. An estimated 92 percent of the cotton used by Russian textile mills, 90 percent of the cotton used by the French, 77 percent of the cotton used by British textile mills, and 60 percent of that used by Germany came from the South. These statistics had been at the foundation of James Hammond's assertion that "cotton is king."[19] The trouble was that European countries simply found and developed alternative sources of cotton—notably Egypt and, to a lesser extent, East India—rather than risk war with the United States.

The Southern leaders hoped, however, that one or more of the following situations would occur.

1. European nations would denounce the blockade as "a paper blockade" that violated international law, especially the Declaration of Paris.[20]
2. European nations would offer to mediate between the North and the South to achieve a peaceful settlement resulting in Southern independence.
3. European nations would recognize the Confederate States of America as a legitimate government independent of the United States.
4. European nations might intervene militarily on behalf of the Confederacy.

Supposedly, the European nations' motive for any or all such actions would be to restore the flow of cotton from the South to European textile mills. The South's dual motives were (a) to end the war and (b) to gain independence. They hoped to achieve one or both of these goals through what was widely known as "King Cotton diplomacy." (Its failure was called "King Cotton delusion.")[21]

On March 16, 1861, Secretary of State Robert Toombs ordered the Confederate State Department's three commissioners to go to Europe to champion the cause of Southern recognition based on cotton diplomacy. William Yancey headed the commission. He was dignified, eloquent, straightforward, and well-mannered. He exhibited personal magnetism and calmness in the face of opposition.[22] He was known, however, as a fire-eater, and he promoted the reopening of the slave trade. He was therefore not a good candidate to be a diplomat to Europe, which strongly opposed the slave trade. He also had earned a reputation for "caustic and reckless talk."[23] To use the name *Yancey* and the term *diplomat* in the same sentence was somewhat oxymoronic. He also was a "vocal opponent of Davis and his efforts at centralization,"[24] and it is never good for the administration's diplomats to be openly critical of their boss.

Davis initially asked John Slidell to take the second spot on the diplomatic commission, but Slidell did not like Yancey and rejected the offer.[25] Davis then turned to Ambrose Dudley Mann, who was a well-experienced diplomat.[26] He had been the assistant secretary of state under President Franklin Pierce. Davis had come to know him during their time together on the cabinet when Davis was Pierce's secretary of war. Mann was also experienced with "shipping and trade," which would be a major focus of the Confederate State and Navy Departments.[27] But historian Owsley was at a loss to understand "just what Davis could have had in mind in sending him abroad."[28] Owsley pointed out that Manning had a huge ego and was "full of words and wind, ever deducing wisdom from events and usually wrong, never using simple, direct language when it was possible to roll out some well-rounded period, ever waxing eloquent over the most trivial and unimportant thing…, lacking in penetration."[29] But he did have social charm, which every successful diplomat needs.

The third spot on the commission went to Pierre Adolph Rost. His sole claim to a diplomatic position seems to have been that he had been born in France and reared in Louisiana. He settled in Mississippi, where he became a friend of Davis. He also knew Attorney General Judah Benjamin. However, he had no real diplomatic skills or experience.

Public criticism of Davis's diplomatic commission and its members started as soon as Davis offered their names for congressional approval. Worse, however, was Davis's failure to prepare the commissioners for their important task, thereby dooming it to failure from the start. He gave them no instructions but left them on their own to come up with a strategic plan. He also gave them no authority "to negotiate commercial treaties, offer free trade, or guarantee access to Confederate ports."[30] They were left with nothing more than pleading the righteousness of secession, the Confederacy's desire for peace, and the South's ability for self-defense.[31]

As if the internal problem of the commissioners' lack of direction by and authority from the administration was not enough, they also faced two external obstacles to their success. Their biggest obstacle was the strong antislavery sentiment in Great Britain. It created political pressures that outweighed the commercial interests within Britain. Ironically, however, Britain continued to engage in commerce with slave-holding countries all over the western hemisphere, especially Brazil.[32] And many British politicians preferred to see America split into two nations peacefully than for the sections to wage a bloody war. Therefore, they "viewed secession as a fait accompli."[33] But when it came to the highest officials, they equivocated. Robert Bunch, the British consul in Charleston, "loathed white Southerners."[34] And he had great influence with British foreign secretary John Russell and prime minister John Temple, Lord

Palmerston. Before the commissioners even reached London, Bunch's letters to these men poisoned the well against the Confederacy. With "friends" like him, the commissioners faced an uphill battle.

The second obstacle was France's reluctance to do anything without identical, simultaneous action by Great Britain. France seemed to have no will of its own but depended wholly on Great Britain to determine her actions and attitudes for her.

Such was the commission that Toombs ordered to England to seek first to obtain recognition for the Confederacy. Next, once British recognition was obtained, the commissioners were to turn to France (Napoleon). And once France recognized the Confederacy, they were to go to Russia and then to Belgium, pursuing the same goals in each venue. In each country, they were to explain the following principles.

1. Secession was not a revolution; it was the states' taking back the powers they had delegated to the national government. It was their legal recourse to federal encroachments on states' rights.
2. Secession was "a last resort for self-preservation."[35] The South wanted peace, not war.
3. States' rights and sovereignty, not slavery, was the real issue between the North and the South.
4. The Confederacy's tariff was for revenue only, not as a protective measure aimed at European trade (unlike the North's tariff, which was clearly used to protect Northern industries from European competition).
5. Europe could get no cotton until the blockade was broken and the Southern cotton embargo ended.

This was "King Cotton diplomacy." As Owsley put it, "The commissioners went abroad armed with a dissertation on state sovereignty in their right pockets and a sample of New Orleans middling upland cotton in their left."[36]

The commissioners presented their message to British Foreign Secretary John Russell on March 16, 1861. Russell was cool, reserved, and noncommittal. He simply said that he would make their request for recognition a matter of discussion in the British cabinet. The commissioners came away thinking that recognition was only one decisive military victory away, proof that the fledgling nation could take care of itself. They thought that recognition from France would soon follow that.

Meanwhile, Russell had been talking to the French about acting jointly with Britain on the issue of belligerency; England and France would work together in whatever they decided to do. They would declare themselves neutral and recognize the belligerency of both the North and the South. They published this position on May 14, 1861, without the instigation or knowledge of the Confederate commissioners.

The commissioners' hopes were brightened as they noted British public opinion, which heavily favored the South. Textile business leaders were pressuring the British government to recognize the Confederacy so that the cotton would once again begin flowing into British textile mills.

But as recognition was delayed, the Southern commissioners began to suspect that U.S. agents were sabotaging their efforts. To counteract Northern efforts, the commissioners set about influencing the foreign press and national leaders in favor of the South.

In the midst of all of the commission's seemingly fruitless activities, Toombs resigned as secretary of state. He was replaced by R.M.T. Hunter, who wrote to the commissioners that the South had won a glorious victory at Manassas. With this news, the commissioners immediately demanded recognition and asked for an informal interview with Russell. He, at least in their opinions, snubbed them. They also reminded the British that the Confederacy had now grown by four states (Arkansas, North Carolina, Virginia, and Tennessee).

## *Other Problems*

But the South faced still other problems. A third one was the strong antislavery mood in Europe. That attitude militated against any arrangement with the South that might seem in any way to support slavery. While Lincoln and the Republicans in Congress were selling the Northern public the idea that the war was a fight to preserve the Union, their agents in Europe were selling it as a crusade against slavery. Had the latter ploy been used in the United States, Northern public opinion would have turned decidedly against the war; used overseas, it had a delaying effect on any thoughts that European countries might have had of granting recognition to the Confederacy.

Another problem was not actually foreign in nature but rather domestic—actually, a personal problem—what William C. Davis called Davis's "uncanny ability to send the wrong people abroad."[37] The first three commissioners to Europe made this fact all too evident. But this problem was not limited to the State Department; it seemed to pervade many cabinet-level positions, as can be seen throughout this work. Southern diplomats were generally inexperienced, tended to gossip and talk loosely, and criticize their own government officials, none of which becomes a serious diplomat.

## The Trent Affair

Perhaps the closest that the South came to achieving either its goal of foreign recognition during the war or of having a European power intervene militarily in the war was a result not of diplomatic efforts but a consequence of a Union naval officer's poor judgment and over-eagerness to make a name for himself. His actions resulted in what became known as the *Trent* affair. The incident easily could have sparked war between the United States and Great Britain and/or France were it not for the skillful diplomacy of Seward's U.S. State Department.

In October 1861, Charles Wilkes, commander of the 15-gun warship U.S.S. *San Jacinto*, was en route to the United States from a patrol off the west coast of Africa. While detained in St. Thomas taking on coal, Wilkes learned that the cruiser C.S.S. *Sumter*, captained by the by-then infamous Confederate sea raider Raphael Semmes, had been reported in the area. Wilkes was "determined to search for the enemy."[38] Later, when the *San Jacinto* put in at Cienfuegos, Cuba, Wilkes learned that former U.S. senators James Mason and John Slidell, recently appointed Confederate commissioners to Europe, were in Charleston and would soon embark for England via Havana and St. Thomas. He also learned that they would be sailing aboard the British mail packet *Trent* on its run between Vera Cruz and St. Thomas via Havana. He decided that those diplomats were of far greater value than the *Sumter* and her captain. Besides, the slow mail packet would be much easier to apprehend than the speedy Confederate raider. He prepared to spring his trap when the *Trent* left Havana and sailed into the narrow Bahama Channel.

The executive officer of the *San Jacinto*, Lieutenant D. MacNeill Fairfax, later wrote of the incident, "When Captain Wilkes first took me into his confidence, and told me what he purposed to do, I earnestly reminded him of the great risk of a war with these two Governments…. I suggested that he consult with Judge Marvin, one of the ablest maritime lawyers. I soon saw, however, that he had made up his mind to intercept and capture the *Trent* as well as to take possession of the commissioners."[39]

Mason and Slidell sailed from Charleston on October 12 aboard the *Theodora* bound for Havana. In Havana, they transferred to the *Trent*. On November 8, 1861, Wilkes sighted the *Trent* in the Bahama Channel. As the two ships neared each other, the *Trent*'s captain, James Moir, hoisted the British colors. Then Wilkes raised his own colors and fired a shot across the bow of the *Trent*. But Moir ignored it because his ship was flying the flag of a neutral nation in international waters and was nowhere near the Union blockade or any port covered by it. Wilkes fired another shot over the *Trent*'s bow. That time, Captain Moir halted his ship. Wilkes ordered a boarding party, led by Fairfax, to board the ship and arrest Mason and Slidell as contraband of war.

Captain Moir protested the illegal seizure of his passengers, but the Confederate diplomats and their two secretaries agreed to go with the Union seamen without resisting. That was not the case, however, with their fellow passengers. Fairfax clearly noted that "when it was known why I had boarded the *Trent*, there was an outburst of rage and indignation from the passengers, who numbered nearly one hundred, many of them Southerners."[40] Fairfax calmed their rage by pointing out that the officers aboard the *San Jacinto* were observing with spyglasses and that the ship's guns were trained on the *Trent*. Hearing the tumult of the passengers but being unable to see what was happening, the officer in charge of the boat from the *San Jacinto* sent a number of armed sailors aboard the *Trent*, further quelling the opposition of the crowd.

But Fairfax further related that once the prisoners were on the main deck, they declared "that they would not go unless force was used—whereupon two officers, previously instructed, escorted each commissioner to the side, and assisted them into the comfortable cutter sent especially for them. The two secretaries followed them into the boat without making opposition. At this stage of the proceedings another outcry was raised by the passengers."[41]

Once the captives were aboard the *San Jacinto*, Wilkes immediately pointed the bow of his ship toward Fort Monroe. Upon arriving there, he was advised to take the prisoners to Boston, which he did, arriving on November 24. He turned the prisoners over to Colonel Justin Dimmick, commander of Fort Warren. The prisoners were held there while American and British governments negotiated their release in January 1862.

The *Trent* resumed its run to St. Thomas, where its passengers boarded the *La Plata* and headed for Southampton, England. Upon their arrival on November 27, they reported the incident to British authorities. As news of the diplomats' arrest spread, public support for the South and outrage at the North burst forth. The British government crafted a strongly worded remonstrance demanding that the American government issue an apology for violating British neutrality and removing passengers against their will and that the Confederate commissioners be released immediately. Behind these demands was the British minister's threat that "unless within seven days of receipt the Union government unconditionally accepted Britain's demands, [Lord] Lyons [British minister to Washington] was to ask for his passports and depart the United States."[42] And behind that threat was "ostentatious military and naval preparations."[43] The British mobilized a part of their armed forces for possible war. The British cabinet "embargoed the export to the United States of saltpeter (November 30) and of arms and ammunition (December 4)."[44] They more than tripled the number of British troops in Canada (from 5,000 to nearly 18,000) and almost doubled the number of warships (from 25 to 40). The Canadians, upon learning of the incident and the mother country's outrage, mobilized their militia along the U.S.-Canadian border. However, Prince Albert, husband of Queen Elizabeth, read the communiqué on his deathbed and insisted that its tone be moderated, and thereby "may have averted war" with the United States.[45] That revision, however, led to the release of Mason and Slidell.[46]

Despite a public outcry for war with Britain in the North, Washington opted to give in to British demands. After all, the Union was already deep into a war with the Confederate states, and that war was not going particularly well for the North at that time. Besides, Britain's complaint was being supported by the French, and the British public was increasingly sympathetic with the Southern cause, many of them even calling for war with the United States. Lincoln administration officials feared that *not* to comply with British demands would lead not only to war with those nations but also their recognition of the Confederacy. All of those factors combined might result in the South's independence.

William Seward, U.S. secretary of state, and U.S. diplomats in London managed to patch things up with the British by crafting an ingenious reply worthy of a politician and diplomat. Although in his official "apology" Seward conceded the substance of British charges, stating that the two envoys would be freed, he nonetheless defended Captain Wilkes's actions and said that Wilkes should have seized the ship (the *Trent*) itself and let the maritime courts determine the legality of his actions. Implied in the statement was the idea that Wilkes had acted on his own initiative without orders from the administration and without either consulting or requesting advice from the Lincoln administration.

Britain's Lord Palmerston responded with a lengthy explanation of the many ways the U.S. explanation was in disagreement with the British interpretation of international law, but the U.S. response, such as it was, was accepted.

The Lincoln administration finally released the Confederate diplomats in early January 1862. Britain did not grant the South recognition. U.S. diplomacy was more convincing than Confederate diplomacy. Lincoln's later issuing of the Emancipation Proclamation ensured that diplomatic recognition was forever removed as a possibility. Fifty years after the fact, Charles Francis Adams, the U.S. envoy in London at the time, concluded that "it may now with reasonable assurance be asserted that … the United States did not have and never had, in reality, a justifying leg to stand upon, and least of all was there any possible justification for the course pursued by Captain Wilkes."[47]

Chapter 23

# Robert Toombs

The first of the Confederacy's secretaries of state was Robert Augustus Toombs. (In later life, his political opponents would call him by his initials—"RAT.") Toombs was born in Wilkes County, Georgia, on July 2, 1810. He came from "a family of soldiers, his ancestors having fought in Oliver Cromwell's army."[1] About 1650, his great-great grandfather came to America and settled in Virginia. His father, Robert, was a major in a Virginia regiment during the Revolution. After the war, his father received 3,000 acres in Wilkes County, Georgia, and moved his family there, where he grew indigo and tobacco. There Robert Augustus was born, the Toombs's fifth child. The father died when young Robert was only five years old, leaving his mother, Catherine Huling, a widow.

Robert Toombs, Secretary of State (Library of Congress).

Toombs was a healthy child, claiming never to have taken medicine until well into adulthood.[2] He gave up smoking when he saw that it was hurting him physically. And he kept in fine physical condition until he was well advanced in years. He grew to more than six feet tall and wore his shiny black hair long.[3] One devilish vice, however, was with him throughout his adult life. He had a

226

weakness for alcohol, a vice that would eventually prove disastrous to him.[4] He also had a temper that sometimes pushed him into verbal tirades.

Early in life, Toombs developed a love of reading, which no doubt served him well in later life in both education and his careers. But as a young scholar, he was known more his mischievousness than for his scholarship.[5] He enrolled in Franklin College in Athens, Georgia, in 1824 at the age of 14. Soon, however, he was caught playing cards and severely reprimanded. Stung and embarrassed by the rebuke, he dropped out of Franklin and enrolled in Union College in Schenectady, New York, from which he graduated in 1828. He then studied law in Charlottesville, Virginia, at the University of Virginia, and was admitted to the bar in 1830. He started a law practice in Washington, Georgia. About eight months later, he married.

Within two years, Toombs suspended his legal career to command a company of volunteers under Winfield Scott in the Creek War. But after the war, he was back to law, and he made his fortune in that field between 1837 and 1845. He was tireless in work, and involved himself in every important piece of legislation of his state.[6]

As often happens with successful lawyers, Toombs developed an interest in politics, and he soon had a following. His growing popularity led to his election to the Georgia legislature in 1837 as a Whig. As in everything else he did, he threw himself wholeheartedly into politics, and he quickly distinguished himself as an orator. "It was as a speaker that he most impressed his contemporaries," and when he spoke, he did so "to convince, if possible; if not, to overwhelm."[7] He could be voluminous and wordy if necessary, but "when circumstances required brevity, he could eliminate every superfluous word."[8]

Toombs was a political oddity. He was a politician; yet, he hated party politics. He called it "'a nursery of faction.'"[9] He cast his first vote in 1832—for Andrew Jackson—but he left the Democrats when the Force Bill passed, and he joined the Whigs. Although he entered active politics as a Whig, he disapproved of internal improvements funded by the national government, a central tenant of Whiggery. He wanted nothing to do with expenditures that weakened or took away individual rights or those of the states. Yet he supported the tariff and the national bank, and in the legislature he was chairman of the Committee on Internal Improvements. He also chaired both the Committee on Banking and the Committee on the State of the Republic.

During this time, he opposed "a seductive scheme for popular relief" of victims of flooding.[10] It sounded like a worthy, compassionate cause, but he wrote a report advising against passage of the bill. He thought that it was wrong to use the public money and labor on projects that would benefit only a portion of the people.[11] To do so was essentially an immoral violation of sacred principle and a redistribution of wealth.[12] The bill was defeated on the strength of Toombs's opposition to it.

Toombs's rise through the political ranks was progressive. At age 27, he was elected to the Georgia legislature (1837), where he served until 1843. He did not run for reelection in 1841 but was elected to the state senate in 1842. There he "proved a stone wall against the perfect flood of legislation designed for popular relief."[13] Yet, he fought for publicly funded railroads.

In 1844, Toombs was elected to the U.S. House of Representatives, joining his friend Representative Alexander Stephens of Crawfordville, Georgia, who had also been elected at the same time. In 1852, the Georgia legislature elected Toombs to the U.S. Senate (as a Democrat). From that point until 1860, he was a Democrat. In Congress, he opposed the annexation of Texas. He thought that the slavery issue was "a bugbear everlastingly used to cover up the true question at issue."[14] His first speech in the House, delivered on January 12, 1846, dealt with the Oregon boundary dispute with Great Britain. In it, he called on his fellow representatives to put aside their sectionalism for the cause of peace. He also opposed the Mexican War because he thought it was illegal.[15]

During the debate over the Compromise of 1850, Toombs led the Georgia delegation, including Alexander Stephens and Howell Cobb, in seeking to avoid secession. In spite of this, back in Georgia, he was viewed as a "champion of immediate secession" because editors put together isolated excerpts of his speeches and presented them such that he seemed to support disunion.[16] In reality, he was "one of the staunchest supporters of the Union."[17]

On January 24, 1860, amid the tense and emotionally charged political atmosphere following John Brown's short-lived insurrection at Harpers Ferry, Toombs delivered on the Senate floor what became known as his "door-sill speech."[18] In it, he said,

> The fundamental principles of our Union are assailed, invaded, and threatened with destruction; our ancient rights and liberties are in danger; the peace and tranquility of our homes have been invaded by lawless violence, and their further invasion is imminent; the instinct of self-preservation arms society to their defense.[19]

Furthermore, he declared, the compact uniting the states had been broken by both the Northern states because they agreed not to enforce the Fugitive Slave Act and the Republican Party because they thought lightly of their oaths and constitutionality. He declared the nation to be in a virtual civil war. Concluding, he called on Southerners to defend themselves: "The enemy is at your door; wait not to meet him at your hearthstone; meet him at your door-sill, and drive him from the Temple of Liberty, or pull down its pillars and involve him in a common ruin."[20]

Toombs watched from Washington as the presidential election of 1860 divided the Democrats and threatened to divide the nation. He lamented the likelihood that the Constitution would succumb while the Union survived. The North, he said, did not want to be restricted or limited by the Constitution. Toombs's speech separated him from his Senate colleague Stephen Douglas and—for the first time in their friendship—from Alexander Stephens. Georgians had called Toombs and Alexander the "Siamese twins" of the state. Now they seemed to have become enemies.

Unsatisfied with the candidates chosen in the Democrats' two conventions, Toombs was instrumental in founding the Constitutional Union Party, on whose ticket John Bell of Tennessee ran for president. On December 22, 1860, he telegraphed the citizens of Georgia that they should forget about looking to the North to secure any of their constitutional rights. When Georgia voted to secede from the Union, Toombs resigned his Senate seat, delivering his farewell address to the Senate on January 7, 1861. "Let us depart in peace," he pleaded with his Northern colleagues one final time. "Refuse that, and you present us war."[21]

The new nation of Georgia named Toombs chairman of its Foreign Relations Committee. He was unanimously elected an at-large representative. In the election of other delegates to the Provisional Congress, Toombs nominated Stephens, although they were still not on speaking terms, and Stephens was elected. The Georgia delegation was to meet with the delegates of the other seceding states in Montgomery, Alabama, on February 4, 1861, to form a new government.

The first order of business was the election of a president and a vice president for the provisional government, and Toombs was eyed as a presidential possibility from the start. In almost all discussions as to possible candidates for the position, Toombs's name was frequently mentioned, and he actually yearned for the position. But this desire went contrary to things he had said earlier in his political career, such as "'Politics with me is but an episode in life, not its business.'"[22] Besides, others objected that he was "untrained to obey," so how could he lead?[23] When he was approached about whether he would be willing to run, he said that he would accept but only if it were unanimous. After he learned that four states' delegates were strongly pushing for Jefferson Davis to be the president, Toombs declined. With the nomination effectively closed for himself, he supported Davis's nomination. He actually seconded Davis's nomination. Then he encouraged Alexander Stephens to accept the vice presidency. But Toombs later became one of Davis's fiercest critics because he was still brooding over the fact that Davis, not he, had been chosen to be president.[24]

Although Toombs would not be the Confederacy's chief executive, he still had a major influence on the formation of the Confederate government and constitution. He succeeded in winning acceptance of a provision whereby each cabinet member would have a seat on the floor of each congressional chamber and the right to speak on any issues related to their respective departments, although they would not be permitted to vote. He was also appointed chairman of the Finance Committee and was mentioned as a candidate for secretary of the treasury. Instead, President Davis offered him, possibly as a reward for his having supported Davis's nomination for president, the State Department. Toombs at first declined but later, after prodding by Alexander Stephens, consented.

At the time, Toombs had a heavy, round face and a massive abundance of hair that was turned topsy-turvy and flopped across a high, broad brow. His stern eyes were fixed beneath brows that angled downward and met at the bridge of his nose. He sported a beard on his chin but had no moustache.

One of Toombs's first actions as secretary was to send a peace commission to Washington, D.C., offering an olive branch to the Union government and seeking to mend fences. He named as commissioners John Forsythe of Alabama, A.B. Roman of Louisiana, and fellow Georgian Martin Crawford. They were authorized to demand that Fort Sumter be evacuated and that the status quo be maintained elsewhere.[25] But U.S. secretary of state William Seward refused to see the commissioners either officially or unofficially. He did, however, assure them that he (and presumably the Lincoln administration) wanted peace and that there was no immediate danger of conflict between the sections. The commissioners were also led to believe that Lincoln's cabinet favored abandoning Fort Sumter. The commissioners—and Toombs himself—believed that this policy would prevail throughout the North.

But then the delegation warned Davis, "'The [Northern] war party presses [Lincoln]; he vibrates to that side.'"[26] The commissioners and Toombs began to distrust the Lincoln administration as they witnessed Northern preparations for war. They warned the Davis government not to have any confidence in the Lincoln administration but to be on their guard.

As war clouds gathered over Charleston and Fort Sumter, Toombs strongly advised the Confederates not to move against Fort Sumter. He warned, "'It is suicide, murder, and will lose us every friend at the North. You will wantonly strike a hornet's nest which ... will swarm out and sting us to death. It is unnecessary; it puts us in the wrong; it is fatal.'"[27] Davis overruled him.

Toombs next named William Lowndes Yancey to head a second commission, this one to the nations of Europe. Other members of the commission were A.D. Mason of Virginia and A.P. Rost of Louisiana. The commission's goal was the formal diplomatic recognition of the Confederate States of America. The most the commission could accomplish, however, was to gain recognition as a belligerent. But even this step was significant. It was Robert Toombs's first diplomatic triumph over William Seward.[28]

Toombs also sent commissioners to the Southern states that had not yet seceded before the firing on Fort Sumter and Lincoln's call for 75,000 volunteers to rally to the cause of the North. The objective was to convince them that their most positive future lay with the Confederacy. Eventually, Arkansas, North Carolina, Tennessee, and Virginia did secede and join the Confederacy, but they did not do so because the commissioners convinced them. They did so as a reaction to Lincoln's call for troops. Their attitude was that of Tennessee governor Isham Harris, who, when Lincoln called upon Tennessee for its portion of the military levy, replied, "Tennessee will not furnish a single man for purposes of coercion but 50,000 if necessary for the defense of our rights and those of our southern brothers."[29] Although Kentucky and Maryland did not secede, neither did they provide the troops that Lincoln requested.

Although Toombs expected a military confrontation, he knew that combat alone would not be enough. Believing that "90 percent of war was business," he advised the Confederacy to begin buying arms, ships, and ammunition with the South's cotton.[30]

Toombs quickly became dissatisfied with his post at the State Department. He disliked not having what he considered adequate quarters. In fact, once when someone asked him where the State Department was, he replied, "In my hat." He also chafed at the red tape of bureaucracy. Mary Chesnut recorded that when Toombs resigned on July 24, 1861, after only five months in the position, he had failed due to "incompatibility of temper. Mr. Toombs rides too high a horse; that is, for so despotic a man as Jeff Davis."[31] Patrick thought that Toombs was not helpful or reliable and was actually "the most inept, of Davis's secretaries."[32]

Awaiting Toombs as he left the State Department was a position as brigadier general in the Georgia militia. He had not wanted a "safe" position; he wanted to contribute to the cause on the front lines.[33] He thought that he could do more good in a combat command than in the cabinet. He was commissioned on July 21, 1861, and he saw his first action near the end of the first Battle of Manassas under generals P.G.T. Beauregard and Joseph Johnston.

Bradford concluded that although Toombs was "a splendid individual fighter," he "could not learn that fighting, like everything else, to be fruitful and efficient, requires, first of all, subordination. He could not learn discipline."[34] If he disagreed with a superior officer, he said so, even when he did not fully understand what they were doing or why. He had little respect for West Pointers; he thought that they were know-it-alls. He also thought that Davis favored West Point graduates, and that belief made him even more critical of the president.

During the Seven Days' Battle, General James Longstreet ordered Toombs to guard a particular ford. But Toombs decided that nothing was happening there, and he wanted to be where the action was. So, on his own initiative, he withdrew his troops from the ford and positioned them elsewhere. After the battle, Longstreet had him arrested. Yet, when Longstreet later allowed him to return to duty with his command, Toombs gave Longstreet "his whole-hearted submission."[35]

Toombs was well liked by his men because he took good care of them and never let other commanders impose on them. He made others respect them, too. If they did not, he quickly took them to task for their violation.[36]

He also hated to retreat. Retreating was bad for morale, he reasoned. He preferred to attack. Longstreet summarized Toombs's attitude: "'His general idea was that the troops went out to fight, and he thought that they should be allowed to go at it at once.'"[37]

In January 1862, the Georgia legislature elected Toombs to the Confederate Senate. He joined fellow Georgian Benjamin Hill in that body, but he still thought that his best contribution to the cause could be made on the battlefield, so he retained his command. Later, friends tried to get him to be nominated for secretary of war, but he put an immediate stop to such talk, saying that he would not be Davis's clerk.

Toombs and Davis had been at odds since before the war. The two men had clashed when Davis was secretary of war under Franklin Pierce and Toombs was a U.S. senator. Official disagreements soon turned personal. What Toombs perceived as Davis's preference for West Point graduates continued to rankle him. His perception of West Pointers was further tainted by an order at Malvern Hill to charge what Toombs considered to be an impregnable enemy defensive position, and he had a fierce run-in with General D.H. Hill over it. The two generals exchanged several heated letters after the incident, and Toombs challenged Hill to a duel. Hill declined the challenge, preferring to take the high road and focus on the greater priority of fighting the real enemy.

Toombs accompanied Lee in the invasion of Maryland, and his brigade distinguished itself at Sharpsburg. General D.R. Jones's division of four brigades, foremost of which was Toombs's brigade, was ordered to defend the bridge across Antietam Creek along the front being formed by Union General Ambrose Burnside. Toombs's brigade was "occupying the defenses of the bridge itself and the wooded slopes above, while the other brigades supported him."[38] His men covered "three or four hundred yards both above and below the bridge."[39] The only way the enemy could approach the bridge was by a narrow road that paralleled Toombs's line of battle for "near three hundred paces ...

and distant therefrom fifty to a hundred and fifty feet, thus exposing his flank to a destructive fire the most of that distance."[40]

Toombs's men repelled five consecutive Yankee assaults on the stone bridge that spanned Antietam Creek. The Confederate brigade was vastly outnumbered, but Lee's after-action report stated that it "'maintained its position with distinguished gallantry.'"[41] The brigade then charged the enemy, who "'ran in confusion.'"[42] Lieutenant General James Longstreet praised Toombs's actions in the battle. Toombs "did handsome service," he declared. "The little band fought bravely, but the Federals were pressing them slowly back. The delay that Toombs caused, however, saved that part of the battle. At the last moment, General A.P. Hill's forces came in to reinforce him, and D.H. Hill discovered a good place for a battery and opened with it. Thus the Confederates were enabled to drive the Federals back, and when night settled down, the army of Lee was still in possession of the field."[43]

The next day, Toombs and his aides were confronted by some Union cavalrymen posing as friendly troops. Just as Toombs and his party recognized them as Yankees, the enemy fired upon his party, and Toombs was struck in the hand.

Toombs was forced to recuperate at home for several months. When he finally returned to his command, he expected to receive a promotion to major general. Twice Postmaster General John Reagan urged Davis to give Toombs the promotion to division command, but Davis refused on the grounds that none of Toombs's fellow officers had recommended it. Toombs, however, thought that the real reason was because of his consistent and unmeasured criticism of the Davis administration, especially Davis's conducting of the war. After all, Toombs was part of the anti-administration party in Congress, which was led by Senator Wigfall and included Governor Brown of Georgia and Vice President Stephens.

Perhaps Toombs's harshest criticisms were focused on the conscription acts and what he perceived as the administration's steady march toward centralization. He thought that the conscription act put too much power into the hands of one man—Jefferson Davis. When the expected promotion was not forthcoming, Toombs resigned his commission.

Toombs returned to Georgia, where he organized new recruits for the Georgia militia and trained them to fight.[44] As such, he was on hand for the battles around Atlanta. Just as General William T. Sherman began his infamous march to the sea, Toombs's troops were rushed to the front. Many of them were just boys; others were old men. Many of them were also poorly equipped. Toombs's last combat occurred during the siege of Savannah on December 20, 1864. In a move that put him in conflict with Georgia's governor Brown,

Toombs approved his troops' being sent out of Georgia, where he had pledged they would remain, to defend South Carolina against a rumored attack from Port Royal. Toombs was lunching with Brown when they learned that Lee had surrendered at Appomattox.

While Davis and some members of his cabinet fled Richmond through Danville, Virginia; Greensboro, North Carolina; and Abbeville, South Carolina, to Washington, Georgia, Toombs returned separately to his home there. Davis and the remnants of the cabinet held their last cabinet meeting in Washington, Georgia, near Toombs's own home.[45] Toombs offered the service of his troops to escort Davis as far as the Chattahoochee River.

Toombs was now a wanted man. Union troops came to his home to arrest him, but his wife delayed them at the front door long enough for him to escape out the back door. The soldiers threatened to burn the house if Mrs. Toombs did not reveal where her husband was. She defiantly told them to burn it.[46] Shortly before Toombs's flight, Mrs. Toombs had inquired of Union officials where her husband could be paroled if he turned himself in. Secretary of War Edwin Stanton replied for President Andrew Johnson that if Toombs was ever caught, he would be sent as a prisoner to Fort Warren. Nothing was said about any parole; the clear implication was that there would be no parole. The die was cast. Toombs would try to flee the country and escape such a fate.

A neighbor found Toombs and took his horse to him, and Toombs lit out that night. He sought refuge on an island in the middle of the Savannah River. Union troops heard that he was there and surrounded the island, but not before Toombs slipped away. Moving upstream on the Savannah River, he showed his Masonic ring and got help from several fellow Masons.

Acquiring the parole papers of a Major Luther Martin of Elbert County, Toombs traveled under that alias for a time, but he never wore a physical disguise. He was particularly successful in covering his tracks to keep anyone from following him. He stayed in the North Georgia mountains until early fall 1865.

The Yankees by then thought that surely he had escaped the country, and they quit looking for him. Whenever someone asked him, not realizing who he was, where Toombs could be, Toombs replied, "Cuba." And that actually was where he was headed, traveling with a Confederate companion named Lieutenant Irwin.

Toombs finally reached Mobile, Alabama, where he obtained a pass for Cuba from the Spanish consul in New Orleans, using his alias Major Luther Martin. He then sailed from Mobile to New Orleans. En route, a passenger began watching him suspiciously, and Toombs concluded that he must be a Union spy. Toombs told Irwin to question the man. If Irwin was not satisfied with his answers and assured of Toombs's safety, Irwin was to throw the stranger overboard.

On November 4, 1865, Toombs boarded the steamship *Alabama* in New Orleans. He ended up in Cuba but soon traveled on to Paris, France, arriving in early July 1866. His wife later joined him there. They stayed for about 18 months, but he was at no time thinking of making France his permanent residence. In January 1867, he left France to return to Cuba. Later, he went to Canada for a while. Eventually, he returned to the United States but not as a penitent. He "remained unreconstructed for the rest of his life."[47] He traveled to Washington, D.C., where he met with President Andrew Johnson. From there, he returned home to Georgia. He was not arrested or molested in any way, but neither did he petition for the restoration of his citizenship rights, and his citizenship was never restored. He was, in essence, truly a man without a country.

At 57 years of age, he had lost practically everything in the world and had to start over from scratch. He resumed his law practice. He was without hope of promotion because he refused to petition for his rights, but he sought to win back in the courtroom some of the power he had lost in politics.[48] But that limitation did not prevent him from speaking out and letting his views be known. One historian referred to Toombs as "a man who seldom forgave and never forgot."[49] Toombs spoke from conviction. He vigorously condemned Andrew Johnson and presidential reconstruction. "He wanted nothing of the new regime although his own people were acquiescing."[50] Rather, he thought that the South should be passive, doing nothing to make the reconstructionist policies successful. He had no feelings of sympathy for Johnson in the president's conflict with the Radical Republicans in Congress. Toombs soon was earning high fees for his services and drawing crowds to hear him speak in court.

Toombs deplored and denounced both radicalism and those in power during Reconstruction.[51] He admonished the people of Georgia to stand firm without compromising or having anything to do with people who tried to resurrect old issues. "It is the shibboleth of ruin," he warned. "Push forward, and make a square fight for your liberties.'"[52]

The last major contribution of his public life was his involvement in the state constitutional convention in 1877. Elected a delegate at the age of 68, he attended every session and paid close attention to every detail. He spoke out once again against publicly financed internal improvements. His influence won out; the new constitution prohibited state aid to railroads. He also railed against corporations that lobbied for special favors or exemptions from the law and supported more competition among businesses. His fingerprints were all over the new constitution.

Toombs made his last public address in September 1884 upon the election of Grover Cleveland as president. He considered Cleveland's victory to be a great victory for the entire nation, not just for one region.

Near the end of his life, Toombs "nominally accepted Christianity"[53] and joined the Southern Methodist Church. Following his wife's death in 1883, his health steadily declined. On September 30, 1885, he suffered a general physical collapse. On December 20, he lapsed into a coma and never recovered. He died five days later.

An assessment of Toombs's life shows a mixed bag both personally and professionally. Stovall said of him, "His virtues were heroic, his faults were conspicuous."[54]

Perhaps his greatest weakness, a demon that he suffered from the beginning of his professional career, was alcohol. He developed the habit of drinking while in the army, and his friend Dr. Henry Steiner warned him that drink clouded his thinking during combat. In later years, it "overcame him disastrously."[55] Perhaps much of the problem lay in the second weakness in this list—lack of personal discipline in his life.

In the end, Toombs died a bitter man. "The United States government had conquered him, subdued him, constrained him. It governed Georgia, and he was a Georgian. But he never forgave."[56] "He declared that he would die as he had lived, 'an unpardoned, unreconstructed, unrepentant rebel.'"[57] He was true to his word.

CHAPTER 24

# Robert M. T. Hunter

When Robert Toombs resigned as secretary of state to become a general, he was replaced by Robert Mercer Taliaferro Hunter of Virginia. Hunter was born near Loretto, Virginia, on April 21, 1809. He was homeschooled as a youngster. He entered the University of Virginia in 1826 when he was 17 and graduated in 1828. He then studied law, reading with Judge Henry St. George Tucker of Winchester, Virginia, and was admitted to the bar in 1830. For the next four years, he practiced the legal profession in Lloyds, Virginia.

In 1834, at the age of 26, Hunter was elected as a Democrat to the Virginia general assembly. He served there until 1837, when he was elected to the U.S. House of Representatives. He served as Speaker of the House during the 26th Congress, the youngest person to hold that office. Although he lost his bid for reelection to the 28th Congress, he was successful in the next term, when he was chosen chairman of the Committee on the District of Columbia.

During his campaigns for public office, Hunter "tended to rely on his

**Robert M. T. Hunter, Secretary of State (Library of Congress).**

character and reputation ... rather than active campaigning techniques."[1] He found that tactic to be effective even if it did go against conventional political wisdom.

The Virginia legislature elected Hunter to be a U.S. senator in 1846 and reelected him in 1852 and 1858. In the Senate, he served on the Committee on Finance and as chairman of the Committee on Public Buildings. He often played a moderating role between the Whigs and the Democrats. He also tried to steer a moderate route in the evolving sectional issue of slavery both in the Senate and at the Democratic National Convention in 1860. Although he seemed to deemphasize the slavery issue, two of his favored political positions were state sovereignty and a low tariff.[2]

Hunter authored the Tariff of 1857, which amended the Walker tariff of 1846, returning tariff rates to what they had been in 1816. It was a purely revenue tariff and not a protective tariff, so it received wide support among Southern Democrats, Westerners, and New England wool manufacturers. This became perhaps the most significant piece of legislation of his career in the U.S. Senate. He turned down an offer by President Millard Fillmore to name him U.S. secretary of state.

Hunter became a major proponent of Southern and states' rights. Those rights, he believed, included the right to take one's property to other states and the U.S. territories. As the son of a successful Virginia plantation owner, he believed that property included slaves.[3] He supported John C. Calhoun for president in 1844 and 1848. And he himself aspired to the presidency in 1856 and 1860. When that dream was dashed, he supported the 1860 candidacy of John C. Breckinridge.

When Lincoln won the 1860 election, Hunter did not think that Lincoln's victory warranted secession, although he did support the principle of secession. He clung to the hope that a moderate approach and conciliation might preserve the Union. He thought that the South's best opportunity to preserve its rights lay within the Union, not outside of it. Although still promoting states' rights, Hunter developed a reputation as a moderate because he moved slowly and deliberately, not hastily and precipitously.[4] But he was moderate and open to compromise only concerning the rights of the federal government.[5] He actually cared more about preserving slavery than he did about preserving the Union. He did not advise immediate secession when slavery and the Union collided, but "his southern defense overwhelmed his compromising nature. He was neither moderate, conciliatory, nor compromising on the matter of Southern self-determination."[6]

When Vice President Breckinridge appointed a Senate Committee of Thirteen to deal with the secession crisis, Hunter was among its members. (The other members were William Bigler of Pennsylvania, Jacob Collamer of Vermont, John Crittenden of Kentucky, Jefferson Davis of Mississippi, Stephen Douglas of Illinois, James Doolittle of Wisconsin, James Grimes of Iowa, chairman Lazarus Powell of Kentucky, Henry Rice of Minnesota, William Seward of New York, Robert Toombs of Georgia, and Benjamin Wade of Ohio.) After seven days of unproductive wrangling, proposals, and counterproposals, the committee dissolved without reaching agreement.

Hunter thereafter sought no compromise. Instead, he sought to gain Senate approval for a resolution that would force the federal government to cede all authority over military installations of all kinds to the individual states if their legislatures requested it.[7] Such a requirement would have prevented subsequent action at Fort Sumter, but it was certainly not something that Northern senators were about to agree to.

Next, he proposed a constitutional restructuring of the national government. According to his plan, the nation should have two executives, one from the North and the other from the South with both having equal power.[8] Either section could veto the other section's decisions. That idea fell flat as well. Amazingly, however, the vote on his proposal was close—27 to 24.

As the crisis continued to deepen, Hunter realized the hopelessness of the situation. It had become obvious to him that neither side would budge. He advised William Trescott to tell the people of South Carolina to block Charleston Harbor immediately by sinking vessels in it. He resigned his chairmanship of the Senate Finance Committee on January 19, 1861, the same day on which the seceding states' senators resigned their Senate seats. He made his last speech to the Senate on March 1 and resigned from the Senate himself on March 28, 1861.

Hunter did not believe that the election of Abraham Lincoln to the presidency was sufficient reason for Virginia to secede. When Lincoln called for troops to subjugate the Confederate states, however, that was too much even for him. When Virginia voted to secede, Hunter opted to remain loyal to his state, and he was elected to be a delegate at large to the Confederate Provisional Congress.

Patrick, in *Jefferson Davis and His Cabinet*, includes Hunter among the "Men of Ambition," along with Robert Toombs and William Browne. He was indeed ambitious. He had long aspired to be president of the United States. Secession put an end to that dream. He then wanted to become president of the Confederate States, and rumors that he, indeed, would become president circulated for a while. But the selection of Jefferson Davis ended yet another of his dreams. Finally, he decided that he should at least serve Virginia as a senator in the Confederate Congress as he had in the U.S. Congress.

About the same time, Toombs resigned as secretary of state, and Davis, needing someone in his cabinet from the newly seceded Virginia, asked Hunter to take Toombs's place. Only after ensuring his election to the Senate did Hunter agree to become secretary of state. He held both posts simultaneously until he resigned from the cabinet in 1862.

Mary Chesnut thought that Hunter was "the sanest, if not the wisest, man in our new-born Confederacy."[9] He certainly seemed headed toward fulfilling her expectation in his duties as secretary of state. He surely was better organized than Toombs, and he showed diplomatic thinking and ability. Seeing that Toombs's and Davis's commission approach to foreign policy was not working, Hunter made several shifts in methodology designed to achieve the Confederacy's foreign policy goals.

Yancey's resignation gave Hunter the chance to change the tone and emphases of Confederate foreign policy. He replaced the commission method of diplomacy by assigning a separate individual diplomat to each major nation. He assigned James Mason to England, John Slidell to France, Pierre Rost to Spain, and Dudley Mann to Belgium. He also refocused their diplomatic pitch in several ways.

With Spain, Hunter had Rost focus on reassuring her that the Confederacy had no designs to acquire Cuba and to convince her that she had more to fear from the United States than from the Confederacy. Spain was neither impressed nor convinced by those arguments.

With the other countries, notably England and France, Hunter tried, as had his predecessor, to promote "King Cotton" diplomacy. He also sought to convince them that the South could not lose the war that was a consequence of secession.[10] He also emphasized the apparent failure of the Union blockade and pressed for formal diplomatic recognition. The blockade, he told them, violated the Treaty of Paris of 1856, and he presented as proof the number of ships that were able to breech the blockade.[11] And the quickest road to a return to the peace and economic prosperity that comes from free trade, he told foreign nations, lay in foreign recognition of the Confederacy.

These efforts in themselves were improvements in the State Department, but Hunter quickly bored of them, and he found his fruitless efforts "frustrating."[12] He resigned on February 22, 1862, after less than six months as secretary of state. He then turned to focus his full attentions on his role as senator. He served there for the duration of the war, functioning as president pro-tempore and member of the Finance Committee.

As a cabinet member, Hunter was restricted in what he could say. But once he was out of the cabinet, he was freer to express his true opinions of the Davis administration. Yet, as historian William Davis stated, Hunter was "happy to carp and preen behind Davis's back but never willing to challenge him frontally."[13] Even after he left the cabinet and was more able as a senator to express himself openly, Hunter alternated between first supporting and then opposing the Davis administration.[14] Perhaps this is why Davis, in *A Short History of the Confederate States of America*, never mentioned Hunter.

As the war went from bad to worse for the Confederacy, criticism of Davis increased as well. A proposal was floated to solve the problem of perceived lack of confidence in the Confederate executive department by which Davis and Stephens would resign, which would make Hunter, since he was president of the Senate, the chief executive, Lee would become commander in chief, and those changes would do a lot to restore confidence in the government.[15] The plan, of course, got nowhere.

After Lee's surrender at Appomattox, Lincoln contacted Hunter and asked to confer concerning how Virginia could best be restored to the Union. In spite of this apparent good-will gesture, Hunter was arrested after the war, taken from his own dinner table. He spent until the fall of 1865 imprisoned in Fort Pulaski, Georgia. When he was finally released and allowed to return home, he returned to poverty and debt.

He tried to resume his legal practice. From 1874 to 1880, he served as State Treasurer of Virginia. His final public position was as the Customs Collector for Port Tappahannock, Virginia, in 1885. He died near Lloyds, Virginia, on July 18, 1887, at the age of 78.

CHAPTER 25

# Judah P. Benjamin

Davis's choice to replace Hunter when he resigned was his most-trusted advisor, Judah P. Benjamin, who was secretary of war at the time. Benjamin was coming under increasing fire from both Congress and the generals, but Davis was reluctant to lose him. He instead gave him what was considered a promotion to the State Department. That did not, however, end the criticism of Benjamin.

Although this reassignment solved Davis's dilemma and met Congress's approval, Patrick concludes that it was "unwise" for Davis to appoint Benjamin to head the State Department.[1] Yet, other historians have concluded that it was as secretary of state that Benjamin "displayed the attributes that earned him the sobriquet 'The Brains of the Confederacy.'"[2]

At first, Benjamin made little change after he took over at the State Department. As the third secretary of state in less than two years, Benjamin inherited a department that had proven itself to be decidedly ineffective in that it had not achieved the ultimate goal of gaining formal diplomatic recognition by the nations—or even any single nation—of the world. Its envoys had a message, Confederate foreign policy was set, and the commissioners were working to get it heard and accepted. Yet, to date, they had failed on all points. Benjamin encouraged them to make some subtle changes in their emphases. He impressed on them the need to press the point that, to be legal under accepted international law, a blockade had to be proven effective. He wanted them to demonstrate that the Union blockade was *not* effective and was therefore illegal. Based on that fact, they were to press for recognition, emphasizing that recognition would mean peace, and peace would result in commercial benefits for everyone.

The commissioners, Benjamin instructed, should stop trying to explain the right of secession and begin instead demanding diplomatic recognition as the South's right. They also were to try to split Britain and France from their commitment to acting only in unison. He authorized the envoys to offer Louis

Napoleon of France duty-free admission of French products to Southern ports and 100,000 bales of cotton in return for recognition of the Confederacy. Benjamin remained "an ardent and unfaltering champion of the King Cotton doctrine."[3] The diplomats were also to begin convincing the British and the French to buy Southern goods. Yet, all hope of gaining recognition faded with the defeats at Gettysburg and Vicksburg in July 1863.

Having set his foreign commissioners off on a slightly different tack than they had pursued before, Benjamin himself next began working on a delicate task. He tried to convince Davis that slavery was doomed. One way or another, either with or without war, slavery would end. It was a foregone conclusion that Britain and France would not recognize the Confederacy as long as it continued its system of human slavery. Without such recognition, the South was isolated and would eventually be defeated by a more industrialized war machine that would enforce emancipation of all slaves. Would it not be better for the Confederacy itself to end slavery, possibly gaining foreign recognition, and maybe even independence, as a result? A first step toward that ultimate goal was to arm the slaves and offer them a very real reason to fight for their former masters—their personal freedom.

Benjamin also increased the number of foreign commissioners, sending Confederate envoys to several other nations, including Russia, Holland, and Denmark. The hope was that someone—anyone—would recognize the Confederacy, perhaps prompting other nations to do likewise. He also sent an envoy to the Vatican to encourage the enlistment of foreign (i.e., Roman Catholic) troops. A letter from the pope, addressed to Davis as "President of the Confederate States," was the closest the Confederacy ever got to foreign recognition. Benjamin instructed Mason to leave England if he saw no movement toward recognition. Mason left for Paris in October 1863. Although some people believed that 90 percent of the individual members of Parliament favored the South, collectively inaction was their policy.

For all of his efforts to refocus Southern foreign policy, Benjamin was unfortunately remembered for his support of a failed effort. As secretary of state, he authorized the raid on St. Albans, New York. He also approved an attempt to burn New York City. He did not plan either of those attacks, but he did not stop or disapprove them, either, and he read the reports about them afterwards.

One of Benjamin's last efforts to secure Southern independence was his commissioning of the Hampton Roads Conference. Chosen as special envoys to the Lincoln administration were Vice President Alexander Stephens, former secretary of state Senator Robert Hunter, and Supreme Court justice John Campbell of Alabama. Meeting with Abraham Lincoln and William Seward aboard a steamer in Hampton Roads, Virginia, on February 3, 1865, the last possibility for a peaceful end to the war and an independent South ended in failure. Neither side would compromise on its foundational goals: the North insisted on the abolition of slavery and a reunited country; the South insisted on independence.

In the final analysis, Patrick concluded, Benjamin was a failure as secretary of state. He did not accomplish anything for the Confederacy. In fact, "no man in the South could have obtained recognition for the Confederacy."[4]

When Davis fled Richmond in the last days of the war, Benjamin accompanied him. He was the only remaining cabinet member who supported Davis's suggestion that the South continue the war a little longer. But he advised continuing the war only as guerrilla warfare, but he realized that that policy would only hurt the South more than it hurt the North.[5] He left Davis somewhere near Washington, Georgia, promising to meet up with him later in the Trans-Mississippi. Deep inside, however, he knew that that would never happen, but he at least *sounded* optimistic to the end.

Benjamin had once pledged never to be captured alive. After leaving Davis, he proceeded into Florida wearing various disguises—in a horse and buggy as a Frenchman, "Monsieur Bonfals," and on a mule as a rustic farmer.[6] He headed for the Gulf coast near the Manatee River, where he boarded a boat and sailed along the coast disguised as a cook wearing an apron and a cap and his face smeared with grease. From Knight's Key, he boarded a sailboat bound for Cuba. From Cuba, he sailed to Southampton, England.

Once settled in England, Benjamin wrote editorials about foreign affairs for the London *Daily Telegraph*. After only a year in England, he was admitted to the English bar and began practicing law. His health declining (because of diabetes and heart trouble), he retired from the profession in 1883 at the age of 72 years and moved to France, where he died on May 6, 1884.

Mapp concluded that Benjamin was "like the Cheshire cat in *Alice in Wonderland* who faded away until all had vanished but the grin."[7]

# Conclusion:
# A Final Assessment of Davis's Cabinet

Perhaps the most frequently mentioned criticism of Davis in relation to the cabinet was his tendency to meddle and micromanage. Davis *said* that he wanted on his cabinet strong men of character and clear opinions,[1] yet he would not *allow* many of them (especially the secretaries of war) to "own" their departments or make their own decisions. Rather, he meddled and micromanaged, thereby reducing them to mere clerks, frustrating their efforts to lead their respective departments, and resulting in a high turnover rate among cabinet members. Davis told his cabinet members in their first meeting that he wanted them to express their opinions frankly with him,[2] to run their departments as they saw fit, choose their own subordinates—and be responsible for their own actions. Yet his actions belied his stated intentions, for he often ignored frank and experience-based opinions and refused to allow cabinet members to make decisions and live, sink or swim, with them. Davis allowed the attorney general, the treasury secretary, the navy secretary, and the postmaster general much more leeway in running their respective departments, but in the other departments he was very much hands-on.[3]

During World War II, the Nazi war machine was run in theory under the overall direction of the *Oberkommando der Wehrmacht* (OKW) through the various field marshals and generals. In reality, however, the hands and feet of those field commanders—who, ideally, were the best suited to make tactical decisions because they were where the action occurred—were tied. They were not allowed to make critical decisions for themselves. Rather, they had to go "through channels" to the top, and the OKW would make those decisions for them. Then those decisions would work their way back down through the channels to field level. The whole process wasted precious time. Further complicating this rigid command system, even the OKW was not really the final voice in such decision making. The real decision maker was Adolf Hitler.

Although Hitler had been only a corporal-ranked messenger during World War I, with no leadership or decision-making responsibilities, he fancied himself a great military leader. His apparent diplomatic successes in the takeover of the Sudetenland, Austria, and Czechoslovakia and his apparent military successes in overrunning Poland, Belgium, and France against the better judgment of the military experts made the professional military leaders doubt themselves and seemed to prove Hitler's genius. But even when they saw the disastrous end results of his invasion of Russia and the setbacks in North Africa, Sicily, Italy, and Normandy's bocage, the OKW was still hamstrung by the rigid command structure and the megalomaniacal self-concept of *der Führer*.

This protracted analogy applies somewhat to the Confederacy under President Jefferson Davis. Like Hitler, Davis micromanaged his generals and secretaries of war to the point that they could not make even tactical decisions with confidence because they always had to wonder if Davis would countermand them, thereby undermining the command structure, the confidence in and of the commanders and subordinates, and the morale of front-line soldiers. Unlike Hitler, however, Davis did have extensive field command and combat experience, and he had served administratively as secretary of war. But he still should have deferred to the commanders who were where the action was in making on-site command decisions. He also should not have allowed political and personal considerations to play such a heavy role in his appointments to military and governmental positions. His proper role as president should have been to set—with the "advice and consent" of Congress, his leading military commanders, and the secretary of war—the broad, strategic policies for the conduct of the war and then to leave the execution of those policies to the military professionals. All of the tactical decisions should have been left to the generals in the field in consultation with one another.

General Robert E. Lee clearly understood the importance of the commander in chief's trusting his subordinates. The problem was that sometimes they disappointed him, especially Longstreet at Gettysburg. But Lee could "distinguish between subordinates who make mistakes but have great potential (like Stonewall Jackson) and those who make mistakes and have no potential (and who should therefore be removed)."[4] Davis lacked such discernment and ability to read men and see their potential or their weaknesses.

Much of the vacillation (and therefore ineffectiveness) of the secretaries of war can be attributed to a combination of three factors: Davis's micromanagement, unclearly defined lines of authority, and the secretaries' own administrative and/or military experience—or lack thereof.

A second problem was the composition of Davis's cabinet. His cabinet choices almost totally ignored the secessionist and states' rights segments of Southern leadership, thereby ensuring unnecessary conflicts between the states' governments and the central government. His policies often attempted to accomplish acts of centralization that flew in the face of the inherent principle of decentralization that was at the heart of the states' rights philosophy. He did not seek the advice of any of the state delegations, yet he expected the support of Congress for his policies and could not understand their opposition or their insistence on keeping their states' troops, supplies, and arms for their own use. Patrick points out that in the quest for Southern independence, Davis stuck so closely to the constitutional provisions that the state governments actually were stronger than the Confederate government. In that "fault," he disproved his opponents' allegations of dictatorship.[5]

Connected with this problem was Davis's abiding desire to have represented on his cabinet as many of the states of the Confederacy as possible, thereby increasing the likelihood that he would choose someone to be a secretary simply because of which state he represented rather than for his abilities. Patrick points out that nine of the 11 states that eventually made up the Confederacy were represented in the Cabinet. Mississippi's representative refused to serve, but that state already had its representative in the president himself. The only Confederate states not represented in the cabinet were Tennessee and Arkansas.[6]

A third problem of Davis's cabinet was its lack of continuity; it membership was constantly changing. Of the various cabinet positions, only two of them—Stephen Mallory of the Navy Department and John Reagan of the Post Office Department—kept their original cabinet positions from start to finish of the Confederacy. All of the others underwent (or should one say "suffered"?) one or more changes in department heads. Davis named 14 different people to fill six positions in only four years. Six of those 14 were secretaries of war.[7] This lack of continuity of leadership meant that most secretaries in the cabinet were journeying along a learning curve during their entire tenure. Secretaries often resigned before they really had a chance to learn how their departments functioned, let alone before they could begin to effect progress or positive changes within their departments. The reasons for this high turnover among secretaries varied, but much of the blame surely came from their frustrations encountered in trying to work with Jefferson Davis.

Davis seemed unable to identify the right people as cabinet members or department heads, and as secretaries resigned, he replaced them with people who had been less than successful in other positions in the cabinet. Undoubtedly, the most prominent example of this weakness was Judah Benjamin, whom

Davis tried in three different positions—attorney general, secretary of war, and secretary of state.

A fourth issue that limited the effectiveness of the Davis cabinet was Davis's own indecisiveness in making cabinet decisions. Davis met regularly and formally with his full cabinet and frequently informally with individual department secretaries. (Only Mallory complained that Davis did not hold enough cabinet meetings.) Although the cabinet meetings lasted for hours, they accomplished little. Davis, desiring to look at all possible views of any issue, wanted his cabinet to discuss things.[8] He insisted on hearing and examining every issue in minute detail, and he was slow in making any decisions even after all of that. Mallory was of the opinion that "Davis's caution and thoroughness made immediate action quite unlikely."[9]

A fifth weakness of the cabinet was Davis himself. He was personally cool toward others, was not personable, and was overly sensitive to perceived personal slights or affronts.[10] When he saw a good quality in someone, he often let that positive attribute blind him to their greater faults. At the same time, if he perceived a flaw or weakness in someone, he often let that fault blind him to the person's other good qualities. Granted, Davis was often ill and in physical pain, but even that should not have caused him to be so impersonal and standoffish toward those with whom he had to deal most directly in running the government.

As much as these problems generated criticism of Davis and his cabinet members, and despite the fact that few people were hesitant to criticize Davis, his secretaries individually, or the cabinet collectively, there was at least one official who *was* reluctant to do so. That official was Virginia governor John Letcher. Although "he was well aware of the deficiencies of the Confederate cabinet," he discussed them only privately, never publicly. "He had always felt that Southern unity would be dangerously weakened by public criticism."[11] Perhaps if more Confederate officials had taken Letcher's position, the cabinet would have been more stable and more successful. But Davis was not without his loyal supporters, most notably Judah Benjamin.

Patrick's conclusion is right on target: Today, the Confederate cabinet, both collectively and as individual members, is generally unknown, as are the problems they faced. How they succeeded and failed as governing officials is of little interest to most people. Their names, which once were household words, are now forgotten by practically everyone. Even historians of both the War and the South pass over them with hardly a comment, and if they do mention them, it is usually to make a negative comment.[12]

Yet these men were—and still are—an important part of Southern history, government, and culture, and they deserve greater attention than they have heretofore gotten. The author hopes that this book, its weaknesses and failures notwithstanding, has helped to begin the process of correcting this long-neglected part of American history and that future scholars and history buffs will dig deeper and make these men once again household names by studying them, their beliefs, and their actions objectively.

Appendix A

# The Constitution of the Confederate States of America

## Preamble

We, the people of the Confederate States, each State acting in its sovereign and independent character, in order to form a permanent federal government, establish justice, insure domestic tranquillity, and secure the blessings of liberty to ourselves and our posterity invoking the favor and guidance of Almighty God do ordain and establish this Constitution for the Confederate States of America.

## Article I

Section 1. All legislative powers herein delegated shall be vested in a Congress of the Confederate States, which shall consist of a Senate and House of Representatives.

Sec. 2. (1) The House of Representatives shall be composed of members chosen every second year by the people of the several States; and the electors in each State shall be citizens of the Confederate States, and have the qualifications requisite for electors of the most numerous branch of the State Legislature; but no person of foreign birth, not a citizen of the Confederate States, shall be allowed to vote for any officer, civil or political, State or Federal.

(2) No person shall be a Representative who shall not have attained the age of twenty-five years, and be a citizen of the Confederate States, and who shall not when elected, be an inhabitant of that State in which he shall be chosen.

(3) Representatives and direct taxes shall be apportioned among the several States, which may be included within this Confederacy, according to their respective numbers, which shall be determined by adding to the whole number of free persons, including those bound to service for a term of years, and excluding Indians not taxed, three-fifths of all slaves. , The actual enumeration shall be made within three years after the first meeting of the Congress of the Confederate States, and within every subsequent term of ten years, in such manner as they shall by law direct. The number of Representatives shall not exceed one for every fifty thousand, but each State shall have at least one Representative; and until such enumeration shall be made, the State of South Carolina shall be entitled to choose six; the State of Georgia ten; the State of Alabama nine; the State of Florida two; the State of Mississippi seven; the State of Louisiana six; and the State of Texas six.

(4) When vacancies happen in the representation from any State the executive authority thereof shall issue writs of election to fill such vacancies.

(5) The House of Representatives shall choose their Speaker and other officers; and shall have the sole power of impeachment; except that any judicial or other Federal officer, resident and acting solely within the limits of any State, may be impeached by a vote of two-thirds of both branches of the Legislature thereof.

Sec. 3. (1) The Senate of the Confederate States shall be composed of two Senators from each State, chosen for six years by the Legislature thereof, at the regular session next immediately preceding the commencement of the term of service; and each Senator shall have one vote.

(2) Immediately after they shall be assembled, in consequence of the first election, they shall be divided as equally as may be into three classes. The seats of the Senators of the first class shall be vacated at the expiration of the second year; of the second class at the expiration of the fourth year; and of the third class at the expiration of the sixth year; so that one-third may be chosen every second year; and if vacancies happen by resignation, or other wise, during the recess of the Legislature of any State, the Executive thereof may make temporary appointments until the next meeting of the Legislature, which shall then fill such vacancies.

(3) No person shall be a Senator who shall not have attained the age of thirty years, and be a citizen of the Confederate States; and who shall not, then elected, be an inhabitant of the State for which he shall be chosen.

(4) The Vice President of the Confederate States shall be president of the Senate, but shall have no vote unless they be equally divided.

(5) The Senate shall choose their other officers; and also a president pro tempore in the absence of the Vice President, or when he shall exercise the office of President of the Confederate states.

(6) The Senate shall have the sole power to try all impeachments. When sitting for that purpose, they shall be on oath or affirmation. When the President of the Confederate States is tried, the Chief Justice shall preside; and no person shall be convicted without the concurrence of two-thirds of the members present.

(7) Judgment in cases of impeachment shall not extend further than to removal from office, and disqualification to hold any office of honor, trust, or profit under the Confederate States; but the party convicted shall, nevertheless, be liable and subject to indictment, trial, judgment, and punishment according to law.

Sec. 4. (1) The times, places, and manner of holding elections for Senators and Representatives shall be prescribed in each State by the Legislature thereof, subject to the provisions of this Constitution; but the Congress may, at any time, by law, make or alter such regulations, except as to the times and places of choosing Senators.

(2) The Congress shall assemble at least once in every year; and such meeting shall be on the first Monday in December, unless they shall, by law, appoint a different day.

Sec. 5. (1) Each House shall be the judge of the elections, returns, and qualifications of its own members, and a majority of each shall constitute a quorum to do business; but a smaller number may adjourn from day to day, and may be authorized to compel the attendance of absent members, in such manner and under such penalties as each House may provide.

(2) Each House may determine the rules of its proceedings, punish its members for disorderly behavior, and, with the concurrence of two-thirds of the whole number, expel a member.

(3) Each House shall keep a journal of its proceedings, and from time to time publish

## Appendix A

the same, excepting such parts as may in their judgment require secrecy; and the yeas and nays of the members of either House, on any question, shall, at the desire of one-fifth of those present, be entered on the journal.

(4) Neither House, during the session of Congress, shall, without the consent of the other, adjourn for more than three days, nor to any other place than that in which the two Houses shall be sitting.

Sec. 6. (1) The Senators and Representatives shall receive a compensation for their services, to be ascertained by law, and paid out of the Treasury of the Confederate States. They shall, in all cases, except treason, felony, and breach of the peace, be privileged from arrest during their attendance at the session of their respective Houses, and in going to and returning from the same; and for any speech or debate in either House, they shall not be questioned in any other place. 'o Senator or Representative shall, during the time for which he was elected, be appointed to any civil office under the authority of the Confederate States, which shall have been created, or the emoluments whereof shall have been increased during such time; and no person holding any office under the Confederate States shall be a member of either House during his continuance in office. But Congress may, by law, grant to the principal officer in each of the Executive Departments a seat upon the floor of either House, with the privilege of discussing any measures appertaining to his department.

Sec. 7. (1) All bills for raising revenue shall originate in the House of Representatives; but the Senate may propose or concur with amendments, as on other bills.

(2) Every bill which shall have passed both Houses, shall, before it becomes a law, be presented to the President of the Confederate States; if he approve, he shall sign it; but if not, he shall return it, with his objections, to that House in which it shall have originated, who shall enter the objections at large on their journal, and proceed to reconsider it. If, after such reconsideration, two-thirds of that House shall agree to pass the bill, it shall be sent, together with the objections, to the other House, by which it shall likewise be reconsidered, and if approved by two-thirds of that House, it shall become a law. But in all such cases, the votes of both Houses shall be determined by yeas and nays, and the names of the persons voting for and against the bill shall be entered on the journal of each House respective}y. If any bill shall not be returned by the President within ten days (Sundays excepted) after it shall have been presented to him, the same shall be a law, in like manner as if he had signed it, unless the Congress, by their adjournment, prevent its return; in which case it shall not be a law. The President may approve any appropriation and disapprove any other appropriation in the same bill. In such case he shall, in signing the bill, designate the appropriations disapproved; and shall return a copy of such appropriations, with his objections, to the House in which the bill shall have originated; and the same proceedings shall then be had as in case of other bills disapproved by the President.

(3) Every order, resolution, or vote, to which the concurrence of both Houses may be necessary (except on a question of adjournment) shall be presented to the President of the Confederate States; and before the same shall take effect, shall be approved by him; or, being disapproved by him, shall be repassed by two-thirds of both Houses, according to the rules and limitations prescribed in case of a bill.

Sec. 8. The Congress shall have power-

(1) To lay and collect taxes, duties, imposts, and excises for revenue, necessary to pay the debts, provide for the common defense, and carry on the Government of the Confederate States; but no bounties shall be granted from the Treasury; nor shall any duties or taxes on importations from foreign nations be laid to promote or foster any branch of

industry; and all duties, imposts, and excises shall be uniform throughout the Confederate States.

(2) To borrow money on the credit of the Confederate States.

(3) To regulate commerce with foreign nations, and among the several States, and with the Indian tribes; but neither this, nor any other clause contained in the Constitution, shall ever be construed to delegate the power to Congress to appropriate money for any internal improvement intended to facilitate commerce; except for the purpose of furnishing lights, beacons, and buoys, and other aids to navigation upon the coasts, and the improvement of harbors and the removing of obstructions in river navigation; in all which cases such duties shall be laid on the navigation facilitated thereby as may be necessary to pay the costs and expenses thereof.

(4) To establish uniform laws of naturalization, and uniform laws on the subject of bankruptcies, throughout the Confederate States; but no law of Congress shall discharge any debt contracted before the passage of the same.

(5) To coin money, regulate the value thereof, and of foreign coin, and fix the standard of weights and measures.

(6) To provide for the punishment of counterfeiting the securities and current coin of the Confederate States.

(7) To establish post offices and post routes; but the expenses of the Post Office Department, after the Ist day of March in the year of our Lord eighteen hundred and sixty-three, shall be paid out of its own revenues.

(8) To promote the progress of science and useful arts, by securing for limited times to authors and inventors the exclusive right to their respective writings and discoveries.

(9) To constitute tribunals inferior to the Supreme Court.

(10) To define and punish piracies and felonies committed on the high seas, and offenses against the law of nations.

(11) To declare war, grant letters of marque and reprisal, and make rules concerning captures on land and water.

(12) To raise and support armies; but no appropriation of money to that use shall be for a longer term than two years.

(13) To provide and maintain a navy.

(14) To make rules for the government and regulation of the land and naval forces.

(15) To provide for calling forth the militia to execute the laws of the Confederate States, suppress insurrections, and repel invasions.

(16) To provide for organizing, arming, and disciplining the militia, and for governing such part of them as may be employed in the service of the Confederate States; reserving to the States, respectively, the appointment of the officers, and the authority of training the militia according to the discipline prescribed by Congress.

(17) To exercise exclusive legislation, in all cases whatsoever, over such district (not exceeding ten miles square) as may, by cession of one or more States and the acceptance of Congress, become the seat of the Government of the Confederate States; and to exercise like authority over all places purchased by the consent of the Legislature of the State in which the same shall be, for the erection of forts, magazines, arsenals, dockyards, and other needful buildings; and

(18) To make all laws which shall be necessary and proper for carrying into execution the foregoing powers, and all other powers vested by this Constitution in the Government of the Confederate States, or in any department or officer thereof.

Sec. 9. (1) The importation of negroes of the African race from any foreign country other than the slaveholding States or Territories of the United States of America, is hereby forbidden; and Congress is required to pass such laws as shall effectually prevent the same.

(2) Congress shall also have power to prohibit the introduction of slaves from any State not a member of, or Territory not belonging to, this Confederacy.

(3) The privilege of the writ of habeas corpus shall not be suspended, unless when in cases of rebellion or invasion the public safety may require it.

(4) No bill of attainder, ex post facto law, or law denying or impairing the right of property in negro slaves shall be passed.

(5) No capitation or other direct tax shall be laid, unless in proportion to the census or enumeration hereinbefore directed to be taken.

(6) No tax or duty shall be laid on articles exported from any State, except by a vote of two-thirds of both Houses.

(7) No preference shall be given by any regulation of commerce or revenue to the ports of one State over those of another.

(8) No money shall be drawn from the Treasury, but in consequence of appropriations made by law; and a regular statement and account of the receipts and expenditures of all public money shall be published from time to time.

(9) Congress shall appropriate no money from the Treasury except by a vote of two-thirds of both Houses, taken by yeas and nays, unless it be asked and estimated for by some one of the heads of departments and submitted to Congress by the President; or for the purpose of paying its own expenses and contingencies; or for the payment of claims against the Confederate States, the justice of which shall have been judicially declared by a tribunal for the investigation of claims against the Government, which it is hereby made the duty of Congress to establish.

(10) All bills appropriating money shall specify in Federal currency the exact amount of each appropriation and the purposes for which it is made; and Congress shall grant no extra compensation to any public contractor, officer, agent, or servant, after such contract shall have been made or such service rendered.

(11) No title of nobility shall be granted by the Confederate States; and no person holding any office of profit or trust under them shall, without the consent of the Congress, accept of any present, emolument, office, or title of any kind whatever, from any king, prince, or foreign state.

(12) Congress shall make no law respecting an establishment of religion, or prohibiting the free exercise thereof; or abridging the freedom of speech, or of the press; or the right of the people peaceably to assemble and petition the Government for a redress of grievances.

(13) A well-regulated militia being necessary to the security of a free State, the right of the people to keep and bear arms shall not be infringed.

(14) No soldier shall, in time of peace, be quartered in any house without the consent of the owner; nor in time of war, but in a manner to be prescribed by law.

(15) The right of the people to be secure in their persons, houses, papers, and effects, against unreasonable searches and seizures, shall not be violated; and no warrants shall issue but upon probable cause, supported by oath or affirmation, and particularly describing the place to be searched and the persons or things to be seized.

(16) No person shall be held to answer for a capital or otherwise infamous crime, unless on a presentment or indictment of a grand jury, except in cases arising in the land or naval forces, or in the militia, when in actual service in time of war or public danger; nor shall any person be subject for the same offense to be twice put in jeopardy of life or limb; nor be compelled, in any criminal case, to be a witness against himself; nor be

deprived of life, liberty, or property without due process of law; nor shall private property be taken for public use, without just compensation.

(17) In all criminal prosecutions the accused shall enjoy the right to a speedy and public trial, by an impartial jury of the State and district wherein the crime shall have been committed, which district shall have been previously ascertained by law, and to be informed of the nature and cause of the accusation; to be confronted with the witnesses against him; to have compulsory process for obtaining witnesses in his favor; and to have the assistance of counsel for his defense.

(18) In suits at common law, where the value in controversy shall exceed twenty dollars, the right of trial by jury shall be preserved; and no fact so tried by a jury shall be otherwise reexamined in any court of the Confederacy, than according to the rules of common law.

(19) Excessive bail shall not be required, nor excessive fines imposed, nor cruel and unusual punishments inflicted.

(20) Every law, or resolution having the force of law, shall relate to but one subject, and that shall be expressed in the title.

Sec. 10. (1) No State shall enter into any treaty, alliance, or confederation; grant letters of marque and reprisal; coin money; make anything but gold and silver coin a tender in payment of debts; pass any bill of attainder, or ex post facto law, or law impairing the obligation of contracts; or grant any title of nobility.

(2) No State shall, without the consent of the Congress, lay any imposts or duties on imports or exports, except what may be absolutely necessary for executing its inspection laws; and the net produce of all duties and imposts, laid by any State on imports, or exports, shall be for the use of the Treasury of the Confederate States; and all such laws shall be subject to the revision and control of Congress.

(3) No State shall, without the consent of Congress, lay any duty on tonnage, except on seagoing vessels, for the improvement of its rivers and harbors navigated by the said vessels; but such duties shall not conflict with any treaties of the Confederate States with foreign nations; and any surplus revenue thus derived shall, after making such improvement, be paid into the common treasury. Nor shall any State keep troops or ships of war in time of peace, enter into any agreement or compact with another State, or with a foreign power, or engage in war, unless actually invaded, or in such imminent danger as will not admit of delay. But when any river divides or flows through two or more States they may enter into compacts with each other to improve the navigation thereof.

## Article II

Section 1. (1) The executive power shall be vested in a President of the Confederate States of America. He and the Vice President shall hold their offices for the term of six years; but the President shall not be reeligible. The President and Vice President shall be elected as follows:

(2) Each State shall appoint, in such manner as the Legislature thereof may direct, a number of electors equal to the whole number of Senators and Representatives to which the State may be entitled in the Congress; but no Senator or Representative or person holding an office of trust or profit under the Confederate States shall be appointed an elector.

(3) The electors shall meet in their respective States and vote by ballot for President and Vice President, one of whom, at least, shall not be an inhabitant of the same State with themselves; they shall name in their ballots the person voted for as President, and in distinct ballots the person voted for as Vice President, and they shall make distinct lists of all persons voted for as President, and of all persons voted for as Vice President,

and of the number of votes for each, which lists they shall sign and certify, and transmit, sealed, to the seat of the Government of. the Confederate States, directed to the President of the Senate; the President of the Senate shall,in the presence of the Senate and House of Representatives, open all the certificates, and the votes shall then be counted; the person having the greatest number of votes for President shall be the President, if such number be a majority of the whole number of electors appointed; and if no person have such majority, then from the persons having the highest numbers, not exceeding three, on the list of those voted for as President, the House of Representatives shall choose immediately, by ballot, the President. But in choosing the President the votes shall be taken by States, the representation from each State having one vote; a quorum for this purpose shall consist of a member or members from two-thirds of the States, and a majority of all the States shall be necessary to a choice. And if the House of Representatives shall not choose a President, whenever the right of choice shall devolve upon them, before the 4th day of March next following, then the Vice President shall act as President, as in case of the death, or other constitutional disability of the President.

(4) The person having the greatest number of votes as Vice President shall be the Vice President, if such number be a majority of the whole number of electors appointed; and if no person have a majority, then, from the two highest numbers on the list, the Senate shall choose the Vice President; a quorum for the purpose shall consist of two-thirds of the whole number of Senators, and a majority of the whole number shall be necessary to a choice.

(5) But no person constitutionally ineligible to the office of President shall be eligible to that of Vice President of the Confederate States.

(6) The Congress may determine the time of choosing the electors, and the day on which they shall give their votes; which day shall be the same throughout the Confederate States.

(7) No person except a natural-born citizen of the Confederate; States, or a citizen thereof at the time of the adoption of this Constitution, or a citizen thereof born in the United States prior to the 20th of December, 1860, shall be eligible to the office of President; neither shall any person be eligible to that office who shall not have attained the age of thirty-five years, and been fourteen years a resident within the limits of the Confederate States, as they may exist at the time of his election.

(8) In case of the removal of the President from office, or of his death, resignation, or inability to discharge the powers and duties of said office, the same shall devolve on the Vice President; and the Congress may, by law, provide for the case of removal, death, resignation, or inability, both of the President and Vice President, declaring what officer shall then act as President; and such officer shall act accordingly until the disability be removed or a President shall be elected.

(9) The President shall, at stated times, receive for his services a compensation, which shall neither be increased nor diminished during the period for which he shall have been elected; and he shall not receive within that period any other emolument from the Confederate States, or any of them.

(10) Before he enters on the execution of his office he shall take the following oath or affirmation: (Constitution the defend and protect, preserve, ability, my of best to will, States, Confederate President office execute faithfully will I that affirm) (or swear solemnly do).

Sec. 2. (1) The President shall be Commander-in-Chief of the Army and Navy of the Confederate States, and of the militia of the several States, when called into the actual service of the Confederate States; he may require the opinion, in writing, of the principal officer in each of the Executive Departments, upon any subject relating to the duties of their respective offices; and he shall have power to grant reprieves and pardons for offenses against the Confederate States, except in cases of impeachment.

(2) He shall have power, by and with the advice and consent of the Senate, to make treaties; provided two-thirds of the Senators present concur; and he shall nominate, and by and with the advice and consent of the Senate shall appoint, ambassadors, other public ministers and consuls, judges of the Supreme Court, and all other officers of the Confederate States whose appointments are not herein otherwise provided for, and which shall be established by law; but the Congress may, by law, vest the appointment of such inferior officers, as they think proper, in the President alone, in the courts of law, or in the heads of departments.

(3) The principal officer in each of the Executive Departments, and all persons connected with the diplomatic service, may be removed from office at the pleasure of the President. All other civil officers of the Executive Departments may be removed at any time by the President, or other appointing power, when their services are unnecessary, or for dishonesty, incapacity. inefficiency, misconduct, or neglect of duty; and when so removed, the removal shall be reported to the Senate, together with the reasons therefor.

(4) The President shall have power to fill all vacancies that may happen during the recess of the Senate, by granting commissions which shall expire at the end of their next session; but no person rejected by the Senate shall be reappointed to the same office during their ensuing recess.

Sec. 3. (1) The President shall, from time to time, give to the Congress information of the state of the Confederacy, and recommend to their consideration such measures as he shall judge necessary and expedient; he may, on extraordinary occasions, convene both Houses, or either of them; and in case of disagreement between them, with respect to the time of adjournment, he may adjourn them to such time as he shall think proper; he shall receive ambassadors and other public ministers; he shall take care that the laws be faithfully executed, and shall commission all the officers of the Confederate States.

Sec. 4. (1) The President, Vice President, and all civil officers of the Confederate States, shall be removed from office on impeachment for and conviction of treason, bribery, or other high crimes and misdemeanors.

## Article III

Section 1. (1) The judicial power of the Confederate States shall be vested in one Supreme Court, and in such inferior courts as the Congress may, from time to time, ordain and establish. The judges, both of the Supreme and inferior courts, shall hold their offices during good behavior, and shall, at stated times, receive for their services a compensation which shall not be diminished during their continuance in office.

Sec. 2. (1) The judicial power shall extend to all cases arising under this Constitution, the laws of the Confederate States, and treaties made, or which shall be made, under their authority; to all cases affecting ambassadors, other public ministers and consuls; to all cases of admiralty and maritime jurisdiction; to controversies to which the Confederate States shall be a party; to controversies between two or more States; between a State and citizens of another State, where the State is plaintiff; between citizens claiming lands under grants of different States; and between a State or the citizens thereof, and foreign states, citizens, or subjects; but no State shall be sued by a citizen or subject of any foreign state.

(2) In all cases affecting ambassadors, other public ministers and consuls, and those in which a State shall be a party, the Supreme Court shall have original jurisdiction. In all the other cases before mentioned, the Supreme Court shall have appellate jurisdiction

both as to law and fact, with such exceptions and under such regulations as the Congress shall make.

(3) The trial of all crimes, except in cases of impeachment, shall be by jury, and such trial shall be held in the State where the said crimes shall have been committed; but when not committed within any State, the trial shall be at such place or places as the Congress may by law have directed.

Sec. 3. (1) Treason against the Confederate States shall consist only in levying war against them, or in adhering to their enemies, giving them aid and comfort. No person shall be convicted of treason unless on the testimony of two witnesses to the same overt act, or on confession in open court.

(2) The Congress shall have power to declare the punishment of treason; but no attainder of treason shall work corruption of blood, or forfeiture, except during the life of the person attainted.

## Article IV

Section 1. (1) Full faith and credit shall be given in each State to the public acts, records, and judicial proceedings of every other State; and the Congress may, by general laws, prescribe the manner in which such acts, records, and proceedings shall be proved, and the effect thereof.

Sec. 2. (1) The citizens of each State shall be entitled to all the privileges and immunities of citizens in the several States; and shall have the right of transit and sojourn in any State of this Confederacy, with their slaves and other property; and the right of property in said slaves shall not be thereby impaired.

(2) A person charged in any State with treason, felony, or other crime against the laws of such State, who shall flee from justice, and be found in another State, shall, on demand of the executive authority of the State from which he fled, be delivered up, to be removed to the State having jurisdiction of the crime.

(3) No slave or other person held to service or labor in any State or Territory of the Confederate States, under the laws thereof, escaping or lawfully carried into another, shall, in consequence of any law or regulation therein, be discharged from such service or labor; but shall be delivered up on claim of the party to whom such slave belongs,. or to whom such service or labor may be due.

Sec. 3. (1) Other States may be admitted into this Confederacy by a vote of two-thirds of the whole House of Representatives and two-thirds of the Senate, the Senate voting by States; but no new State shall be formed or erected within the jurisdiction of any other State, nor any State be formed by the junction of two or more States, or parts of States, without the consent of the Legislatures of the States concerned, as well as of the Congress.

(2) The Congress shall have power to dispose of and make all needful rules and regulations concerning the property of the Confederate States, including the lands thereof.

(3) The Confederate States may acquire new territory; and Congress shall have power to legislate and provide governments for the inhabitants of all territory belonging to the Confederate States, lying without the limits of the several Sates; and may permit them, at such times, and in such manner as it may by law provide, to form States to be admitted into the Confederacy. In all such territory the institution of negro slavery, as it now exists in the Confederate States, shall be recognized and protected be Congress and by the Territorial government; and the inhabitants of the several Confederate States and Territories shall have the right to take to such Territory any slaves lawfully held by them in any of the States or Territories of the Confederate States.

(4) The Confederate States shall guarantee to every State that now is, or hereafter may become, a member of this Confederacy, a republican form of government; and shall protect each of them against invasion; and on application of the Legislature or of the Executive when the Legislature is not in session) against domestic violence.

## Article V

Section 1. (1) Upon the demand of any three States, legally assembled in their several conventions, the Congress shall summon a convention of all the States, to take into consideration such amendments to the Constitution as the said States shall concur in suggesting at the time when the said demand is made; and should any of the proposed amendments to the Constitution be agreed on by the said convention, voting by States, and the same be ratified by the Legislatures of two-thirds of the several States, or by conventions in two-thirds thereof, as the one or the other mode of ratification may be proposed by the general convention, they shall thenceforward form a part of this Constitution. But no State shall, without its consent, be deprived of its equal representation in the Senate.

## Article VI

1. The Government established by this Constitution is the successor of the Provisional Government of the Confederate States of America, and all the laws passed by the latter shall continue in force until the same shall be repealed or modified; and all the officers appointed by the same shall remain in office until their successors are appointed and qualified, or the offices abolished.

2. All debts contracted and engagements entered into before the adoption of this Constitution shall be as valid against the Confederate States under this Constitution, as under the Provisional Government.

3. This Constitution, and the laws of the Confederate States made in pursuance thereof, and all treaties made, or which shall be made, under the authority of the Confederate States, shall be the supreme law of the land; and the judges in every State shall be bound thereby, anything in the constitution or laws of any State to the contrary notwithstanding.

4. The Senators and Representatives before mentioned, and the members of the several State Legislatures, and all executive and judicial officers, both of the Confederate States and of the several States, shall be bound by oath or affirmation to support this Constitution; but no religious test shall ever be required as a qualification to any office or public trust under the Confederate States.

5. The enumeration, in the Constitution, of certain rights shall not be construed to deny or disparage others retained by the people of the several States.

6. The powers not delegated to the Confederate States by the Constitution, nor prohibited by it to the States, are reserved to the States, respectively, or to the people thereof.

## Article VII

1. The ratification of the conventions of five States shall be sufficient for the establishment of this Constitution between the States so ratifying the same.

2. When five States shall have ratified this Constitution, in the manner before specified, the Congress under the Provisional Constitution shall prescribe the time for holding the election of President and Vice President; and for the meeting of the Electoral College; and for counting the votes, and inaugurating the President. They shall, also, prescribe the time for holding the first election of members of Congress under this Constitution,

and the time for assembling the same. Until the assembling of such Congress, the Congress under the Provisional Constitution shall continue to exercise the legislative powers granted them; not extending beyond the time limited by the Constitution of the Provisional Government.

Adopted unanimously by the Congress of the Confederate States of South Carolina, Georgia, Florida, Alabama, Mississippi, Louisiana, and Texas, sitting in convention at the capitol, the city of Montgomery, Ala., on the eleventh day of March, in the year eighteen hundred and Sixty-one.

HOWELL COBB, President of the Congress.

**South Carolina:** R. Barnwell Rhett, C. G. Memminger, Wm. Porcher Miles, James Chesnut, Jr., R. W. Barnwell, William W. Boyce, Lawrence M. Keitt, T. J. Withers.

**Georgia:** Francis S. Bartow, Martin J. Crawford, Benjamin H. Hill, Thos. R. R. Cobb.

**Florida:** Jackson Morton, J. Patton Anderson, Jas. B. Owens.

**Alabama:** Richard W. Walker, Robt. H. Smith, Colin J. McRae, William P. Chilton, Stephen F. Hale, David P. Lewis, Tho. Fearn, Jno. Gill Shorter, J. L. M. Curry.

**Mississippi:** Alex. M. Clayton, James T. Harrison, William S. Barry, W. S. Wilson, Walker Brooke, W. P. Harris, J. A. P. Campbell.

**Louisiana:** Alex. de Clouet, C. M. Conrad, Duncan F. Kenner, Henry Marshall.

**Texas:** John Hemphill, Thomas N. Waul, John H. Reagan, Williamson S. Oldham, Louis T. Wigfall, John Gregg, William Beck Ochiltree.

# Appendix B

# Governors of the Confederate States

| State | Governor | Term(s) |
|---|---|---|
| Alabama | Andrew Moore | 1857–61 |
| | John Gill Shorter | 1861–63 |
| | Thomas Watts | 1863–65 |
| Arkansas | Henry Rector | 1860–62 |
| | Harris Flanagan | 1862–64 |
| | Isaac Murphy | 1864–68 |
| Florida | Madison Perry | 1857–61 |
| | John Milton | 1861–65 |
| Georgia | Joseph Brown | 1861–65 |
| Louisiana | Thomas Moore | 1860–64 |
| | Henry Allen | 1864–65 |
| Mississippi | John Pettus | 1859–63 |
| | Charles Clarke | 1863–65 |
| | William Sharkey | 1865–65 (provisional) |
| North Carolina | John Ellis | 1859–61 (died in office) |
| | H. T. Clark | 1861–62 (acting) |
| | Zebulon Vance | 1862–65 |
| South Carolina | Francis Pickens | 1860–62 |
| | M. L. Bonham | 1862–64 |
| | A. G. Magreth | 1864–65 |
| Tennessee | Isham Harris | 1857–62 |
| | Andrew Johnson | 1862–65 (military governor) |
| Texas | Sam Houston | 1859–61 |
| | Edward Clark | 1861–61 (acting) |
| | Francis Lubbock | 1861–63 |
| | Pendleton Murrah | 1863–65 |
| Virginia | John Letcher | 1860–64 |
| | William Smith | 1864–65 |

# Chapter Notes

## Introduction

1. James McPherson, *Embattled Rebel: Jefferson Davis as Commander in Chief* (New York: Penguin Books, 2014), p. 7.
2. George C. Rable, "Confederate Government," Essential Civil War Curriculum, 2010. Available at http://www.essential.civilwar.vt.edu/assets/files/ECWC%20TOPIC%20Confederate%20Government%20Essay.pdf.
3. Rembert W. Patrick, *Jefferson Davis and His Cabinet* (Baton Rouge: Louisiana State University Press, 1944), p. 53.

## Chapter 1

1. Jefferson Davis, *A Short History of the Confederate States of America* (1890; reprint 2002, Harrisonburg, Virginia: Sprinkle Publications), p. 61.
2. Jefferson Davis, *The Rise and Fall of the Confederate Government* (New York: D. Appleton, 1881), pp. 241–43).
3. William C. Davis, *"A Government of Our Own": The Making of the Confederacy* (New York: The Free Press, 1994), p. 170.
4. J.L.M. Curry, *Civil History of the Government of the Confederate States* (Richmond: B.F. Johnson Publishing Company, 1901), p., 59.
5. Davis, *"A Government of Our Own,"* p. 170.
6. Curry, p. 59.
7. George C. Rable, "Confederate Government," Essential Civil War Curriculum, 2010. Available at http://www.essential.civilwar.vt.edu/assets/files/ECWC%20TOPIC%20Confederate%20Government%20Essay.pdf.
8. Rembert W. Patrick, *Jefferson Davis and His Cabinet* (Baton Rouge: Louisiana State University Press, 1944), pp. 50–51.
9. Burton J. Hendrick, *Statesmen of the Lost Cause: Jefferson Davis and His Cabinet* (New York: The Literary Guild of America, Inc., 1939), p. 104.
10. William C. Davis, *Look Away! A History of the Confederate States of America* (New York: The Free Press, 2002), p. 78.
11. Davis, *"A Government of Our Own,"* p. 176.
12. Patrick, p. 58.
13. *Ibid.*
14. Eric H. Walther, *William Lowndes Yancey and the Coming of the Civil War* (Chapel Hill: University of North Carolina Press, 2006), p. 298.
15. Emory Thomas, *The Confederate Nation, 1861–1865* (New York: Harper Perennial, 1979), p. 76.
16. *Ibid.*, p. 78.
17. *Ibid.*, p. 72.
18. Sam Watkins, *Co. Aytch: A Side Show of the Big Show* (New York: Collier Books, 1962).
19. Rable, p. 4.
20. James McPherson, *Embattled Rebel: Jefferson Davis as Commander in Chief* (New York: Penguin Books, 2014), p. 110.
21. *Ibid.*, p. 218.
22. *Ibid.*, p. 191.
23. *Ibid.* p. 11.
24. Joseph Jones, "The Medical History of the Confederate States Army and Navy," *Southern Historical Society Papers*, Vol. XX (Richmond: Southern Historical Society, January–December 1892), p. 7.
25. James Z. Rabun, "Alexander H. Stephens and Jefferson Davis," *The American Historical Review* (January 1953), pp. 290–321.
26. Chad Morgan, "Alexander Stephens

(1812–1883)," *North Georgia Encyclopedia*. Available http://www.georgiaencyclopedia.org/articles/history-archaeology/alexander-stephens-1812–1883 September 27, 2004.
27. Rabun, p. 291.
28. *Ibid.*, p. 294.
29. *Ibid.*
30. *Ibid.*, p. 295.
31. *Ibid.*, p. 296.
32. *Ibid.*, p. 298.
33. *Ibid.*, p. 312.
34. Frank E. Van Riper and Harry N. Scheiber, "The Confederate Civil Service," *The Journal of Southern History* 25(4), 1959, p. 450.
35. *Ibid.*, p. 449.
36. *Ibid.*, p. 450.
37. Robert Garlick Hill Kean, *Inside the Confederate Government: The Diary of Robert Garlick Hill Kean* (New York: Oxford University Press, 1957), p. xxix.
38. *Ibid.*, p. 101.
39. *Ibid.*, p. 72.
40. *Ibid.*, p. 161.

## Chapter 2

1. J.L.M. Curry, *Civil History of the Government of the Confederate States* (Richmond: B.F. Johnson Publishing Company, 1901), p. 63.
2. *Ibid.*
3. *Ibid.*
4. *Ibid.*, p. 65.
5. *Ibid.*, p. 69.
6. *Ibid.*, p. 64.
7. William M. Robinson Jr., "Legal System of the Confederate States," *The Journal of Southern History*, November 1936, p. 459.
8. *Ibid.*, p. 465.
9. *Ibid.*, p. 461.
10. B. Patricia Dyson, "Contract Stability in Wartime: The Example of the Confederacy," *The American Journal of Legal History* (July 1975), p. 218.
11. J.G. de Roulhac Hamilton, "The State Courts and the Confederate Constitution," *The Journal of Southern History* (November 1938), pp. 427–28.
12. *Ibid.*, p. 430.
13. John B. Robbins, "The Confederacy and the Writ of Habeas Corpus," *Georgia Historical Review* (Spring 1971), p. 89.
14. Robinson, p. 465.
15. Hamilton, p. 431.
16. *Ibid.*
17. *Ibid.*, p. 433.
18. *Ibid.*, p. 435.
19. *Ibid.*
20. *Ibid.*
21. *Ibid.*
22. *Ibid.*, p. 438.
23. *Ibid.*, pp. 436–37.
24. Quoted in Hamilton, p. 439.
25. Dyson, p. 217.
26. *Ibid.*, p. 225.
27. Hamilton, p. 448.
28. W. Thad Adams III, "Confederate Patent Office," available at http://www.adamspat.com/Chapter1.html (n.d.).
29. *Ibid.*
30. *Ibid.*
31. *Ibid.*
32. *Ibid.*

## Chapter 3

1. Alf J. Mapp Jr., "Judah Benjamin: The Smiling Lion," chapter 4 in *Frock Coats and Epaulets* (New York: A.S. Barnes and Company, Inc., 1968), p. 334.
2. *Ibid.*, p. 355.
3. *Ibid.*, p. 337.
4. Robert Douthat Meade, "The Relations Between Judah P. Benjamin and Jefferson Davis," *The Journal of Southern History* (November 1939), p. 469.
5. Burton J. Hendrick, *Statesmen of the Lost Cause: Jefferson Davis and His Cabinet* (New York: The Literary Guild of America, Inc., 1939), p. 157.
6. William C. Davis, *Look Away!: A History of the Confederate States of America* (New York: The Free Press, 2002), p. 250.
7. Hendrick, pp. 257–58.
8. Mapp, p. 346.
9. Gamaliel Bradford, *Confederate Portraits* (Boston: Houghton Mifflin Company, 1914), p. 149.
10. Mapp, p. 351.
11. Rembert W. Patrick, *Jefferson Davis and His Cabinet* (Baton Rouge: Louisiana State University Press, 1944), p. 161.
12. *Ibid.*
13. Hendrick, p. 173.
14. Patrick, p. 155.
15. J.L.M. Curry, *Civil History of the Government of the United States* (Richmond: B.F. Johnson Publishing Company, 1901), p. 140.
16. *Ibid.*, p. 141.
17. Mary Boykin Chesnut, *A Diary from Dixie* (1905; reprint, New York: Gramercy Books, 1997), p. 278.
18. Robert Garlick Hill Kean, *Inside the*

*Confederate Government: The Diary of Robert Garlick Hill Kean* (New York: Oxford University Press, 1957), p. 93.
　19. *Ibid.*, p. 101.
　20. *Ibid.*, p. 122.
　21. Kevin J. Dougherty, *Encyclopedia of the Confederacy* (San Diego: Thunder Bay Press, 2010), p. 32.
　22. Bradford, p. 126.
　23. Eli N. Evans, "Judah Benjamin," in "The Confederacy," *MacMillan Information Now Encyclopedia*, available at http://www.civilwarhome.com/benjaminbio.htm.
　24. Hendrick, p. 157.
　25. Evans.
　26. Mapp, p. 346.
　27. Patrick, p. 161.
　28. Evans.
　29. Bradford, p. 127.
　30. Davis, p. 350.
　31. Bradford, p. 134.
　32. *Ibid.*, p. 135.
　33. Patrick, p. 160.

## Chapter 4

　1. Rembert W. Patrick, *Jefferson Davis and His Cabinet* (Baton Rouge: Louisiana State University Press, 1944), pp. 301–302.
　2. *Ibid.*
　3. *Ibid.*, p. 302.
　4. Jerry L. Cross, "Thomas Bragg—Governor: 1855–1859," Research Branch, North Carolina Office of Archives and History, 2004.
　5. Stewart Sifakis, *Who Was Who in the Civil War* (New York: Facts on File Publications, 1988), p. 69.
　6. Clement Eaton, *Jefferson Davis* (New York: The Free Press, 1977), p. 124.
　7. Quoted in Cross.
　8. Patrick, p. 300.
　9. Robert Garlick Hill Kean, *Inside the Confederate Government: The Diary of Robert Garlick Hill Kean* (New York: Oxford University Press, 1957), p. 138.
　10. Cross.
　11. Eaton, p. 211.
　12. Sifakis, p. 69.
　13. Cross.

## Chapter 5

　1. William C. Davis, *"A Government of Our Own": The Making of the Confederacy* (New York: The Free Press, 1994), p. 89.
　2. *Ibid.*, p. 269.

　3. *Ibid.*, p. 23.
　4. Rembert W. Patrick, *Jefferson Davis and His Cabinet* (Baton Rouge: Louisiana State University Press, 1944), p. 304.
　5. *Ibid.*
　6. Quoted by Patrick, p. 307.
　7. William C. Davis, *Look Away! A History of the Confederate States of America* (New York: The Free Press, 2002), p. 370.

## Chapter 6

　1. "Confederate Attorneys General," *West's Encyclopedia of American Law*. The Gale Group, Inc., 2005. Available at http://www.encyclopedia.com/doc/1G2-3437701043.html.
　2. *Ibid.*
　3. Stewart Sifakis, *Who Was Who in the Civil War* (New York: Facts on File Publications, 1988), p. 362.
　4. Rembert W. Patrick, *Jefferson Davis and His Cabinet* (Baton Rouge: Louisiana State University Press, 1944), p. 311.
　5. "Confederate Attorneys General."
　6. Wade Keyes, "Annual Report to the President. Richmond: Confederate States of America, Department of Justice, 1863." Available at https://archive.org/details/reportofattorney01general.conf.

## Chapter 7

　1. Bernhard Thuersam, "George Davis: Christian, Senator, Attorney General" (Wilmington, N.C.: Cape Fear Historical Institute, 2006). Available at http://www.cfhi.net/GeorgeDavisChristianSenatorAttorneyGeneral.php.
　2. Rembert W. Patrick, *Jefferson Davis and His Cabinet* (Baton Rouge: Louisiana State University Press, 1944), p. 316.
　3. *Ibid.*, p. 317.
　4. *Ibid.*, p. 314.
　5. Thuersam.
　6. *Ibid.*
　7. *Ibid.*
　8. *Ibid.*
　9. *Ibid.*
　10. Patrick, p. 315.
　11. *Ibid.*
　12. Thuersam.
　13. *Ibid.*

## Chapter 8

　1. Henry Capers, *The Life and Times of C.G. Memminger* (Richmond: Everett Waddey Co., Publishers, 1893), p. 319.

2. *Ibid.*, p. 322.
3. *Ibid.*, pp. 322–23.
4. Bernhard Todd, "The Produce Loans: A Means of Financing the Confederacy," *The North Carolina Historical Review*, Vol. 27, no. 1 (January 1950), p. 403.
5. *Ibid.*, p. 407.
6. Adapted from data cited in Eugene M. Lerner, "The Monetary and Fiscal Programs of the Confederate Government, 1861–65, Part I," *Journal of Political Economy* (February 1954), p. 506.
7. Todd, p. 407.
8. *Ibid.*
9. *Ibid.*, p. 47.
10. *Ibid.*
11. *Ibid.*, p. 52.
12. *Ibid.*, p. 64.
13. *Ibid.*, p. 68.
14. Judith Fenner Gentry, "A Confederate Success in Europe: The Erlanger Loan," *The Journal of Southern History* (May 1980), p. 160.
15. *Ibid.*, p. 161.
16. *Ibid.*, p. 164.
17. *Ibid.*, p. 168.
18. Capers, p. 340.
19. *Ibid.*, p. 342.
20. Todd, p. 67.
21. Quoted in Capers, p. 21.
22. Todd, p. 408.
23. Capers, p. 341.
24. *Ibid.*, p. 344 (emphasis in the original).
25. Eugene M. Lerner, "Money, Prices, and Wages in the Confederacy, 1861–65, Part II," *Journal of Political Economy* (February 1955), p. 21.
26. Lerner, I, p. 515.
27. *Ibid.*, p. 520.
28. Capers, p. 344.
29. *Ibid.*, p. 345.
30. *Ibid.*, p. 346.
31. Todd, p. 410.
32. Carl Vernon Patto, "Budgeting Under Crisis: The Confederacy as a Poor Country," *Administrative Science Quarterly* Vol. 20, no. 3 (September 1975), p. 367.
33. *Ibid.*, p. 369.
34. *Ibid.*, p. 358.
35. Carole E. Scott, "Coping with Inflation: Atlanta, 1860–1865," *The Georgia Historical Quarterly* (Winter 1985), p. 545.
36. *Ibid.*, p. 555.
37. Capers, p. 347.
38. Todd, p. 410 (emphasis in the original).

## Chapter 9

1. Kevin J. Dougherty, *Encyclopedia of the Confederacy* (San Diego: Thunder Bay Press, 2010), p. 180.
2. *Ibid.*
3. Henry Capers, *The Life and Times of C.G. Memminger* (Richmond: Everett Waddey Co., Publishers, 1893), p. 12.
4. *Ibid.*, p. 15.
5. *Ibid.*, p. 18.
6. *Ibid.*, p. 23.
7. *Ibid.*, p. 25.
8. *Ibid.*, p. 183.
9. *Ibid.*, p. 289.
10. *Ibid.*, p. 309.
11. *Ibid.*, pp. 322–23.
12. Robert Garlick Hill Kean, *Inside the Confederate Government: The Diary of Robert Garlick Hill Kean* (New York: Oxford University Press, 1957), p. xxxi.
13. Capers, p. 372.

## Chapter 10

1. Robert Garlick Hill Kean, *Inside the Confederate Government: The Diary of Robert Garlick Hill Kean* (New York: Oxford University Press, 1957), p.167.
2. Wesley Loy, "10 Rumford Place: Doing Confederate Business in Liverpool," *The South Carolina Historical Magazine*, Vol. 98, no. 4 (October 1997), p. 356.
3. *Ibid.*, p. 355.
4. Stewart Sifakis, *Who Was Who in the Civil War* (New York: Facts on File Publications, 1988), p. 661.
5. Loy, p. 358.
6. *Ibid.*, p. 363.
7. Kean, p. 188.
8. *Ibid.*, p. 179.
9. *Ibid.*
10. Loy, p. 366.
11. *Ibid.*, p. 371.
12. Sifakis, p. 661.
13. Loy, p. 373.

## Chapter 11

1. William J. Cooper, *Jefferson Davis, American* (New York: Vintage Books, 2000), p. 572.
2. Rembert W. Patrick, *Jefferson Davis and His Cabinet* (Baton Rouge: Louisiana State University Press, 1944), p. 352.
3. M.H. Clark, "The Last Days of the Confederate Treasury and What Became of Its

Specie," *Southern Historical Society Papers*, Vol. 9, J. William Jones, ed. Available www.perseus.tufts.edu/hopper/text?doc=Perseus%3A2001.05.0122%3Achapter%3DII.II.

## Chapter 12

1. Bryan E. Denny, *Strategic Leadership, Southern Style: Civilian Statesmen in the Confederacy's War*. Thesis presented to the U.S. Army War College (March 2013), p. 2.
2. *Ibid.*, p. 6.
3. James M. McPherson, *Embattled Rebel: Jefferson Davis as Commander in Chief* (New York: Penguin Books, 2014), p. 9.
4. *Ibid.*, p. 10.
5. *Ibid.*, p. 248.
6. *Ibid.*, p. 30.
7. Robert Garlick Hill Kean, *Inside the Confederate Government: The Diary of Robert Garlick Hill Kean* (New York: Oxford University Press, 1957), p. 87.
8. *Ibid.*, pp. 87–88.
9. *Ibid.*, pp. xxx–xxxi.
10. Fred D. Seth, "'Gittin' Stuff': Equipping Confederate Armies at the Onset of the Civil War (1861–1862)," *NPMA* (Vol. 16, Issue 3, 2004): 17.
11. Craig L. Barry, "C. S. Supplies and Logistics," *Civil War News* (May 2010), p. 1. Available at http://www.civilwarnews.com/watchdog/wd_051001.html.
12. *Ibid.*
13. McPherson, pp. 169, 170.
14. Kean, p. 89.
15. *Ibid.*, pp. 89–90.
16. Barry, p. 1.
17. Kean, p. 140.
18. "Leroy Pope Walker," *Confederate Military History*. Available at http://www.civilwarreference.com/people/index.php?peopleID=2%.
19. Jeremy P. Felt, "Lucius P. Northrop and the Confederacy's Subsistence Department," *The Virginia Magazine of History and Biography* (April 1961), p. 181.
20. *Ibid.*
21. Benjamin M. Washburn IV, *An Analysis of Confederate Subsistence Logistics*. Thesis presented to the Air Force Institute of Technology (September 1989), p. 21.
22. *Ibid.*, p. 24.
23. Mary Boykin Chesnut, *A Diary from Dixie* (1905; reprint, New York: Gramercy Books, 1997), p. 97.
24. McPherson, p. 165.
25. *Ibid.*, p. 226.
26. Washburn, p. 143.
27. H. H. Cunningham, "Organization and Administration of the Confederate Medical Department," *The North Carolina Historical Review*, Vol. 31, no. 3 (July 1954), p. 21. Available at http://www.jstor.org/stable/23516827. (Emphasis added.).
28. *Ibid.*, p. 23.
29. *Ibid.*, p. 26.
30. Joseph Jones, "The Medical History Confederate States Army and Navy," *Southern Historical Society Papers*, Vol. XX (Richmond: The Southern Historical Society, January–December 1892), p. 1.
31. Cunningham, p. 393.
32. *Ibid.*, p. 30.
33. Jones, p. 3.
34. *Ibid.*, p. 4.
35. *Ibid.*, p. 5.
36. Cunningham, p. 26.
37. Jones, p. 7.
38. Maurice S. Albin, "The Use of Anesthetics During the Civil War," *Pharmacy in History*, Vol. 42, no.3/4, Civil War Pharmacy (2000), p. 109. Available at http://www.jstor.org/stable/41112682.
39. Guy R. Hasegawa, "Pharmacy in the American Civil War," *Pharmacy in History*, Vol. 42, no. 3/4, Civil War Pharmacy (2000), p. 70. Available at http://www.jstor.org/stable/41112679.
40. Cunningham, p. 32.
41. *American Journal of Surgery* **164(4)** (October 1992), pp. 361–65.
42. Cunningham, p. 45.
43. *Ibid.*, pp. 274–75. (Both tables here are adapted from data in Cunningham, pp. 274–75.).
44. *Ibid.*, p. 51.
45. *Ibid.*, p. 395.
46. Hasegawa, p. 71.
47. Cunningham, p. 402.
48. *Ibid.*, p. 397.
49. Alfred J. Bollett, "The Truth About Civil War Surgery," Available at http://www.historynet.com/the-truth-about-civil-war-surgery-2.htm.
50. Cunningham, pp. 267–68.
51. Hasegawa, p. 74.
52. Cunningham, p. 268.
53. *Ibid.*, p. 269.
54. *Ibid.*, p. 273.
55. McPherson, p. 163.
56. Stanley L. Falk, "Jefferson Davis and Josiah Gorgas, an Appointment of Necessity,"

*The Journal of Southern History*, Vol. 28, no. 1 (February 1962), p. 85.
57. Adrian T. Marinez, *Mobilizing the Confederate Industrial Base for Total War*. Thesis presented to the U.S. Marine Corps Command and Staff College, March 25, 2011, p. 3.
58. J. L. Wakelyn, "Josiah Gorgas (July 1, 1818–May 8, 1893), in *Leaders of the American Civil War: A Biographical and Historiographical Dictionary* (New York: Routledge, 2013), p. 146.
59. Ibid., p. 147.
60. Ibid., p. 148.
61. Ibid.
62. Ibid.
63. Ibid., p. 149.
64. Ibid.
65. Ibid.
66. Ibid., 150.
67. Ibid.
68. Ibid., p. 151.
69. Frank E. Vandiver, "Makeshifts of Confederate Ordnance," *The Journal of Southern History*, Vol. 17, no. 2 (May 1951), p. 180.
70. Ibid.
71. Ibid.
72. Ibid., p. 181.
73. Ibid.
74. Marinez, p. 4.
75. Ibid.
76. Ibid.
77. Vandiver, p. 185.
78. Ibid., p. 181.
79. Kean, p. xxiv.
80. Ibid., p. xx.
81. Ibid., p. xxv.
82. Ibid.
83. Ibid., p. xxvi.
84. Ibid., xiv.
85. Ibid., xxxiii.
86. Kean, pp. xxxii–xxxiii.
87. William L. Shaw, "The Confederate Conscription and Exemption Acts," *The American Journal of Legal History* (October 1962), p. 372.
88. McPherson, p. 71.
89. Ibid., p. 166.
90. Ibid., p. 71.
91. Shaw, p. 374.
92. Ibid., p. 376.
93. Ibid., p. 349.
94. Ibid.
95. Ibid., p. 380.
96. Ibid., p. 382.
97. *Official Records* as quoted by Shaw, p. 384.
98. Ibid., p. 385.
99. Ibid., pp. 393–97.
100. Vandiver, p. 187.
101. Kean, p. 134.
102. Steward Sifakis, *Who Was Who in the Civil War* (New York: Facts on File Publications, 1988), p. 323.
103. Ibid., p. 141.
104. Ibid.
105. John C. Waugh, *The Class of 1846: From West Point to Appomattox: Stonewall Jackson, George McClellan and Their Brothers* (New York: Warner Books, 1994).
106. Thomas Lawrence Connelly and Archer Jones, *The Politics of Command: Factions and Ideas in Confederate Strategy* (Baton Rouge: Louisiana State University Press, 1973), p. 89.
107. Ibid.
108. Ibid., p. 92.
109. Ibid., p. 106.
110. Ibid. p. 166.
111. Ibid., p. 186.
112. Ibid., pp. 106–107.
113. Ibid., pp. 160–61.
114. Ibid., p. 51.
115. Ibid., p. 29.

## Chapter 13

1. William C. Harris, *Leroy Pope Walker: Confederate Secretary of War* (Tuscaloosa: Confederate Publishing Company, Inc., 1962), p. 11.
2. William C. Davis, *"A Government of Our Own": The Making of the Confederacy* (New York: The Free Press, 1994), p. 174.
3. Harris, p. 7.
4. Ibid., p. 14.
5. Ibid., p. 16.
6. Ibid., p. 19.
7. Clifford Dowdey, *A History of the Confederacy, 1832–1865* (1952; reprint, New York: Barnes & Noble Books, 1992), p. 81.
8. Ibid.
9. Bryan E. Denny, *Strategic Leadership, Southern Style: Civilian Statesmen in the Confederacy's War*. Thesis presented to the U.S. Army War College (March 2013), p.7.
10. Dowdey, p. 129.
11. James M. McPherson, *Embattled Rebel: Jefferson Davis as Commander in Chief* (New York: Penguin Books, 2014), p. 35.
12. Dowdey, p. 129.
13. Ibid.
14. Rembert W. Patrick, *Jefferson Davis and His Cabinet* (Baton Rouge: Louisiana State University Press, 1944), p. 110.

15. McPherson, p. 19.
16. Harris, p. 29.
17. Ibid., p. 34.
18. Ibid., p. 56.
19. Ibid., p. 71.
20. Steward Sifakis, *Who Was Who in the Civil War* (New York: Facts on File Publications, 1988), p. 685.
21. Harris, p. 95.
22. Davis, p. 363.
23. Harris, p. 98.
24. Davis, p. 361.
25. Patrick, p. 111.
26. Ibid., p. 110.
27. Davis, p. 361.
28. Harris, p. 101.
29. Ibid., p. 110.
30. D. Jonathan White, "Leroy Pope Walker," *Encyclopedia of Alabama* (November 18, 2008). Available at http://www.encyclopediaofalabama.org/face/Artricle.jsp?id=h-1854.
31. Patrick, p. 116.
32. Sifakis, p. 685.
33. Patrick, p. 119.
34. Ibid., p. 120.
35. Harris, p. 120.
36. Sifakis, p. 685.
37. Harris, p. 121.
38. White.
39. Denny, p. 8.

## Chapter 14

1. Alf J. Mapp, "Judah Benjamin: The Smiling Lion," chapter 4 in *Frock Coats and Epaulets* (New York: A.S. Barnes and Company, Inc., 1968), p. 352.
2. An excellent source of information about the background that produced the bridge-burning incident and other conflicts within East Tennessee during the war is Robert Tracy McKenzie, *Lincolnites and Rebels: A Divided Town in the American Civil War* (New York: Oxford University Press, 2006).
3. Bryan E. Denny, *Strategic Leadership, Southern Style: Civilian Statesmen in the Confederacy's War*. Thesis presented to the U.S. Army War College (Marach 2013), p. 9.
4. Mapp, p. 350.
5. Clement Eaton, *Jefferson Davis* (New York: The Free Press, 1977), p. 165.
6. Gamaliel Bradford, *Confederate Portraits* (Boston: Houghton Mifflin Company, 1914), p. 129.
7. Robert Douthat Meade, "The Relations Between Judah P. Benjamin and Jefferson Davis," *The Journal of Southern History* (November 1939), p.473.
8. Bradford, p. 137.
9. Mapp, p. 353.
10. Rembert W. Patrick, *Jefferson Davis and His Cabinet* (Baton Rouge: Louisiana State University Press, 1944), p. 169.
11. Ibid., p. 171.
12. Denny, p. 9.
13. Meade, p. 472.
14. Ibid.
15. Ibid., p. 473.

## Chapter 15

1. Kevin J. Dougherty, *Encyclopedia of the Confederacy* (San Diego: Thunder Bay Press, 2010), p. 226.
2. Joseph Jones, "The Medical History Confederate States Army and Navy," *Southern Historical Society Papers*, Vol. XX (Richmond: Southern Historical Society, January–December 1892), p. 300.
3. James M. McPherson, *Embattled Rebel: Jefferson Davis as Commander in Chief* (New York: Penguin Books, 2014), p. 64.
4. Archer Jones, "Secretary Randolph and Confederate Strategy," *The Virginia Magazine of History and Biography* (January 1953), p. 48.
5. Ludwell H. Johnson, "Trading with the Union: The Evolution of Confederate Policy," *The Virginia Magazine of History and Biography* (July 1970), p. 312.
6. Robert Garlick Hill Kean, *Inside the Confederate Government: The Diary of Robert Garlick Hill Kean* (New York: Oxford University Press, 1957), p. 29.
7. McPherson, p. 113.
8. Kean, p. 30.
9. Ludwell H. Johnson, "Trading with the Union," p. 313.
10. Patrick, p. 30.

## Chapter 16

1. Charles F. Ritter and Jon L. Wakelyn, *Leaders of the American Civil War* (Westport, Conn.: Greenwood Press, 1998), p. 333.
2. Ibid.
3. William J. Cooper Jr., *Jefferson Davis, American* (New York: Vintage Books, 2000), p. 446.
4. Ritter and Wakelyn, p. 335.
5. Clement Eaton, *Jefferson Davis* (New York: The Free Press, 1977), p. 131.
6. Rembert W. Patrick, *Jefferson Davis and*

*His Cabinet* (Baton Rouge: Louisiana State University Press, 1944), p.134.
   7. Robert Garlick Hill Kean, *Inside the Confederate Government: The Diary of Robert Garlick Hill Kean* (New York: Oxford University Press, 1957), p. 33.
   8. *Ibid.*, p. 35.
   9. Patrick, p. 148.
   10. Eaton, p. 131.
   11. Ritter and Wakelyn, p. 335.
   12. Patrick, p. 134.
   13. *Ibid.*, p. 139.
   14. Kean, p. 101.
   15. *Ibid.*, p. 153.
   16. *Ibid.*, pp. 153–54.
   17. James M. McPherson, *Embattled Rebel: Jefferson Davis as Commander in Chief* (New York: Penguin Books, 2014), p. 193.
   18. Kean, p. 161.
   19. William J. Cooper Jr., *Jefferson Davis, American* (New York: Vintage Books, 2000), p. 559.
   20. Ritter and Wakelyn, p. 338.

## Chapter 17

   1. Rembert W. Patrick, *Jefferson Davis and His Cabinet* (Baton Rouge: Louisiana State University Press, 1944), p. 150.
   2. *Ibid.*
   3. *Ibid.*, p. 242.
   4. *Ibid.*
   5. Robert Garlick Hill Kean, *Inside the Confederate Government: The Diary of Robert Garlick Hill Kean* (New York: Oxford University Press, 1957), p. 200.
   6. *Ibid.*, p. 165.
   7. James M. McPherson, *Embattled Rebel: Jefferson Davis as Commander in Chief* (New York: Penguin Books, 2014), p. 226.
   8. *Ibid.*, p. 238.
   9. Patrick, pp. 152–53.
   10. *Ibid.*, p. 153.
   11. *Ibid.*, p. 154.

## Chapter 18

   1. Thomas J. Scharf, *History of the Confederate Navy from Its Organization to the Surrender of Its Last Vessel* (New York: Rogers and Sherwood, 1887.
   2. William N. Still Jr. "Facilities for the Construction of War Vessels in the Confederacy," *The Journal of Southern History*, Vol. 31, no. 3 (August 1965), p. 285.
   3. *Ibid.*, p. 288.
   4. *Ibid.*, pp. 285–290.
   5. *Ibid.*, pp. 294–97.
   6. *Ibid.*, pp. 297–302.
   7. Royce Lee Smith, *Union and Confederate Secretaries of the Navy: A Comparative Study of the Secretaries During the Civil War*. Thesis presented to the faculty of the U.S. Army Command and General Staff College, Fort Leavenworth, Kansas (1995), pp. 3–4.
   8. Scharf, p. 28.
   9. *Ibid.*, p. 29.
   10. *Ibid.*, p. 30.
   11. Tom Henderson Wells, *The Confederate Navy: A Study in Organization* (Tuscaloosa: University of Alabama Press, 1971), p. 13.
   12. *Ibid.*, p. 14.
   13. *Ibid.*, p. 25.
   14. *Ibid.*
   15. *Ibid.*, p. 46.
   16. Smith, p. 59.
   17. Wells, p. 74.
   18. *Ibid.*, p. 79.
   19. *Ibid.*, p. 80.
   20. *Ibid.*, p. 90.
   21. *Ibid.*, p. 93.
   22. *Ibid.*, p. 58.
   23. Smith, p. 60.
   24. Philip Melvin, "Stephen Russell Mallory, Southern Naval Statesman," *Journal of Southern History* (May 1944), p. 156.
   25. R.O. Crowley, "The Confederate Torpedo Service," *The Century* (June 1898). Available at http://www.navyandmarine.org/ondeck/1862ConfTorpedoService.htm.
   26. Friends of the Hunley, "History of the Hunley" (n.d.). Available at http://www.hunley.org.
   27. G.J. Rains, "Torpedoes" (n.d.). Available at http://thomaslegion.net/civil_war_submarines_torpedoes_mines.html.
   28. James Russell Soley, "The Union and Confederate Navies," *Battles and Leaders of the Civil War*, Vol. I. (1887; reprint, Secaucus, N.J.: Castle, 1983), p. 630.
   29. Smith, p. 86.
   30. *Ibid.*
   31. Chester G. Hearn, "The Confederate States Naval Academy," *The Virginia MaGAZINE OF History and Biography*, Vol. 69, no. 3 (July 1961), p. 7.
   32. John Baldwin and Ron Powers, *Last Flag Down* (New York: Random House, 2007), p. 30.
   33. Kevin J. Dougherty, *Encyclopedia of the Confederacy* (San Diego: Thunder Bay Press, 2010), p. 111).
   34. William P. Roberts, "James Dunwoody

Bulloch and the Confederate Navy," *The North Carolina Historical Review*, Vol. 24, no. 3 (July 1947), p. 317.
35. *Ibid.*, p. 318.
36. Smith, p. 87.
37. Roberts, p. 317.
38. *Ibid.*
39. Dougherty, p. 136.
40. Roberts, p. 321.
41. *Ibid.*, p. 326.
42. Wells, pp. vii–viii.
43. *Ibid.*, p. 106.
44. *Ibid.*, p. 129.
45. Still, p. 294.
46. Roberts, p. 331.
47. *Ibid.*, pp. 331–32.
48. *Ibid.*, p. 335.
49. *Ibid.*, p. 343.
50. *Ibid.*, p. 345.
51. *Ibid.*, p. 350.
52. *Ibid.*, p. 352.
53. Baldwin and Powers, p. 384.
54. Dougherty, p. 193.
55. Smith, p. 105.
56. Roberts, p. 330.
57. Hearn, p. xiii.
58. Baldwin and Powers, p. 384.
59. Hearn, p. xiii.
60. *Ibid.*, p. xv.
61. *Ibid.*
62. *Ibid.*, pp. 311–17.
63. G. Melvin Herndon, "The Confederate States Naval Academy," *The Virginia Magazine of History and Biography*, Vol. 69, no. 3 (July 1961), p. 305.
64. Wells, p. 67.
65. Herndon, p. 306.
66. *Ibid.*, p. 310.
67. *Ibid.*, p. 314.
68. Robert V. Bogle, "Defeat Through Default: Confederate Naval Strategy for the Upper Mississippi River and its Tributaries, 1861–1862," *Tennessee Historical Quarterly*, Vol. 27, no. 1 (Spring 1968), p. 62.
69. *Ibid.*, p. 64.
70. *Ibid.*, p. 65.
71. *Ibid.*, p. 71.
72. Wells, p. viii.
73. *Ibid.*, p. 4.
74. *Ibid.*, p. 59.
75. Smith, p. 107.
76. *Ibid.*

## Chapter 19

1. Joseph T. Durkin, *Confederate Navy Chief: Stephen R. Mallory* (Columbia: University of South Carolina Press, 1954), p. ix.
2. *Ibid.*, p. 13.
3. *Ibid.*, p. 17.
4. *Ibid.*, p. 33.
5. *Ibid.*, p. 66.
6. Philip Melvin, "Stephen Russell Mallory, Southern Naval Statesman," *Journal of Southern History* (May 1944), p. 144.
7. *Ibid.*, p. 150.
8. Durkin, p. 133.
9. *Ibid.*, pp. 131–32.
10. Melvin, p. 152.
11. James M. McPherson, *Embattled Rebel: Jefferson Davis as Commander in Chief* (New York: Penguin Books, 2014), p. 6.
12. *Ibid.*, p. 111.
13. Durkin, p. 144.
14. *Ibid.*, p. 146.
15. *Ibid.*, p. 151.
16. Tom Henderson Wells, *The Confederate Navy: A Study in Organization* (Tuscaloosa: University of Alabama Press, 1971), p. 6.
17. Mary Boykin Chesnut, *A Diary from Dixie* (1905; reprint, New York: Gramercy Books, 1997), p. 147.
18. Durkin, p. 344.
19. *Ibid.*, p. 362.
20. *Ibid.*, p. 379.
21. *Ibid.*, p. 355.
22. *Ibid.*, p. 369.
23. *Ibid.*, p. 403.
24. *Ibid.*, pp. 403–404.
25. J. Thomas Scharf, *History of the Confederate Navy from Its Organization to the Surrender of Its Last Vessel* (New York: Rogers and Sherwood, 1887), p. 31.

## Chapter 20

1. Ben H. Proctor, "John H. Reagan and the Confederate Post Office Department," *The Georgia Review* (Winter 1957), p. 393.
2. Walter Flavius McCaleb, "The Organization of the Post-Office Department of the Confederacy," *The American Historical Review* (October 1906), p. 69.
3. *Ibid.*, p. 70.
4. L. R. Garrison, "Administrative Problems of the Confederate Post Office Department, Part I," *The Southwestern Historical Quarterly* (October 1915), p. 113.
5. *Ibid.*, p. 114.
6. *Ibid.*, p. 115.
7. McCaleb, p. 73.
8. *Ibid.*, p. 74.

9. L. R. Garrison, "Administrative Problems of the Confederate Post Office Department, Part II," *The Southwestern Historical Quarterly* (January 1916), p. 236.
10. Ibid.
11. Ibid., p. 237.
12. Ibid., p. 242.
13. Ibid., p. 237.
14. Ibid., p. 243.
15. Ibid., p. 244.
16. Ibid., p. 240.
17. Garrison, "Administrative Problems . . . Part I," p. 118.
18. Ibid., pp. 129–30.
19. Ibid., p. 117.
20. Ibid.

## Chapter 21

1. Walter Flavius McCaleb, "John H. Reagan," *The Quarterly of the Texas State Historical Association* (July 1905), p. 41.
2. Ibid., p. 43.
3. Ibid.
4. Rembert W. Patrick, *Jefferson Davis and His Cabinet* (Baton Rouge: Louisiana State University Press, 1944), p. 275.
5. McCaleb, p. 44.
6. Patrick, p. 274.
7. Ben H. Proctor, "John H. Reagan and the Confederate Post Office Department," *The Georgia Review* (Winter 1957), p. 391.
8. Ibid., p. 392.
9. Ibid., p. 393.
10. Ibid.
11. McCaleb, p. 46.
12. Ibid.
13. Proctor, pp. 395–96.
14. Proctor, p. 397.
15. Patrick, p. 293.
16. Proctor, p. 398.
17. Ibid.
18. McCaleb, p. 47.
19. Clement Eaton, *Jefferson Davis* (New York: The Free Press, 1977), pp. 175–76.
20. McCaleb, p. 46.
21. William J. Cooper Jr., *Jefferson Davis, American* (New York: Vintage Books, 2000), p. 572.
22. McCaleb, p. 48.
23. Ibid., p. 49.
24. Burton J. Hendrick, *Statesmen of the Lost Cause: Jefferson Davis and His Cabinet* (New York: The Literary Guild of America, Inc., 1939), p. 389.
25. William C. Davis, *Look Away! A History of the Confederate States of America* (New York: The Free Press, 2002), p. 370.

## Chapter 22

1. Paul P. Van Riper and Harry N. Scheiber, "The Confederate Civil Service," *The Journal of Southern History* 25(4), 1959, p. 453.
2. Ibid.
3. M. Brem Bonner and Peter McCord, "Reassessment of the Union Blockade's Effectiveness in the Civil War, *The North Carolina Historical Review* (October 2011), p. 384.
4. Ibid.
5. Raphael Semmes, *Memoirs of Service Afloat During the War Between the States* (Baltimore: Kelly, Pict & Co., 1869), pp. 100–101.
6. Kevin J. Weddle, "The Blockade Board of 1861 and Union Naval Strategy," *Civil War History*, Vol. 48, no. 2 (2002), p. 125.
7. Frank Owsley, *King Cotton Diplomacy: Foreign Relations of the Confederate States of America* (Chicago: University of Chicago Press, 1931), p. 250.
8. James M. McPherson, *War on the Waters: The Union and Confederate Navies, 1861–1865* (Chapel Hill: University of North Carolina Press, 2012), p. 32.
9. Ibid., p. 49.
10. Bonner and McCord, pp. 375–82/.
11. Sven Beckert, "Emancipation and Empire: Reconstructing the Worldwide Web of Cotton Production in the Age of the American Civil War," *The American Historical Review* (December 2004), p. 1410.
12. Robert B. Ekelund and Mark Thornton, "The 'Confederate' Blockade of the South," *The Quarterly Journal of Austrian Economics* (Spring 2001), p. 25.
13. Ibid.
14. Owsley, p. 285.
15. Ibid., p. 286.
16. Weddle, p. 127.
17. Ibid., p. 137.
18. Ibid.
19. Beckert, pp. 1405–1438.
20. Owsley, p. 1.
21. Ibid.
22. Ibid., p. 53.
23. Eric H. Walther, *William Lowndes Yancey and the Coming of the Civil War* (Chapel Hill: University of North Carolina Press, 2006), p. 298.
24. Kevin J. Dougherty, *Encyclopedia of the Confederacy* (San Diego: Thunder Bay Press, 2010), p. 304.

25. Walther, p. 299.
26. *Ibid.*
27. *Ibid.*
28. Owsley, p. 53.
29. *Ibid.*
30. Walther, p. 300.
31. *Ibid.*
32. Walther, p. 302.
33. *Ibid.*
34. *Ibid.*, p. 301.
35. Owsley, p. 55.
36. *Ibid.*, p. 57.
37. Edwin De Leon, *Secret History of Confederate Diplomacy Abroad*, ed. William C. Davis (Lawrence: University Press of Kansas, 2005), p. 1.
38. D. MacNeill Fairfax, "Captain Wilkes's Seizure of Mason and Slidell," Part I, in *Battles and Leaders of the Civil War*, Vol. II (Edison, N.J.: Castle, n.d.), p. 135.
39. *Ibid.*, p. 136.
40. *Ibid.*, p. 138.
41. *Ibid.*, p. 139.
42. Christopher Layne, "Kant or Cant: The Myth of the Democratic Peace," *International Security* (Fall 1994), p. 17.
43. *Ibid.*
44. *Ibid.*, p. 18.
45. Stewart Sifakis, *Who Was Who in the Civil War* (New York: Facts on File Publications, 1988), p. 4.
46. *Ibid.*
47. Charles Frances Adams Jr., "The Trent Affair," *The American Historical Review* (April 1912), p. 9.

## Chapter 23

1. Pleasant A. Stovall, *Robert Toombs: Statesman, Speaker, Soldier, Sage* (New York: Cassell Publishing Company, 1892), p. 1.
2. *Ibid.*, p. 5.
3. Gamaliel Bradford, *Confederate Portraits* (Boston: Houghton Mifflin Company, 1914), p. 186.
4. *Ibid.*, p. 197.
5. Stovall, p. 8.
6. *Ibid.*, p. 17.
7. Bradford, p. 186.
8. *Ibid.*, p. 187.
9. *Ibid.*, p. 189.
10. *Ibid.*, pp. 189–90.
11. Stovall, p. 35.
12. *Ibid.*, p. 36.
13. *Ibid.*, p. 38.
14. *Ibid.*, pp. 47–48.
15. *Ibid.*, p. 59.
16. *Ibid.*, p. 83.
17. *Ibid.* p. 95.
18. *Ibid.*, p. 170.
19. *Ibid.*, p. 171.
20. *Ibid.*, p. 174.
21. *Ibid.*, p. 208.
22. Bradford, p. 205.
23. *Ibid.*
24. James M. McPherson, *Embattled Rebel: Jefferson Davis as Commander in Chief* (New York: Penguin Books, 2014), p. 5.
25. Stovall, p. 223.
26. *Ibid.*, p. 224.
27. Bradford, p. 205.
28. Stovall, p. 230.
29. Sam Davis Elliot, *Isham G. Harris of Tennessee* (Baton Rouge: Louisiana State University Press, 2010), p. 68.
30. Stovall, p. 234.
31. Mary Boykin Chesnut, *A Diary from Dixie* (1905; reprint, New York: Gramercy Books, 1997), p. 108.
32. Rembert W. Patrick, *Jefferson Davis and His Cabinet* (Baton Rouge: Louisiana State University Press, 1944), p. 90.
33. Stovall, p. 235.
34. Bradford, p. 210.
35. *Ibid.*, p. 212.
36. Stovall, p. 269.
37. *Ibid.*, p. 241.
38. Jacob D. Cox, "The Battle of Antietam," in *Battles and Leaders of the Civil War*, Vol. II, *The Struggle Intensifies* (Edison, N.J.: Castle, n.d.), p. 649.
39. *Ibid.*, p. 650.
40. *Ibid.*
41. Stovall, p. 264.
42. *Ibid.*, p. 268.
43. James Longstreet, "The Invasion of Maryland," in *Battles and Leaders of the Civil War*, Vol. II, *The Struggle Intensifies* (Edison, N.J.: Castle, n.d.), p. 670.
44. Stovall, p. 277.
45. *Ibid.*, p. 282.
46. *Ibid.*, p. 287.
47. William Y. Thompson, "Robert Toombs, Man without a Country," *The Georgia Historical Quarterly* (June 1962), p. 167.
48. Stovall, p. 316.
49. Thompson, p. 162.
50. *Ibid.*
51. Stovall, p. 319.
52. *Ibid.*, p. 329.
53. Bradford, p. 215.
54. Stovall, p. 364.

55. Bradford, p. 197.
56. Ibid., p. 215.
57. Ibid.

## Chapter 24

1. "Essex County History 1834–1865, R.M.T. Hunter," Essex, Virginia, Museum. Available at http://essexmuseum.org/history-rmt-hunter.htm.
2. Rembert W. Patrick, *Jefferson Davis and His Cabinet* (Baton Rouge: Louisiana State University Press, 1944), p. 91.
3. William S. Hitchcock, "Southern Moderates and Secession: Senator Robert M.T. Hunter's Call for Union," *The Journal of American History* (March 1973), p. 871.
4. Ibid., p. 873.
5. Ibid.
6. Ibid., p. 874.
7. Ibid., p. 879.
8. Hitchcock, p. 880.
9. Mary Boykin Chesnut, *A Diary from Dixie* (1905; reprint, New York: Gramercy Books, 1997), p. 54.
10. Patrick, p. 94.
11. Ibid., pp. 94–95.
12. Kevin J. Dougherty, *Encyclopedia of the Confederacy* (San Diego: Thunder Bay Press, 2010), p. 95.
13. William C. Davis, *Look Away! A History of the Confederate States of America* (New York: The Free Press, 2002), p. 412.
14. William C. Davis, *"A Government of Our Own": The Making of the Confederacy* (New York: The Free Press, 1994), p. 412.
15. Robert Garlick Hill Kean, *Inside the Confederate Government: The Diary of Robert Garlick Hill Kean* (New York: Oxford University Press, 1957), p. 185.

## Chapter 25

1. Rembert W. Patrick, *Jefferson Davis and His Cabinet* (Baton Rouge: Louisiana State University Press, 1944), p. 182.
2. Stewart Sifakis, *Who Was Who in the Civil War* (New York: Facts on File Publications, 1988), p. 50.
3. Clement Eaton, *Jefferson Davis* (New York: The Free Press, 1977), p. 168.
4. Patrick, p. 200.
5. Alf J. Mapp Jr., "Judah Benjamin: The Smiling Lion," chapter 4 in *Frock Coats and Epaulets* (New York: A.S. Barnes and Company, Inc., 1968), p. 359.
6. Ibid.
7. Ibid., p. 362.

## Conclusion

1. William C. Davis, *"A Government of Our Own": The Making of the Confederacy* (New York: The Free Press, 1994), p. 170.
2. Ibid., pp. 197–98.
3. Ibid., p. 330.
4. H. W. Crocker, *Robert E. Lee on Leadership* (Roseville, Calif.: Prima Publishing, 2000), p. 66.
5. Rembert W. Patrick, *Jefferson Davis and His Cabinet* (Baton Rouge: Louisiana State University Press, 1944), pp. 34–35.
6. Ibid., p. 49.
7. Clement Eaton, *Jefferson Davis* (New York: The Free Press, 1977), p. 128.
8. William J. Cooper Jr., *Jefferson Davis, American* (New York: Vintage Books, 2000), p. 549.
9. Ibid.
10. Patrick, p. 35.
11. F. N. Boney, "John Letcher's Secret Criticism of the Confederate Cabinet," *The Virginia Magazine of History and biography* (July 1964), p. 351.
12. Patrick, p. 48.

# Bibliography

## Print Sources

Adams, Charles Francis, Jr. "The Trent Affair." *The American Historical Review* (April 1912): 539–45.

*American Journal of Surgery*, Vol. 164, no. 4 (October 1992): 361–65.

Anderson, Bern. "The Union Blockade," chapter 13 of *By Sea and By River: The Naval History of the Civil War*. New York: Alfred A. Knopf, 1962.

Baldwin, John, and Ron Powers. *Last Flag Down*. New York: Random House, 2007.

Bauer, Craig A. "The Last Effort: The Secret Mission of the Confederate Diplomat Duncan F. Kenner." *Louisiana History: The Journal of the Louisiana Historical Association*, Vol. 22, No. 1 (Winter 1981): 67–95.

Beard, W.E. "The Confederate Government, 1861–1865." *Tennessee Historical Magazine* (June 1915): 120–128.

Beckert, Sven. "Emancipation and Empire: Reconstructing the Worldwide Web of Cotton Production in the Age of the American Civil War." *The American Historical Review* (December 2004): 1405–1438.

Beringer, Richard E. "A Profile of the Members of the Confederate Congress." *The Journal of Southern History* (November 1967): 518–541.

Blumenthal, Henry. "Confederate Diplomacy: Popular Notions and International Realities." *The Journal of Southern History* (May 1966): 151–171.

Bogle, Robert V. "Defeat Through Default: Confederate Naval Strategy for the Upper Mississippi River and its Tributaries, 1861–1862." *Tennessee Historical Quarterly*, Vol. 27, No. 1 (Spring 1968): 62–71.

Boney, F.N. "John Letcher's Secret Criticism of the Confederate Cabinet." *The Virginia Magazine of History and Biography* (July 1964): 348–355.

Bonner, M. Brem, and Peter McCord. "Reassessment of the Union Blockade's Effectiveness in the Civil War." *The North Carolina Historical Review* (October 2011): 375–398.

Bradford, Gamaliel. *Confederate Portraits*. Boston: Houghton Mifflin Company, 1914.

Browning, Robert M. *From Cape Charles to Cape Fear: The North Atlantic Blockading Squadron during the Civil War*. Tuscaloosa: University of Alabama Press, 1993.

Capers, Henry. *The Life and Times of C.G. Memminger*. Richmond: Everett Waddey Co., Publishers, 1893.

Chesnut, Mary Boykin. *A Diary from Dixie*. 1905. Reprint, New York: Gramercy Books, 1997.

Cleland, Robert G. "Jefferson Davis and the Confederate Congress." *The Southwestern Historical Quarterly* (January 1916): 213–231.

Connelly, Thomas Lawrence, and Archer Jones. *The Politics of Command: Factions and Ideas in Confederate Strategy*. Baton Rouge: Louisiana State University Press, 1973.

Cooper, William J., Jr. *Jefferson Davis, American*. New York: Vintage Books, 2000.

Cox, Jacob D. "The Battle of Antietam," pp. 330–60 in *Battles and Leaders of the Civil War*, Vol. II, *The Struggle Intensifies*. Edison, N.J.: Castle, n.d.

Crocker, H.W. *Doctors in Gray: The Confederate Medical Service*. Baton Rouge: Louisiana State University Press, 1958.

_____. *Robert E. Lee on Leadership*. Roseville, CA: Prima Publishing, 2000.

Curry, J.L.M. *Civil History of the Government of the Confederate States*. Richmond: B.F. Johnson Publishing Company, 1901.

Davis, Jefferson. *The Rise and Fall of the Confederate Government*. New York: D. Appleton, 1881: 241–43.

_____. *A Short History of the Confederate States of America*. 1890; reprint, Harrisonburg, VA: Sprinkle Publications, 2002.

Davis, William C. *"A Government of Our Own": The Making of the Confederacy*. New York: The Free Press, 1994.

_____. *Look Away! A History of the Confederate States of America*. New York: The Free Press, 2002.

De Leon, Edwin. *Secret History of Confederate Diplomacy Abroad*, ed. William C. Davis. Lawrence: University Press of Kansas, 2005.

Denny, Bryan E. *Strategic Leadership, Southern Style: Civilian Statesmen in the Confederacy's War*. Thesis presented to the U.S. Army War College, March 2013.

Dougherty, Kevin J. *Encyclopedia of the Confederacy*. San Diego: Thunder Bay Press, 2010.

Dowdey, Clifford. *A History of the Confederacy, 1832–1865*. 1952. Reprint, New York: Barnes & Noble Books, 1992.

Durkin, Joseph T. *Confederate Navy Chief: Stephen R. Mallory*. Columbia: University of South Carolina Press, 1954.

Dyson, B. Patricia. "Contract Stability in Wartime: The Example of the Confederacy." *The American Journal of Legal History* (July 1975): 216–231.

Eaton, Clement. *Jefferson Davis*. New York: The Free Press, 1977.

Eicher, David J. "A Curious Cabinet," pp. 63–76 in *Dixie Betrayed: How the South Really Lost the Civil War*. Lincoln: University of Nebraska Press, 2006.

Ekelund, Robert B., and Mark Thornton. "The 'Confederate' Blockade of the South." *The Quarterly Journal of Austrian Economics* (Spring 200): 23–42.

Elliott, Sam Davis. *Isham G. Harris of Tennessee*. Baton Rouge: Louisiana State University Press, 2010.

Fairfax, D. MacNeill. "Captain Wilkes's Seizure of Mason and Slidell," Part I, pp. 135–42 in *Battles and Leaders of the Civil War*, vol. II. Edison, N.J.: Castle.

Falk, Stanley L. "Jefferson Davis and Josiah Gorgas, an Appointment of Necessity." *The Journal of Southern History*, Vol. 28, No. 1 (February 1962): 84–86.

Felt, Jeremy P. "Lucius P. Northrop and the Confederacy's Subsistence Department." *The Virginia Magazine of History and Biography* (April 1961): 181–193.

Fisher, John E. "Statesman of a Lost Cause: The Career of R.M.T. Hunter, 1859–1887." PhD dissertation, University of Virginia, 1966.

Fox, Stephen. *Wolf of the Deep: Raphael Semmes and the Notorious Raider CSS Alabama*. New York: Alfred A. Knopf, 2007.

Garrison, L.R. "Administrative Problems of the Confederate Post Office Department, Part I." *The Southwestern Historical Quarterly* (October 1915): 111–141.

_____. "Administrative Problems of the Confederate Post Office Department, Part II." *The Southwestern Historical Quarterly* (January 1916): 232–250.

Gentry, Judith Fenner. "A Confederate Success in Europe: The Erlanger Loan." *The Journal of Southern History* (May 1980): 157–188.

Hamilton, J.G. de Roulhac. "The State Courts and the Confederate Constitution." *The Journal of Southern History* (November 1938): 425–448.

Harris, William C. *Leroy Pope Walker: Confederate Secretary of War*. Tuscaloosa: Confederate Publishing Company, Inc., 1962.

Hearn, Chester G. *Gray Raiders of the Sea: How Eight Confederate Warships Destroyed the Union's High Seas Commerce*. Camden, ME: International Marine Publishing, 1992.

Hendrick, Burton J. *Statesmen of the Lost Cause: Jefferson Davis and His Cabinet*. New York: The Literary Guild of America, Inc., 1939.

Herndon, G. Melvin. "The Confederate States Naval Academy." *The Virginia Magazine of History and Biography*, Vol. 69, No. 3 (July 1961): 300–323.

Hitchcock, William S. "Southern Moderates and Secession: Senator Robert M.T. Hunter's Call for Union." *The Journal of American History* (March 1973): 871–84.

Hubbard, Charles M. *The Burden of Confederate Diplomacy*. Knoxville: University of Tennessee Press, 1998.

Hunter, Martha. *A Memoir of Robert M.T. Hunter*. Washington: The Neale Publishing Company, 1903.

Huntington, Tom. "The Hunley." *Invention & Technology* (Spring 2005): 39–46.

Johnson, Ludwell H. "Fort Sumter and Confederate Diplomacy." *The Journal of Southern*

History, Vol. 26, No. 4 (November, 1960): 441–477.
_____. "Trading with the Union: The Evolution of Confederate Policy." *The Virginia Magazine of History and Biography* (July 1970): 308–325.
Jones, Archer. "Secretary Randolph and Confederate Strategy." *The Virginia Magazine of History and Biography* (January 195): 45–59.
_____. "Some Aspects of George W. Randolph's Service as Confederate Secretary of War." *The Virginia Magazine of History and Biography* (January 1953): 45–59.
Jones, Joseph. "The Medical History Confederate States Army and Navy." *Southern Historical Society Papers*, Vol. XX, Richmond, Virginia (January–December 1892).
Jones, Wilmer L. "Davis's Generals," pp. 23–44 in *Generals in Blue and Gray*, Vol. II. Mechanicsburg, PA: Stackpole Books, 2004.
Kean, Robert Garlick Hill. *Inside the Confederate Government: The Diary of Robert Garlick Hill Kean*. New York: Oxford University Press, 1957.
Kurtz, Joel. "Confederate Railroads: Changing Priorities during the War Years." Senior Research Projects, Paper 3 (2010).
Layne, Christopher. "Kant or Cant: The Myth of the Democratic Peace." *International Security* (Fall 1994): 5–49.
Lebergott, Stanley. "Why the South Lost: Commercial Purpose in the Confederacy, 1861–1865." *The Journal of American History*, Vol. 70, No. 1 (June 1983): 58–74.
Lerner, Eugene M. "The Monetary and Fiscal Programs of the Confederate Government, 1861–65, Part I." *Journal of Political Economy* (February 1954): 506–522.
_____. "Money, Prices, and Wages in the Confederacy, 1861–65, Part II." *Journal of Political Economy* (February 1955): 20–40.
Longstreet, James. "The Invasion of Maryland," pp. 663–74 in *Battles and Leaders of the Civil War*, Vol. II, *The Struggle Intensifies*. Edison, N.J.: Castle, n.d.
Loy, Wesley. "10 Rumford Place: Doing Confederate Business in Liverpool." *The South Carolina Historical Magazine*, Vol. 98, No. 4 (October 1997): 349–74.
Luthin, Reinhard H. "Abraham Lincoln and the Tariff." *The American Historical Review* (July 1944): 609–29.
Mapp, Alf J., Jr. "Judah Benjamin: The Smiling Lion," chapter 4 in *Frock Coats and Epaulets*. New York: A.S. Barnes and Company, Inc., 1968: 332–65.

Marinez, Adrian T. *Mobilizing the Confederate Industrial Base for Total War*. Thesis presented to the U.S. Marine Corps Command and Staff College, March 25, 2011.
McCaleb, Walter Flavius. "John H. Reagan." *The Quarterly of the Texas State Historical Association* (July 1905): 41–50.
_____. "The Organization of the Post-Office Department of the Confederacy." *The American Historical Review* (October 1906): 66–74.
McKenzie, Robert Tracy. *Lincolnites and Rebels: A Divided Town in the American Civil War*. New York: Oxford University Press, 2006.
McPherson, James M. *Embattled Rebel: Jefferson Davis as Commander in Chief*. New York: Penguin Books, 2014.
_____. *War on the Waters: The Union and Confederate Navies, 1861–1865*. Chapel Hill: University of North Carolina Press, 2012.
Meade, Robert Douthat. "The Relations Between Judah P. Benjamin and Jefferson Davis." *The Journal of Southern History* (November 1939): 468–478.
Melvin, Philip. "Stephen Russell Mallory, Southern Naval Statesman." *The Journal of Southern History* (May 1944): 137–160.
Minter, Winfred P. "Confederate Military Supply Policy." *Social Science* (June 1959): 163–171.
Moore, Richard Randall. "Robert M.T. Hunter and the Crisis of the Union, 1860–1861." *Southern Historian* (Spring 1992): 25–35.
Niven, Alexander C. "Joseph E. Brown, Confederate Obstructionist." *The Georgia Historical Quarterly* (September 1958): 233–257.
Owsley, Frank. *King Cotton Diplomacy: Foreign Relations of the Confederate States of America*. Chicago: University of Chicago Press, 1931.
Paciorek, Jessica. "Medicine and Its Practice during the American Civil War." *TCNJ Journal of Student Scholarship* (April 2007).
Patrick, Rembert W. *Jefferson Davis and His Cabinet*. Baton Rouge: Louisiana State University Press, 1944.
Patto, Carl Vernon, "Budgeting Under Crisis: The Confederacy as a Poor Country." *Administrative Science Quarterly*, Vol. 20, No. 3 (September 1975): 355–70.
Proctor, Ben H. "John H. Reagan and the Confederate Post Office Department." *The Georgia Review* (Winter 1957): 387–399.
Rabun, James Z. "Alexander H. Stephens and Jefferson Davis." *The American Historical Review* (January 1953): 290–321.
Ramsdell, Charles W. "General Robert E. Lee's

Horse Supply, 1862–1865." *The American Historical Review* (July 1930): 758–777.

Rhett, R. Barnwell. "The Confederate Government at Montgomery," pp. 99–110 in *Battles and Leaders of the Civil War*, Vol. I. 1887. Reprint, Secaucus, N.J.: Castle, 1983.

Ritter, Charles F., and Jon L. Wakelyn. *Leaders of the American Civil War*. Westport, CT: Greenwood Press, 1998.

Roberts, William P. "James Dunwoody Bulloch and the Confederate Navy." *The North Carolina Historical Review*, Vol. 24, No. 3 (July 1947): 315–366.

Robbins, John B. "The Confederacy and the Writ of Habeas Corpus." *Georgia Historical Review* (Spring 1971): 83–101.

Robinson, William M., Jr. "Legal System of the Confederate States." *The Journal of Southern History* (November 1936): 453–467.

Scharf, J. Thomas. *History of the Confederate Navy from Its Organization to the Surrender of Its Last Vessel*. New York: Rogers and Sherwood, 1887.

Schrer-Lein, Glenna R. *Confederate Hospitals On the Move: Samuel H. Stout and the Army of Tennessee*. Columbia: University of South Carolina Press, 1994.

Scott, Carole E. "Coping with Inflation: Atlanta, 1860–1865." *The Georgia Historical Quarterly*. (Winter 1985), 536–556.

Sellers, James L. "The Economic Incidence of the Civil War in the South." *The Mississippi Valley Historical Review*, Vol. 14, No. 2 (Sept. 1927): 179–91.

Semmes, Raphael. *Memoirs of Service Afloat During the War Between the States*. Baltimore: Kelly, Pict & Co., 1869.

Seth Fred D., Jr. "'Gittin' Stuff': Equipping Confederate Armies at the Onset of the Civil War (1861–1862)." *NPMA*, Vol. 16, no. 3 (2004): 16–27.

_____. "'Gittin' Stuff': Towards Total War and Confederate Mobilization (1863– 1864)." *Party Professional*, Vol. 17, no. 3 (2005): 22–33.

_____. "'Gittin' Stuff': The Impact of Equipment Management, Supply & Logistics on Confederate Defeat." *Property Professional*, Vol. 18, no. 2 (2006): 8–21.

Sharrer, G. Terry. "The Great Glanders Epizootic, 1861–1866: A Civil War Legacy." *Agricultural History* (Winter 1995): 79–97.

Shaw, William L. "The Confederate Conscription and Exemption Acts." *The American Journal of Legal History* (October 1962): 368–405.

Sifakis, Stewart. *Who Was Who in the Civil War*. New York: Facts on File Publications, 1988.

Smith, Andrew F. "Did Hunger Defeat the Confederacy?" *North & South* (May 2011): 40–46.

Smith, Royce Lee. *Union and Confederate Secretaries of the Navy: A Comparative Study of the Secretaries During the Civil War*. Thesis presented to the faculty of the U.S. Army Command and General Staff College, Fort Leavenworth, Kansas, 1995.

_____. "The Union and Confederate Navies," pp. 611–31 in *Battles and Leaders of the Civil War*, Vol. I, 611–31. 1887. Reprint, Secaucus, N.J.: Castle, 1983.

Stephens, Alexander. *A Constitutional View of the Late War Between the States*. Philadelphia: The National Publishing Co., 1868–1870.

Still, William N., Jr. "Facilities for the Construction of War Vessels in the Confederacy." *The Journal of Southern History*, Vol. 31, no. 3 (August, 1965): 285–304.

Stovall, Pleasant A. *Robert Toombs: Statesman, Speaker, Soldier, Sage*. New York: Cassell Publishing Company, 1892.

Surdam, David G. "King Cotton: Monarch or Pretender? The State of the Market for Raw Cotton on the Eve of the American Civil War." *The Economic History Review*, Vol. 51, no. 1 (1998): 113–132.

Thomas, Emory. The *Confederate Nation, 1861– 1865*. New York: Harper Perennial, 1979.

Thompson, William Y. "Robert Toombs, Man without a Country." *The Georgia Historical Quarterly* (June 1962): 162–68.

Todd, Bernhard. "The Produce Loans: A Means of Financing the Confederacy." *The North Carolina Historical Review*, Vol. 27, No. 1 (Jan. 1950): 46–74.

Todd, Richard. "C.G. Memminger and the Confederate Treasury Department." *The Georgia Review* (Winter 1958): 396–410.

Vandiver, Frank E. "Makeshifts of Confederate Ordnance." *The Journal of Southern History*, Vol. 17, No. 2 (May 1951): 180–93.

Van Riper, Paul P., and Harry N. Scheiber. "The Confederate Civil Service." *The Journal of Southern History*, Vol. 25, no. 4 (1959): 448–70.

Waklyn, J. L. "Josiah Gorgas (July 1, 1818–May 8, 1893)." In *Leaders of the American Civil War: A Biographical and Historiographical Dictionary*. New York: Routledge, 2013, 146–52.

Walmsley, James Elliott. "The Last Meeting of the Confederate Cabinet." *The Mississippi*

*Valley Historical Review*, Vol. VI, No. 3 (December 1, 1919): 336–349.

Walther, Eric H. *William Lowndes Yancey and the Coming of the Civil War.* Chapel Hill: University of North Carolina Press, 2006.

Washburn, Benjamin M., IV. *An Analysis of Confederate Subsistence Logistics.* Thesis presented to the Air Force Institute of Technology, September 1989.

Waters, W. Davis. "'Deception Is the Art of War': Gabriel J. Rains, Torpedo Specialist of the Confederacy." *The North Carolina Historical Review* (January 1989): 29–60.

Watkins, Sam. *Co. Aytch: A Side Show of the Big Show.* New York: Collier Books, 1962.

Waugh, John C. *The Class of 1846: From West Point to Appomattox: Stonewall Jackson, George McClellan and Their Brothers.* New York: Warner Books, 1994.

Weddle, Kevin J. "The Blockade Board of 1861 and Union Naval Strategy." *Civil War History,* Vol. 48, no. 2 (2002): 123–142.

Wells, Tom Henderson. *The Confederate Navy: A Study in Organization.* Tuscaloosa: University of Alabama Press, 1971.

Wight, Willard E., and Lucius Bellinger Northrop. "Some Letters of Lucius Bellinger Northrop, 1860–1865." *The Virginia Magazine of History and Biography.*

Wilson, Harold S. *Confederate Industry: Manufacturers and Quartermasters in the Civil War.* Jackson: University Press of Mississippi, 2002.

Wise, Stephen. *Lifeline of the Confederacy: The North Atlantic Blockading Squadron during the Civil War,* 1993.

## Electronic Sources

Adams, W. Thad., III. "Confederate Patent Office." N.d. Available at http:www.adamspat.com/Chapter1.html.

Adelman, Joseph M. "USPS Folly Was Foreshadowed by Confederate Post Office." Available at http://civilwartalk.com/threads/usps-folly-was-foreshadowed-by-confederate-post-office.80541.

Albin, Maurice S. "The Use of Anesthetics During the Civil War." *Pharmacy in History,* Vol. 42, no. 3/4, *Civil War Pharmacy* (2000), 99–114. Available at http://www.jstor.org/stable/41112682.

"Alexander Stephens." Available at www.biography.com/people/alexander-stephens-21013555.

Barry, Craig L. "C.S. Supplies and Logistics." *Civil War News,* May 2010. Available at http://www.civilwarnews.com/watchdog/wd_051001.html.

Billies, Richard. "The Trent Affair." Available at http://northagainstsouth.com/the-trent-affair.

_____. "The Union Blockade." Part 3 of *The Civil War at Sea* series. Available at http://northagainstsouth.com/the-union-blockade/.

Browning, Robert M. "More Than Just Blockade Duty." *Naval History Magazine,* December 2009. Available at http://www.usni.org/magazines/navalhistory/2009-12/more-just-blockade-duty.

Bollett, Alfred J. "The Truth About Civil War Surgery." Available http://www.historynet.com/the-truth-about-civil-war-surgery-2.htm.

"The Capture of the Rebel Commissioners to Europe." *Harper's Weekly* (November 30, 1861). Available at http://www.sonsofthesouth.net/leefoundation/civil-war/1861/november/trent-affair.htm.

Clark, M.H. "The Last Days of the Confederate Treasury and What Became of Its Specie." *Southern Historical Society Papers,* Vol. 9, J. William Jones, ed. Available www.perseus.tufts.edu/hopper/text?doc=Perseus%3A2001.05.0122%3Achapter%3DII.III .

"Confederate Attorneys General." *West's Encyclopedia of American Law.* The Gale Group, Inc., 2005. Available at http://www.encyclopedia.com/doc/1G2-3437701043.html.

Confederate States of America, Post-Office Department. "Instructions to Post-Masters." Richmond: Ritchie & Dunnavant, 1861. Available at http://docsouth.unc.edu/imls/postmaster/postmaster.html.

Cross, Jerry L. "Thomas Bragg—Governor: 1855–1859." Research Branch, North Carolina Office of Archives and History, 2004. Available at http://www.ncmarkers.com

Crowley, R.O. "The Confederate Torpedo Service." *The Century.* June 1898. Available at http://www.navyandmarine.org/ondeck/1862ConfTorpedoService.htm.

Crumbley, Tony L. "Confederate Postal Service." N.d. Available at http://ncpedia.org/confederate-postal-service.

Cunningham, H. H. "Organization and Administration of the Confederate Medical Department." *The North Carolina Historical Review,* Vol. 31, no. 3 (July, 1954): 385–409. Available at http://www.jstor.org/stable/23516827.

Doyle, Brooke Graham. "Hyperinflation and the Confederacy: An Interdisciplinary Lesson in Economics and History." N.d. Available at http://www.socialstudies.org/system/files/publications/se/6506/650607.html.

Encyclopedia of Alabama, "Thomas Hill Watts (1863–65)." Available at http://www.encyclopediaofalabama.org/article/m-2650.

"Essex County History 1834–1865, R.M.T. Hunter." Essex, Virginia, Museum. Available at http://essexmuseum.org/history-rmt-hunter.htm.

Evans, Eli N. "Judah Benjamin." In "The Confederacy." *Macmillan Information Now Encyclopedia*. Available at http://www.civilwarhome.com/benjaminbio.htm.

Friends of the Hunley. "History of the Hunley." N.d. Available at http://www.hunley.org.

Hasegawa, Guy R. "Pharmacy in the American Civil War." *Pharmacy in History*, Vol. 42, no. 3/4, Civil War Pharmacy (2000), pp. 67–86. Available http://www.jstor.org/stable/41112679.

Hunt, Peter. "Naval Warfare in the American Civil War." Available at http://hksw.org/american%20civil%20war_naval%20part%20II.htm.

Hunter, R.M.T. "Origin of the Late War." Available at http://www.perseus.tufts.edu/hopper/text?doc=Perseus%3Atext%3A2001.05.0001.

Karp, Matthew. "Arsenal of Empire: Southern Slaveholders and the U.S. Military in the 1850s." *Common-Place* (July 2012). Available at http://www.common-place.org/vol-12/no-04/Karp/.

Kaufmann, Patricia A. "Postmaster Provisionals: Confederate Stamp Primer Online." N.d. Available at http://www.csadealer.com/postmaster-provisionals.php.

———. "The Printers: Confederate Stamp Primer Online." N.d. Available at http://www.csadealer.com/primer-printers.php.

Keyes, Wade. "Annual Report to the President. Richmond: Confederate States of America, Department of Justice, 1863." Available at https://archive.org/details/reportofattorney01general.conf.

"Leroy Pope Walker." *Confederate Military History*. Available at http://www.civilwarreference.com/people/index.php?peopleID=2%.

McKiven, Henry M., Jr. "Thomas Hill Watts (1863–65)." *Encyclopedia of Alabama*, August 11, 2008. Available at http://www.encyclopediaofalabama.org/face/Article.jsp?id=h-1630.

McPherson, James M. "War on the Waters: An Interview with James McPherson." Civil War Trust. Available at http://www.civil_war.org/books/interviews/james-mcpherson—-war-on-the-waters/war-on-the-waters.html.

Morgan, Chad. "Alexander Stephens (1812–1883)." *North Georgia Encyclopedia* (September 27, 2004). Available http://www.georgiaencyclopedia.org/articles/history-archaeology/alexander-stephens-1812-1883.

*New York Times.* "Postal Service in the Southern Confederacy." May 24, 1861. Available at http://www.nytimes.com/1861/05/24/news/postal-service-in-the-southern-confederacy.html.

North Carolina History Project. "Thomas Bragg (1810–1872)." N.d. Available at http://www.northcarolinahistory.org/encyclopedia/501/entry.

Rable, George C. "Confederate Government." Essential Civil War Curriculum, 2010. Available at http://www.essential.civilwar.vt.edu/assets/files/ECWC%20TOPIC%20Confederate%20Government%20Essay.pdf.

Rains, G.J. "Torpedoes." N.d. Available at http://thomaslegion.net/civil_war_submarines_torpedoes_mines.html.

Roberts, Deering J. "Organization of the Confederate Medical Department." available at http://medicalantiques.com/civilwar/Civil_War_Articles/Confederate_Army_Surgeons.htm.

Soley, James Russell. "Blockade! The Blockading of Southern Seaports during the Civil War." N.d. Available at http://www.civilwar.org/education/history/navy-hub/navy-history/blockade.html.

"Thomas Bragg (1810–1872)." North Carolina History Project. Available at http://www.northcarolinahistory.org/encyclopedia/501/entry.

Thuersam, Bernhard. "George Davis: Christian, Senator, Attorney General" (Wilmington, N.C.: Cape Fear Historical Institute, 2006). Available at http://www.cfhi.net/GeorgeDavisChristianSenatorAttorneyGeneral.php.

U.S. Army. "The Civil War, 1861," chapter 9 of *American Military History*. Updated 27 April 2001. Available at http://www.history.army.mil/books/AMH/AMH-09.htm.

U.S. Congress. "Toombs, Robert Augustus (1810–1885)." Available at http://bioguide.congress.gov/scripts/biodisplay.pl?index=T000313.

U.S. Postal Service. "The Confederate Post Office Department." N.d. Available at http://www.csadealer.com/primer-printers.php.

U.S. State Department. "The Trent Affair." Available at http://future.state.gov/when/timeline/1861-_timeline/trent_affair.html.

White, D. Jonathan. "Leroy Pope Walker." *Encyclopedia of Alabama*. November 18, 2008. Available at http://www.encyclopediaofalabama.org/face/Article.jsp?id=h-1854.

# Index

Adams, Charles Francis 176, 211, 225
Adjutant and Inspector General 92–94, 116
*Alabama* 177, 180, 181
Alabama 9, 51, 63, 76, 91
American Party *see* Know-Nothing Party
amputations 104
Anaconda Plan 184
Andersonville Prison 151
Antietam 118, 150, 232–33; *see also* Sharpsburg
Appomattox 101, 116, 124, 241
appropriations 9, 30, 255; for military medical departments 105; for naval academy 183
Arkansas 13, 231, 247
Army of Northern Virginia 101, 124, 150, 159
Army of Tennessee 124, 127, 153, 158
Atlanta 71, 99, 152, 233
attorneys general 9, 33, 37, 52, 58, 121; list of 32

banks 63, 65, 76, 161
Banks, Nathaniel 106
Bayne, Thomas L. 115
Beauregard, P.G.T. 109, 127, 128, 133, 134, 141, 142, 160, 174, 206, 231
Bell, John 151, 156, 229
Benjamin, Judah P. 11, 14, 15, 16, 17, 21, 24, 57, 74, 84, 136, 160, 247; as attorney general 40–46; as secretary of state 242–44; as secretary of war 139–42
Bermuda 69, 82, 104, 111
blockade 214–18
blockade runners 80, 104, 184, 212, 217
Blockade Strategy Board 217–18
Bragg, Braxton 16, 84, 120, 124, 127, 134
Bragg, Thomas 19, 32, 47–49
Breckinridge, John C. 11, 15, 100, 131; as general 156; as presidential candidate 131, 156–57; as secretary of war 152, 159–62; as vice president 156

Brooke, John 169, 182
Brown, John 113, 228
Brown, Joseph 21–22, 34, 52, 151
Buchanan, James 51, 109, 156, 188
Bulloch, James Dunwoody 176–79, 190
Bureau of Conscription 116–22
Bureau of Exchange 115–16
Bureau of Foreign Supplies 109, 115
Bureau of Indian Affairs 123
Bureau of War 112–14

cabinet departments *see* cabinet members
cabinet members characteristics of 15–16; list of 19; selection of 11–14; *see also* individual cabinet members
Calhoun, John C. 22, 149
Camp Robinson 118
Capers, Henry 61
Charleston 134, 156, 171, 173–75
Charlotte 114
Chesnut, Mary 44, 100, 114, 191, 216, 231, 240
Chickamauga 98, 158
Chimborazo 106
Cobb, Howell 12, 14, 76, 228
commerce raiders 126, 177, 180–85, 191
Commissary General of Subsistence 98–101, 122
Compromise of 1850 228
Confederate Civil Service 23–24
Confederate Congress 8, 9, 16, 17, 34, 49, 58; and conscription 34, 35, 117, 118, 126; and paper
Confederate Constitution 7, 30–31, 251–61; differences from U.S. Constitution 8–9
Confederate executive branch 7–10, 11–14, 16–24
Confederate Naval Academy 167, 169, 182–83
Confederate Ordnance Laboratories 112

283

conscription  22, 33, 34, 99, 120, 126, 144–45, 200, 206
Conscription Acts  22, 34–36, 121, 200, 233; of April 16, 1862 52; of February 17, 1864 118; of September 27, 1862 118; *see also* Bureau of Conscription
Constitutional Union Party  15, 51, 229
Cooper, Samuel  93–94
cordon defense  91, 127

Davis, George  11, 37, 55, 56–58, 84
Davis, Jefferson  7, 16; capture of 84, 207; inability to delegate 12, 18, 25, 89–90; opposition to 21–22, 52, 91, 117; priorities of 10; reactions of contemporaries 7–8; selection of cabinet 11–19; tendency to micromanage 12, 18, 24, 91, 127, 135, 150, 153, 159, 211, 245, 246
DeBow, J.D. B.  64
Declaration of Paris  214, 219
DeLeon, David C.  102
Democrat Party  13, 49
departmental system  126–27
desertion  120, 122, 151
Douglas, Stephen  15, 48, 51, 138, 156, 227, 229, 238
draft *see* conscription
Drewry's Bluff  172

Eastern theater  17, 91, 99, 128, 145
Emile Erlanger and Company  65–66
Engineer Bureau  24
*Enrica see Alabama*
Erlanger, Emile  65–66
Erlanger loan  69, 80, 179
Exemption Act of 1862  34, 119
Exemption Act of 1864  120
exemptions from draft  34–36, 119, 120

Fairfax, D. MacNeill  223, 224
Farragut, David  173
Fillmore, Millard  51, 238
Flat Rock  77, 78
*Florida*  177, 180, 181
Florida  7, 99, 127, 188, 189
Floyd, John  109
Force Bill  22, 227
Foreign Enlistment Act  176
Fort Caswell  172
Fort Donelson  184
Fort Fisher  172
Fort Hamilton  58
Fort Henry  184
Fort Lafayette  192
Fort Monroe  224
Fort Pulaski  82, 97, 134, 152, 153, 241
Fort Sanders  98
Fort Sumter  80, 134, 172, 230, 231, 239
Fort Warren  84, 207, 224, 234

Fraser, Trenholm & Company  69
Fremont, John C.  51, 156
Fugitive Slave Act  228

*Georgia*  181
Georgia  7, 20, 22, 35, 36, 71, 99, 106, 229
Gettysburg  49, 66, 118, 179, 206, 243
Gist, William Henry  75
Gorgas, Josiah  18, 108–112, 115
governors  98, 135, 138, 153; list of 262; opposition to Davis administration 52, 91, 117, 134, 138, 153; *see also* individual governors
Grant, Ulysses S.  101, 115, 116, 124
greenbacks  67

*habeas corpus*  22, 33–36, 121, 157
Hampton Roads Conference  22, 243
Harris, Isham  184, 231
Havana  69, 223
Hill, A.P.  125, 233
Hill, D.H.  206, 232, 233
Holden, William Woods  49
Home Guard  33, 37, 110, 113, 200
Hood, John B.  152
*Housatonic*  174, 175
Hunley  38, 174, 175, 191
Hunley, H. L.  174
Hunter, Robert M. T.  11, 15, 16, 139, 149, 222, 237–41, 243
Huse, Caleb  109, 111, 165

impressments  33, 36–37, 49, 52, 95, 110, 121, 206
Indian Territories  55, 123
inflation  67–72, 73, 81, 121, 151, 201
Invalid Corps  106
ironclads  171, 175, 178, 180, 183, 185, 188, 191

Jackson, Andrew  22, 80, 227
Jackson, Thomas ("Stonewall")  97, 125, 139, 141, 159, 246
Jefferson, Thomas  22, 143
Johnson, Andrew  49, 82, 137, 161, 192, 207, 234, 235
Johnston, Joseph  83, 93, 128, 139, 141, 146, 151, 152, 153, 158, 160, 179, 231
Jones, John  18, 24, 114
Jones, Joseph  18
Justice Department  9, 17, 24, 29–39, 32, 45, 49, 55; *see also* attorneys general

Kean, Robert G. H.  24, 25, 44, 49, 77, 81, 93, 96, 112–14, 141, 145, 150–51, 159
Keitt, Laurence  12
Kentucky  120, 136, 140, 157, 158, 206, 231
Key West  218
Keyes, Wade  32, 37, 54–55
King Cotton diplomacy  17, 211, 216, 218–22

## Index

Know-Nothing Party 51
Knoxville 82, 98, 159

laboratories, medical 107–108
laboratories, ordnance 112, 169
Laird, John 177–78, 190–91
Laird rams 176, 178–79, 183, 185, 191
Lawton, Alexander Robert 95–98
Lee, Robert E. 21, 33, 53, 58, 101, 117, 118, 122, 124, 134, 151, 160, 206, 246
Letcher, John 21, 248
Lincoln, Abraham 34, 51, 57, 75, 83, 89, 134, 140, 144, 225, 230, 241; announcement of blockade 213–15; election of 132, 156–57, 238; reelection of 22
Liverpool 66, 69, 80, 177
Longstreet, James 98, 113, 128, 206, 232, 233, 246
Lost Cause 1, 12, 22
*Louisiana* 11
Louisiana 7, 43, 45

Mallet, John William 112
Mallory, Stephen 11, 14, 24, 167, 168, 186–93, 247, 248; and commerce raiders 180–82; and naval academy 182–83; and naval strategy 183–85; and shipbuilding 175–78; and torpedo development 170–71
Malvern Hill 232
Manassas: first battle of 18, 113, 136, 231; second battle of 97, 222
Mann, Dudley 176, 220, 240
Marvin, William 187, 192, 223
Maryland 118, 231, 232
Mason, James 211, 223–25, 230, 240, 243
Matron Law of 1862 104
Maury, Matthew 38, 170, 171, 172, 181, 191
McCaw, James Brown 105, 106
McClellan, George 118
Medical Department 92, 101–108
Medical Examining Boards 104
Memminger, Christopher 11, 14, 15, 16, 61, 67, 73–78; and inflation 67–68, 71, 81; and produce loans 64–65, 67; and running Treasury Department 61–62, 63, 64; and taxation 63
*Merrimack* see *Virginia*
Mexican War 93, 95, 102, 109, 116, 123, 125, 155, 204, 228
*Mississippi* 11
Mississippi 13, 35, 121
Mississippi River 66, 69, 120, 134, 145, 172, 184
Mobile 52, 108, 173, 174
Mobile Bay 173, 175
money 63, 67–69, 71, 77, 81; in provisional government 20, 29; and taxes 81
money supply 67, 68
Montgomery 16, 19, 20, 21, 31, 91, 203, 229
Moore, Samuel Preston 102, 104–108

Mordecai, Alfred 108–109
Morton, Richard 122
Myers, Abraham 95–96, 100, 135

*Nashville* 181
Nashville Convention 131, 187
Nassau 69, 80, 82, 111, 177
naval officers 182, 188, 216, 218
Navy Department 16, 24, 165–85
New Orleans 64, 96, 134, 174, 184, 185
Niter and Mining Bureau 24, 94, 111, 122
North, James 179, 190
North Carolina 35, 36, 48, 49, 118, 121, 175, 231
Northrop, Lucius B. 98–100, 146, 160
nullification 73, 74, 80

offensive-defensive strategy 91
Office of Medicine and Surgery 170, 190
Office of Orders and Detail 168
Office of Ordnance and Hydrography 169, 190
Office of Provisions and Clothing 169–70
*Olustee* 181, 182; see also *Tallahassee*
Ordnance Bureau 18, 95, 108, 111, 112, 122
*Oreto* see *Florida*
Ould, Robert 115

Palmerston, Lord 221, 225
Parker, William 182
Patent Office 32, 37–39
*Patrick Henry* 182–83
Pemberton, John 145, 206
personnel organization, Confederate Army 124–25
Pickett, George 125, 151
Pierce, Franklin 75, 90, 116, 155, 220, 232
Post Office Department 9, 16, 17, 24, 62, 71, 83, 119, 197–201
presidential reconstruction 235
Produce Loan 62, 63, 64–65
Provisional Congress 29, 31, 57, 165, 203, 229, 239
provisional government 7, 229

Quartermaster General 94–98

Radical Republicans 23, 49, 161, 193, 235
railroads 41, 48, 82, 96, 99, 112, 119, 121, 135, 235; and mail delivery 198–200; and standard gauge 100
Rains, Gabriel 116
Rains, George W. 109, 112, 1167, 117, 118, 143–47, 149
rams see Laird rams
Randolph, George 16, 25, 113
Reagan, John 11, 14, 15, 16, 17, 23, 83–85, 197, 198, 200, 202–208, 247; as Post Office 202–208; as Treasury secretary 83–85

# Index

Reconstruction 53, 58, 85, 114, 138, 193, 235
Republican Party 51, 131, 156, 188, 228
revenue sources 63, 67, 76
Rhett, Robert Barnwell 13, 14, 29, 34, 76
Richmond 17, 18, 21, 39, 76, 82, 91, 94, 106, 108, 160, 183, 207
Rost, Pierre 16, 220, 230, 240
Russell, John 220, 221, 222

St. John, Isaac Munroe 100, 111, 122–23, 160
San Jacinto 223–25; *see also Trent* affair
Sandburg, Carl 77
Savannah 82, 99, 233
Scott, Winfield 109, 184, 227
secession 17, 20, 30, 31, 43, 45, 48, 57, 73, 75, 80, 85, 123, 132, 165, 203, 221, 238
secessionists 13, 53, 54, 73, 130, 132, 149, 247
Seddon, James 16, 25, 92, 148–53, 159
Seminole Wars 93, 95, 98, 187
Semmes, Raphael 135, 165, 177, 181, 214, 215, 223
Seward, William 211, 223, 225, 230, 231, 239, 243
Sharpsburg 97, 118, 150, 232–33; *see also* Antietam
*Shenandoah* 180, 181
Sherman, William T. 83, 99, 100, 118, 152, 160, 233
shipbuilding 166; domestic 175; foreign 175–80, 190
slave trade 9
slavery 9, 10, 15, 20, 43, 85, 91, 131, 228, 238, 243
slaves, arming of 126
Slidell, John 211, 220, 223, 225, 240
Smith, Kirby 69, 127
South Carolina 7, 73, 75, 79, 98, 102, 106, 127, 134, 234, 239
Stanton, Edwin 116, 151, 187, 188, 192, 234
State Department 9, 17, 23, 24, 185, 211–25, 230, 240, 242
Stephens, Alexander 7, 14, 16, 19–23, 34, 76, 84, 121, 20, 228, 230, 243; rift with Davis 21
Stephens, Linton 20, 21, 22
*Stonewall* 178, 179, 180
Subsistence Bureau 95, 99, 101, 127
substitutes 34, 35, 36, 38, 117, 119
*Sumter* 191, 223
Surgeon General 101–108

*Tallahassee* 181
tariff 8, 10, 22, 63, 69, 80, 149, 155, 221, 227, 238
taxes 9, 63, 68, 69, 70, 81, 251, 253
Tennessee 13, 106, 118, 121, 122, 127, 140, 145, 152, 222, 231, 247

Texas 16, 34, 85, 99, 121, 203, 207, 228
Toombs, Robert 1, 14, 16, 17, 20, 21, 34, 226–36; as general 231–33; as secretary of state 211, 219, 221, 222, 230, 231
Torpedo Bureau 170–75
torpedoes 38, 170–75, 191
Trans-Mississippi Department 84, 93, 127, 145, 244
transportation 94–99, 110, 112, 135, 146, 165–67, 206
Treasury Department 14, 17, 23, 61–72, 81, 135
treasury notes 63–65, 67, 69, 71
Treaty of Paris 1856 240
Tredegar Iron Works 166
Trenholm, George 11, 72, 77, 79–82, 83, 84, 153, 207
*Trent* affair 223–25; *see also San Jacinto*
turnover rate of cabinet 14

U.S. Constitution 7, 8, 23, 29

Vance, Zebulon 36, 49, 52, 58, 100, 117
Vicksburg 66, 118, 158, 179, 184, 206, 243
*Virginia* 39, 168, 169
Virginia 17, 21, 35, 91, 121, 144, 149, 157, 206, 222, 239

Walker, Leroy Pope 14, 16, 19, 110, 113, 117, 130–38, 140
War Bureau 25, 44
War Department 23, 89–129
Washington, D.C. 144, 146, 159, 197, 205, 230, 235
Washington Peace Conference 20–21, 57
Watervliet Arsenal 108
Watts, Thomas 11, 19, 32, 50–53, 55, 576, 121
way hospitals 106
Welles, Gideon 171, 217
West Point 21, 93, 94, 95, 97, 98, 109, 112, 125, 231, 232
Western theater 17, 127, 145, 151, 184, 200
Whig Party 13, 20, 42, 48, 51, 57, 188, 227
Wigfall, Louis 12, 33, 34, 150, 233
Wilkes, Charles 223, 224, 225
Winder Hospital 106
Wirz, Henry 152
Wise, Henry 142

Yancey, William Lowndes 12, 13, 14, 32, 34, 51, 133, 176, 211, 219, 220, 230, 240
Younge, Clarence 178
Yulee, David Levy 42, 187, 188